Stealth Democracy

Americans often complain about the current operation of their government, but scholars have never developed a complete picture of people's preferred type of government. In this provocative and timely book, John Hibbing and Elizabeth Theiss-Morse, employing an original national survey and focus groups, report the specific governmental procedures Americans desire. Their results are surprising. Contrary to the prevailing view that people want greater involvement in politics, most citizens do not care about most policies and therefore are content to turn over decision-making authority to someone else. People's most intense desire for the political system is that decision makers be empathetic and, especially, non-self-interested, not that they be responsive and accountable to the people's largely nonexistent policy preferences or, even worse, that the people be obligated to participate directly in decision making. In light of these findings, Hibbing and Theiss-Morse conclude by cautioning communitarians, direct democrats, social capitalists, deliberation theorists, and all those who think that greater citizen involvement is the solution to society's problems.

John R. Hibbing is the Foundation Regents Professor of Political Science at the University of Nebraska-Lincoln. He has formerly served as editor of the *Legislative Studies Quarterly,* chair of his department, and president of the American Political Science Association's Legislative Studies Section. He has written widely on legislatures and American public opinion.

Elizabeth Theiss-Morse is Associate Professor of Political Science at the University of Nebraska-Lincoln. She is the coauthor of two award-winning Cambridge University Press books, including *Congress as Public Enemy,* coauthored with Professor John Hibbing and winner of the American Political Science Association's Fenno prize in 1996 for the best book on legislatures. She was the program cochair for the Midwest Political Science Association for 2002.

Cambridge Studies in Political Psychology and Public Opinion

General Editors

James H. Kuklinski, *University of Illinois, Urbana-Champaign*
Dennis Chong, *Northwestern University*

Editorial Board

Stanley Feldman, *State University of New York, Stony Brook*
Roger D. Masters, *Dartmouth College*
William J. McGuire, *Yale University*
Norbert Schwarz, *Zentrum für Umfragen, Methoden und Analysen ZUMA, Mannheim, FRG*
David O. Sears, *University of California, Los Angeles*
Paul M. Sniderman, *Stanford University* and *Survey Research Center, University of California, Berkeley*
James A. Stimson, *University of North Carolina*

This series has been established in recognition of the growing sophistication in the resurgence of interest in political psychology and the study of public opinion. Its focus ranges from the kinds of mental processes that people employ when they think about democratic processes and make political choices to the nature and consequences of macro-level public opinion.

Some of the works draw on developments in cognitive and social psychology and relevant areas of philosophy. Appropriate subjects include the use of heuristics, the roles of core values and moral principles in political reasoning, the effects of expertise and sophistication, the roles of affect and emotion, and the nature of cognition and information processing. The emphasis is on systematic and rigorous empirical analysis, and a wide range of methodologies are appropriate: traditional surveys, experimental surveys, laboratory experiments, focus groups, and in-depth interviews, as well as others. These empirically oriented studies also consider normative implications for democratic politics generally.

Politics, not psychology, is the primary focus, and it is expected that most works will deal with mass publics and democratic politics, although work on nondemocratic publics is not excluded. Other works will examine traditional topics in public opinion research, as well as contribute to the growing literature on aggregate opinion and its role in democratic societies.

Other books in the series

Asher Arian, *Security Threatened: Surveying Israeli Opinion on Peace and War*
James DeNardo, *The Amateur Strategist: Intuitive Deterrence Theories and the Politics of the Nuclear Arms Race*
Robert S. Erikson, Michael B. MacKuen, and James A. Stimson, *The Macro Polity*
John Hibbing and Elizabeth Theiss-Morse, *Congress as Public Enemy: Public Attitudes Toward American Political Institutions*

Series list continues on page following the Index

Stealth Democracy

AMERICANS' BELIEFS ABOUT HOW
GOVERNMENT SHOULD WORK

John R. Hibbing
University of Nebraska-Lincoln

Elizabeth Theiss-Morse
University of Nebraska-Lincoln

CAMBRIDGE
UNIVERSITY PRESS

PUBLISHED BY THE PRESS SYNDICATE OF THE UNIVERSITY OF CAMBRIDGE
The Pitt Building, Trumpington Street, Cambridge, United Kingdom

CAMBRIDGE UNIVERSITY PRESS
The Edinburgh Building, Cambridge CB2 2RU, UK
40 West 20th Street, New York, NY 10011-4211, USA
477 Williamstown Road, Port Melbourne, VIC 3207, Australia
Ruiz de Alarcón 13, 28014 Madrid, Spain
Dock House, The Waterfront, Cape Town 8001, South Africa

http://www.cambridge.org

First published 2002

Printed in the United Kingdom at the University Press, Cambridge

Typeface ITC New Baskerville 10.5/13 pt.   *System* QuarkXPress [BTS]

A catalog record for this book is available from the British Library.

Library of Congress Cataloging in Publication data available

ISBN   0 521 81138 4   hardback
ISBN   0 521 00986 3   paperback

To our advisors,
Samuel C. (Pat) Patterson and John L. Sullivan,
role models and friends

Contents

Figures

Tables

Acknowledgments

While we wish, as always, that we had additional data, we nonetheless have been able to compile an unusually extensive and varied collection of information on Americans' preferred governmental procedures. The reason we were able to do so was the generous financial support of the National Science Foundation (SES-97-09934), which allowed us to conduct a major national survey and eight focus groups across the nation. Especially in light of the topic, we believe this multimethod approach to be valuable, and we deeply appreciate the NSF making it possible for us to attack the topic from several sides. The survey itself was conducted with impressive efficiency by the Gallup Organization. We thank Ron Aames, Max Larsen, and the others at Gallup for their cooperation and their good work. We also had valuable assistance in arranging the logistics of the focus groups. Thanks to Amy Fried, Matt Moen, Staci Beavers, Eliza Cheesman, Richard Serpe, Sandy Babcock, the Social and Behavioral Research Institute at California State University, San Marcos, and Debbie Diehl and TDM Research in Birmingham, Alabama. We also appreciate the help we received from Paul Ordal, Elice Hubbert, J. T. Smith, Chris Sommerich, Nancy Heltzel, Cameron Otopalik, Kathy Lee, and Jan Edwards and her compatriots. Throughout the entire project, Jody Bennett provided unbelievable support. She was much more than a research assistant.

We feel tremendous gratitude toward the many colleagues across the nation who agreed to read earlier drafts of chapters and often the entire book. While it may be the norm for authors to acknowledge such cooperation, it is especially apt for us since many of the readers have taken positions in print that differ at one point or another from our findings and interpretations. That so many of them were willing to offer wonderfully constructive suggestions in light of these occasional differences certainly speaks well of them. We are extremely fortunate that such an all-star cast was willing to help in this fashion. The identities of these saints? John Alford, Steve Ansolabehere, Jack Citrin, Steve Finkel, Mo Fiorina, Rick Hall, Jennifer Hochschild, Jon Krosnick, Jane Mansbridge, Diana Mutz, Alan Rosenthal, Jeff Spinner-Halev, Tom Tyler, and Gerald Wright.

We continue to enjoy our relationship with Cambridge University Press, particularly the two editors with whom we have worked: Alex Holzman and Lewis Bateman. Finally, and most important, we thank our families for their unflagging support and patience.

Lincoln, Nebraska   John R. Hibbing
November 2001   Elizabeth Theiss-Morse

Stealth Democracy

Introduction

For the past decade we have been studying Americans' attitudes toward their government. Since dissatisfaction is common and since we believe dissatisfaction with government can be dangerous, we were moved to ask people about the particular type of government that might increase levels of satisfaction. Their answers, properly interpreted, directly contradict standard elite interpretations of popular desires. Specifically, pundits, politicians, and even many social scientists believe that Americans are populists, that they distrust any decision maker who is not an ordinary person or who is not at least intimately connected to ordinary people. Americans prefer to rule themselves, the argument goes, and will support any reform that empowers the people at the expense of elites. Only if direct democracy is not feasible will they accept a representative system and even then only if representatives act simply as mouthpieces for the people's wishes – wishes that individuals are eager to offer to elected officials if only those officials would listen.

THE BOOK'S THESIS

But this conventional description has been put together with remarkably little direct input from ordinary Americans. When we started listening to the people and taking seriously what they had to say, we were led to conclude that this conventional wisdom was not just somewhat misguided, it was backward. The last thing people want is to be more involved in political decision making: They do not want to make political decisions themselves; they do not want to provide much input to those who are assigned to make these decisions; and they would rather not know all the details of the decision-making process. Most people have strong feelings on few if any of the issues the government needs to address and would much prefer to spend their time in nonpolitical pursuits.

Rather than wanting a more active, participatory democracy, a remarkable number of people want what we call stealth democracy. Stealth aircraft such as B-2 bombers are difficult to see with standard radar techniques, yet everyone knows they exist. Similarly, the people want democratic procedures to exist but not to be visible on a routine basis. But how can people in a stealth democracy hold government accountable for its policy decisions? The focus of this question is actually off the mark. The people as a whole tend to be quite indifferent to policies and therefore are not eager to hold government accountable for the policies it produces. This does not mean people think no mechanism for government accountability is necessary; they just do not want the mechanism to come into play except in unusual circumstances. The people want to be able to make democracy visible and accountable on those rare occasions when they *are* motivated to be involved. They want to know that the opportunity will be there for them even though they probably have no current intention of getting involved in government or even of paying attention to it. Just as stealth bombers can be made to show up on radar when desired, the people want to know that their government will become visible, accountable, and representative should they decide such traits are warranted. Until that time, however, most people prefer not to be involved and therefore desire unobtrusive accountability.

How could conventional wisdom have gone so wrong? Easy. Although the people dislike a political system built on sustained public involvement, there is something they dislike even more: a political system in which decision makers – for no reason other than the fact that they are in a position to make decisions – accrue benefits at the expense of non-decision makers. Just as children are often less concerned with acquiring a privilege than with preventing their siblings from acquiring a privilege, citizens are usually less concerned with obtaining a policy outcome than with preventing others from using the process to feather their own nests. Since the people constitute one obvious check on the ability of decision makers to be self-serving, it often appears as though the people want more political influence for themselves, when in fact they just do not want decision makers to be able to take advantage of them.

As we write these words, efforts continue to be made to form a stable new government in Afghanistan subsequent to the military defeat of the Taliban. The American press is filled with references to the need to bring democracy to Afghanistan. Our suspicion is that the Afghani people have little desire for democracy. Instead, the Uzbekis primarily want a government in which it will be impossible for the Hazaras to get the upper hand; the Hazaras want to be assured the Tajiks will not be able to take advantage of them; the Tajiks are worried about certain Pashtun tribes; those Pashtun tribes seek protection against the use of power by other Pashtun tribes; and so on. In the United States, traditional allegiance to individual rights and a more established ability to enforce those rights have obviously given some observers the impression that Americans desire something more from their political arrangements, but in truth those who think Americans lack the Afghanis' basic sensitivity to the perceived power of outgroups are fooling themselves.

Evidence of the people's desire to avoid politics is widespread, but most observers still find it difficult to take this evidence at face value. People must really want to participate but are just turned off by some aspect of the political system, right? If we could only tinker with the problematic aspects of the system, then the people's true participatory colors would shine for all to see, right? As a result of this mindset, when the people say they do not like politics and do not want to participate in politics, they are simply ignored. Elite observers claim to know what the people really want – and that is to be involved, richly and consistently, in the political arena. If people are not involved, these observers automatically deem the system in dire need of repair.

We do not deny that the American political system could be improved in numerous ways, but we do deny that these improvements would generate significant long-term increases in meaningful participation on the part of the public. Participation in politics is low not because of the difficulty of registration requirements or the dearth of places for citizens to discuss politics, not because of the sometimes unseemly nature of debate in Congress or displeasure with a particular public policy. Participation in politics is low because people do not like politics even in the best of circumstances; in other words, they simply do not like the process of openly arriving at a decision in the face of diverse opinions. They do not like politics when they view it from afar and they certainly do not like politics when they participate in it themselves.

After the September 11, 2001, terrorist attack on the Pentagon in Washington and the World Trade Center in New York and during the subsequent war in Afghanistan, Americans' attitudes toward government improved markedly over the (already relatively high) levels of the late 1990s and early 2000s. Nine out of ten people approved of the job being done by President George W. Bush, three out of four approved of the job being done by Congress, and overall trust and confidence in government rose to levels not seen in forty years (Gallup 2001). Of course, the predictable surge of patriotism and the associated rally-around-the-flag effect were the main causes of these remarkable poll numbers, but it would be a mistake to ignore the fact that this was also a time when government was working the way the people think it should work. Objectives in the wake of the attack were widely shared (strike back at Osama bin Laden and the Taliban in Afghanistan and do whatever it takes to secure Americans at home), partisan disputes were practically invisible, special interests were silent, and media interpretations rarely implied that politicians were taking action for self-interested (i.e., political) reasons. Americans shared a common enemy, and except for that brief time when House leaders committed the serious public relations blunder of closing the body in the wake of the anthrax scare, people generally believed that politicians were acting to promote the general interest. This is an important reason attitudes toward government were so favorable in the months after September 11.

Those who persist in claiming that people approve of government only when it becomes more accountable have much more difficulty explaining trends in public opinion after September 11. Did the government become more responsive, more accountable, more sensitive to the people's every whim during this time? Hardly. Did people become more involved in the making of high-level political decisions? Not in the least. If anything, power flowed away from the more accountable parts of government, such as Congress, state governments, and the people themselves and toward more detached elements such as the military, the President, and appointed individuals in the upper levels of the administration. In point of fact, government accountability and responsiveness declined, yet people's attitudes toward government improved dramatically. People do not want responsiveness and accountability in government; they want responsiveness and accountability to be unnecessary.

When people's aversion to politics is accepted as a basic and sensible trait, the normative implications are far-reaching. For at least 150 years, theorists have believed that popular involvement in the political process would lead to better decisions, better people, and a more legitimate political system. But why should getting people to do something they do not want to do make them feel the system is more legitimate? Why should it make them happier people? And why should it make for better policy decisions? The answer, of course, is that none of these improvements should be expected. Moreover, none of them seems to occur. An encouraging but all-too-recent trend is empirical testing of the claims normative theorists have long been making about the benefits of greater public involvement in politics. One searches this empirical literature in vain for credible evidence that participation in real political processes leads participants to be more approving of that process, to be more understanding of other people, or to be better able to produce successful policy decisions. In fact, quite often this empirical work suggests that participation has a negative effect on decisions, the political system, and people. The belief that participatory democracy is preferable to other political processes crumbles with disconcerting ease as soon as people's desire to avoid politics is accepted as fact.

These claims are bold and will not go down well in many quarters. Some people have devoted their lives to finding ways of promoting political participation on the assumption that it would make government and people better. We take no particular pleasure in disagreeing with these well-meaning, dedicated democrats. But the evidence, while certainly open to alternative interpretations, suggests to us that it is time to consider the possibility that political participation is not the universal solution advocates often aver. We hasten to point out that there are situations in which participation can have the beneficial consequences advocates so badly want it to have. As we document below in the book, these situations are likely to occur when the people involved recognize diversity in society and appreciate the frustrations inherent in democratic decision making in the context of this diversity. The consequences of participation that result from this enlightened understanding are completely different from the consequences of untutored participation that is too often grudging and artificially induced.

So our disagreement with those touting the glories of participatory democracy is only over their belief that any participation of any sort is good. We believe a proper reading of the evidence suggests that the consequences of popular participation are often neutral or negative; thus, we believe a key task of future research is determining those limited situations in which participation can be beneficial. The solution to the problems of the political system is not as simple as just getting people involved. Instead, we must encourage involvement that is based on an appreciation of democracy and, as heretical as it may seem, discourage involvement that is not. The naive faith that increased contact with the political process will always be a plus must be abandoned for the empirically sound realization that people's reactions to political participation vary widely. Only under limited circumstances will heightened participation benefit the person and the system.

THE BOOK'S ORGANIZATION

The three parts of this book are quite distinct, and since some readers may be interested in one part more than the others, we now provide brief descriptions of each. The argument we sketched above is predicated on the belief that political processes matter; that is, that people are quite concerned with how government works, not just with what it produces. In this we are encouraging an important shift in thinking, since the study of politics has too long operated under the assumption that people are so concerned with results that the mechanism for obtaining results is largely irrelevant to them. In short, the common belief has been that, as far as the people are concerned, the ends justify the means. We provide evidence in Part I that people actually are concerned with the process as well as the outcome. Contrary to popular belief, many people have vague policy preferences and crystal-clear process preferences, so their actions can be understood only if we investigate these process preferences.

In Part I our dominant concern is in distinguishing process variables from the more commonly employed policy variables and then demonstrating that process variables matter. The details of the particular processes people prefer are left to later. In fact, to the extent we do address people's specific preferences, the presentation in Part I is so undeveloped as to be misleading. For example, in this part we use a simple spectrum that ranges only from decision making exclusively by the people to decision making exclusively by elected officials. By limiting attention to such a basic process distinction (and by not including decision making by non-self-serving elites as an option), we actually leave the inaccurate impression that people do want to be more involved in decision making. Further, in this part we make no distinction among the many different ways in which the people could participate in political decisions, such as being per-

sonally involved in structured or in unstructured deliberative settings, influencing decision makers, voting for decision makers, or
voting on ballot measures (initiatives and referenda). Even so, the
advantage of Part I's overly simplistic process spectrum is that it
allows us to distinguish process preferences from policy preferences
and to demonstrate the importance of process satisfaction in explaining numerous important political phenomena. The message of Part
I, then, is that, contrary to assumptions about the centrality of policy,
process matters, too.

After identifying, measuring, distinguishing, and demonstrating
the importance of process concerns in Part I, the issue in Part II becomes precisely which processes people prefer. If people are concerned with how government works, just how do they want it to work?
To answer this question, we use results from (1) numerous items in
a specially designed national survey conducted in the late spring of
1998, and (2) extensive focus group sessions held around the nation
a few months earlier. This multimethod approach allows us to describe people's views of government, their reactions to particular
reform proposals, their opinions of the political capabilities of ordinary people, and their thoughts on the role of politicians (and other
possible decision makers) in a properly working polity.

In the last chapter of Part II (Chapter 6) these findings are
brought together to make the case summarized above, that the kind
of government people want is one in which ordinary people do not
have to get involved. We show that people want to distance themselves from government not because of a system defect but because
many people are simply averse to political conflict and many others
believe political conflict is unnecessary and an indication that something is wrong with governmental procedures. People believe that
Americans all have the same basic goals, and they are consequently
turned off by political debate and deal making that presuppose an
absence of consensus. People believe these activities would be unnecessary if decision makers were in tune with the (consensual) public
interest rather than with cacophonous special interests. Add to this
the perceived lack of importance of most policies and people tend
to view political procedures as a complete waste of time. The processes people really want would not be provided by the populist
reform agenda they often embrace; it would be provided by a stealth
democratic arrangement in which decisions are made by neutral
decision makers who do not require sustained input from the people
in order to function.

Having established in Part I the importance of understanding the people's process preferences and having established in Part II the particular kind of governmental process desired by the people, we turn in Part III to the issue of whether or not it would be a good idea to modify the workings of government to make them more consistent with the people's process preferences. As such, whereas Parts I and II are largely empirical, Part III contains less data and is more theoretical. The issue shifts to the nature and wisdom of the changes in the polity indicated by people's preference for stealth as opposed to participatory democracy. Readers interested in the more grounded and empirical nature of people's process desires may wish to concentrate on the first two parts of the book, whereas readers more interested in normative arguments flowing from the empirical findings may want to spend more time with Part III, perhaps after reading Chapter 6 to help them get oriented.

Since the empirical findings suggest that people want to withdraw from politics even more than they already have, the central task in Part III is tallying the pros and cons of popular participation in the political process. Only by knowing the likely consequences of reduced participation can we know whether stealth democracy is something that should be encouraged. As noted above, the assumption of theorists has long been that participation is good. We detail their arguments in Chapter 7 before critiquing them in Chapter 8. Our conclusion is that the alleged benefits of more participatory political procedures are based on wishful thinking rather than real evidence. This appears to be true of each of the many proposed styles of popular participation. For example, neither encouraging people to join voluntary community groups nor pushing them into face-to-face discussions of controversial issues with opponents seems to produce useful outcomes, since the former shields people too much from the divisiveness that they need to appreciate and the latter shields them too little. Not only is the evidence lacking for the claim that more participatory involvement in zero-sum politics enhances people, decisions, and system legitimacy, empirical work actually provides evidence that popular involvement can have negative consequences. Though more work needs to be done before such a conclusion is accepted as fact, our findings regarding people's aversion to politics (note that we are not claiming people lack ability) would help to account for why these negative consequences occur.

Should people be given the stealth democratic procedures so many of them crave or should we continue to labor under the false hope, propagated by so many well-intentioned elites, that if we just alter yet another voter registration requirement or invite people to more coffee klatches, if we make Congress more responsive, if we create minipopuli or electronic town hall meetings or citizen fora or deliberative public opinion polls, then people will eagerly participate? In the book's final full-length chapter, Chapter 9, we address this question. As is apparent from the way we phrase the question, we believe that Americans' motivation to avoid politics is deep and not the result of particular defects in the current system. It is politics they do not like, not a particular version of politics. We believe people's intense desire to give decision-making authority to someone else and to give those decision makers wide berth as long as they are barred from taking advantage of their position for personal gain should be taken seriously. After all, avoiding a distasteful activity makes perfect sense and aversion to being played for a sucker is a core trait of human social behavior, if recent work in social psychology and experimental economics is to be believed, as we think it should.

At the same time, while people's preferences for a form of stealth democracy are understandable, we are not convinced they are wise. In our view, elite prescriptions for altering democratic political procedures in the United States are out of touch with the preferences of the people and, as a result, are doomed to failure. But just as it is a mistake to blithely ignore the people's wishes, so too is it a mistake to follow slavishly those wishes. While it is possible to envision political structures capable of preventing decision makers from ever being perceived as acting in their own interest, it is not easy – particularly if these decision makers are to be accorded standard First Amendment rights and particularly in light of people's tendency to suspect self-interest absent clear evidence to the contrary. Moreover, to the extent people have (or can be made to have) any policy preferences at all, stealth democracy becomes more problematic. The implication of people's process preferences, as we have described them, is that people tend to believe that all policy solutions driven by a concern for the general welfare (rather than special interests) are more or less acceptable, or at least not worth arguing about. People's perception seems to be that the common good is not debatable but rather will be apparent if selfishness can be stripped away. In this, we believe the people are wrong.

Disagreements about the best way to promote the common good in general and about individual policy issues are not necessarily an indication that those disagreeing have suddenly gone over to the dark side of pursuing self-interests or special interests. People need to understand that disagreements can occur among people of good heart and that some debating and compromising will be necessary to resolve these disagreements and come to a collective solution. As such, education designed to increase people's appreciation of democracy needs to be a crucial element of efforts to improve the current situation. Stealth democracy is what the people want and as such is preferable to the many permutations of participatory democracy being touted today. But we argue that it is not a particularly feasible form of democracy and its allure rests on erroneous assumptions. Limiting the ability of elected officials to be self-serving is only a partial solution.

But the primary goal of our study is not to advocate certain systemic reforms; it is to discover people's political process preferences. These preferences, properly understood, suggest that the ultimate danger for the American polity is not, after all is said and done, that a populace bent on collecting power in its own hands will destroy any opportunity for Burkean and Madisonian sensibilities to be displayed by suitably detached elected officials. Rather, the deeper danger is that people will seize the first opportunity to tune out of politics in favor of government by autopilot, and, ironically, the main reason they do not is the perception that politicians are self-serving. If people had a greater number of clear policy preferences and if they recognized that other people had different but nonetheless legitimate preferences, political participation, especially deliberation, could have beneficial consequences. But since many people care deeply about only a few policy items on the government's agenda and assume their fellow citizens are the same, people's main political goal is often limited to nothing more than achieving a process that will prevent decision makers from benefiting themselves. Thus, when people are moved to involve themselves in politics, it is usually because they believe decision makers have found a way to take advantage of their positions. Consequently, political participation in the United States is often connected to resentment, dissatisfaction, and puzzlement rather than to legitimacy, trust, and enlightenment.

Before turning to the data, two caveats are in order. First, we readily admit that the evidence we present in support of our interpretations is suggestive, not conclusive. For the time being, we will be content if our work encourages political observers at least to question traditional assumptions such as (1) people care about policy results and not the means by which these results were achieved, (2) people are eager to "reconnect" with politics, and (3) people feel better about themselves, their colleagues, and their political system when they are connected to real-life politics. We believe our interpretations are correct, but issues such as the type of governing procedures the people truly desire are difficult to test directly. These are not the kind of preferences that are at the top of people's heads or, relatedly, that they have practice verbalizing. Focus groups help by allowing people more opportunity to ruminate, but even after utilizing focus groups alongside our national survey, many of our claims are still based on circumstantial evidence. We hope that this evidence is suggestive enough to justify the construction of more direct tests of popular preferences for governmental procedures and of the consequences of those preferences.

Second, throughout the book we make the claim that "the people want this procedure or that." Of course, it is not the case that all Americans have the same preferences for how government should work, but we ask for some poetic license on this point. Using the phrase "relative to what the literature and conventional wisdom imply, more people want this procedure or that" would make for clumsy sentences and we have enough of those as is. We fully recognize that some ordinary Americans love the give and take of politics, feel strongly about a wide range of issues, would prefer to be more involved, and would benefit from additional involvement. What we want to suggest is that, because of understandable biases in research techniques, because politicized citizens make more noise, and because political writers themselves are smitten with politics and care about issues, the number of "politicos" in the general population has been grossly overestimated. When the populists, communitarians, participationists, and direct democrats all claim that "the people want back in" politics, they are wrong. When we claim "the people want out," so are we. But let there be no mistake that our language is intended to convey a belief that process matters to most people and that more people want out of politics than want in.

PART I

The Benefits of Studying the Processes People Want

THIS OPENING SECTION lays the groundwork for the rest of the book. We take issue with the notion that policy concerns alone drive Americans' political attitudes and behaviors. Instead, we argue that people care at most about one or two issues; they do not care about the vast majority of policies addressed by the government. They want to see certain ends – such as a healthy economy, low crime rates, good schools – but they have little interest in the particular policies that lead to those ends. If this is the case, as we claim, then political scientists should not place policy at the center of the public's political universe.

What do people care about if not policies? We argue that people care deeply about process. Understanding people's process preferences helps solve several mysteries, such as why Americans believe the two major political parties are so similar and the government is so unresponsive to their wishes. People think about process in relatively simple terms: the influence of special interests, the cushy lifestyle of members of Congress, the bickering and selling out on principles. Because they suggest decision makers are taking advantage of the people, these perceived process features make people appear eager to take power away from elected officials.

The centrality of process preferences means they are potentially powerful predictors of people's attitudes toward government. We do not contend that process can explain people's conventional participation in politics or their vote choice between the two major parties. After all, both the Democratic and Republican parties are thought to be part of the same nefarious processes. But process concerns can help us better understand dissatisfaction with government, support for third-party candidates who focus on process in their campaigns, support for reforms, and compliance with the law. We show that policy matters, but process is often a better predictor of these attitudes and behaviors than policy.

Part I therefore focuses on the distinction between policy and process. In Chapter 1, we discuss the venerated place policy has held in political science research and criticize this view. Policy stands are often unable to explain many political phenomena. Even more important, people do not care much about policies, which means policies cannot adequately explain their political attitudes or behaviors. We offer an alternative explanation in Chapter 2 where we focus on process. Our view of process in this chapter is oversimplified and deals only with people's beliefs about where the locus of decision-making power ought to lie. Should it be with elected officials and institutions or with the people themselves? In Chapter 3 we use this spectrum to explain a variety of attitudes and behaviors: approval of government, support for Ross Perot's third-party candidacy, support for reforms, and willingness to comply with the law.

1

Policy Space and American Politics

What do people want the government to do? What governmental policies would make the people happy? Questions such as these are apropos in a democracy because public satisfaction, as opposed to the satisfaction of, say, a haughty, distant, and self-serving monarch, is the key goal of democratic governance. The answer to the questions seems obvious, if difficult to achieve – satisfaction increases when governmental policies approximate the policies preferred by the people – and a substantial literature has developed investigating the connection between popular satisfaction with government and the policies government produces. In this chapter, we review much of this literature, but the purpose of this review is to show that, despite the idea's intuitive appeal, people's satisfaction with government is not driven mainly by whether or not they are getting the policies they want – partially yes, but mainly no. Policies and issues are frequently and surprisingly unable to explain variation in people's satisfaction with government. Others have questioned the importance in American politics of the people's issue positions, and we borrow much from them while adding some new evidence of our own.

Theoretically, it is possible to ascertain people's preferences in each and every policy area on the governmental agenda. To measure policy preferences, analysts often present policy options on spectra (rather than as forced-choice dichotomies). For example, a spectrum could run, as it does in the top half of Figure 1.1, from massive cuts in defense spending through a middle ground of no change in current spending levels all the way to massive increases. Such spectra allow individuals to be represented in policy space. Due to logical progressions from, say, more to less spending or fewer to greater

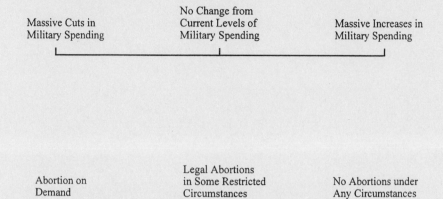

Figure 1.1. Policy space for military spending and for legal abortions.

restrictions on the circumstances in which an abortion can legally take place, analysts can derive meaning and predictions from the relative positions of individuals in this space.

Since there are so many issues being addressed in the political arena, creating a policy space for each of them quickly leads to overload for both the respondents and the analysts. Accordingly, a common practice is to utilize a single, overarching policy space (sometimes called ideological space). Instead of innumerable separate spectra, a composite spectrum running from extremely liberal to moderate to extremely conservative can be used. This practice of treating policy space as unidimensional unavoidably introduces some potentially serious distortions (e.g., liberals on one issue are not necessarily liberals on all issues) and these distortions are discussed in detail below. But the simplification to a single encompassing dimension renders policy space tractable and researchers commonly employ it when studying policy preferences.[1]

USING POLICY SPACE TO DERIVE EXPECTATIONS

Whether dealing with an individual issue or the more overarching concept of political ideology, the relevant idea is that people want the distance between their own policy preferences and the policies

---

[1] Hinich and Munger (1994: 160) even argue that employing a single ideological spectrum is not only simpler, it is analytically preferable. For more on the advantages of a single dimension, see Poole and Rosenthal (1997).

passed by government to be small. Perhaps the most obvious application of policy space is the expectation that people will vote for the candidate closest to them on the issues, assuming they deem the issues important. This basic concept of voters attending to the distance between their issue positions and candidates' issue positions was delineated by Hotelling (1929) and elaborated by Downs (1957).[2] Hotelling's original analogy involved lazy shoppers who were trying to minimize the distance they walked to a store. Just as customers would patronize the nearest store, voters were expected to support the political candidate whose policy position was closest to their own. To stick with one of the examples from Figure 1.1, an ardent "abortion on demand" voter would be expected to vote for whichever candidate favored the fewest restrictions on a woman's right to an abortion. Candidates and parties, being Machiavellian vote maximizers in the spatial world, would adopt the policy position that would attract the most votes just as stores would locate wherever they would attract the most customers.

Just what is the optimal position or location for a party or a candidate? In the United States, it is in the middle, since Americans tend to adopt centrist positions on most policy issues. Usually, a relatively small number of people prefer massive increases or massive decreases in military spending, with most favoring either no or minor alterations in current spending levels. Even on abortion, which many take to be the quintessential divisive issue, most Americans actually support the middling position of permitting abortions but under a number of restrictive conditions. Fiorina (1996) believes this is why divided government is so common. Most American voters view themselves as residing in the middle of policy space *and* see the parties as being on each side of the middle, Republicans to the right and Democrats to the left. Fiorina claims that the separation of powers system we have in the United States allows people to obtain the centrist policies that neither party would provide if left entirely to its own devices. People do so, of course, by electing one party to one institution (the Congress) and the other party to the other major elective institution (the presidency), thereby ingeniously minimizing the distance between their policy preferences and actual policies.

A widely invoked corollary of the notion that voters select candidates whose policy stands are most consistent with their own

---

[2]For good summaries, see Enelow and Hinich (1984); Merrill and Grofman (1999).

preferences is that people will vote for incumbents when the government is producing the "right" kind of policies. Often, analysts test this expectation not by determining the precise policy-space location of an incumbent politician relative to voters but by assuming voters desire peace, a prosperous economy, low crime rates, and so on, and then determining whether incumbents are more likely to win votes when these favorable conditions apply (see, esp., Tufte 1975; Fiorina 1981). This shift from policy positions to policy outcomes is an important one, although analysts are still assuming policy-goal-directed behavior on the part of voters.

However policy satisfaction is measured, analysts believe it influences far more than whether they vote for candidate A or candidate B, the incumbent or the challenger. Barely half of those eligible take the opportunity to vote in even the most publicized and salient of American elections, and many more people are not eligible, so a focus on voting behavior ignores the sentiments of half of the adult population. All people, on the other hand, make decisions about whether or not to support the government and its various parts, whether or not to participate in politics (conventionally or otherwise), and whether or not to comply with governmental edicts, and these are the topics that are of most concern to us.

In many respects, we should expect policy space to be strongly related to public attitudes toward government. After all, it makes sense that those dissatisfied with the outputs of government would also be dissatisfied with the government itself. This was certainly the thinking of Gamson (1968: 178), who contended that political distrust could be traced to undesirable policy decisions and outcomes. As Alesina and Wacziarg (2000: 166) put it, "greater voter dissatisfaction could also originate from increased discrepancies between the preferences of the median voter and the policies actually implemented." Citrin (1974), Miller (1974), and virtually all others who have written on the topic have assumed the same. Citrin (1974: 973) summarizes the core hypothesis nicely: "Political elites 'produce' policies; in exchange, they receive trust from citizens satisfied with these policies and cynicism from those who are disappointed." Citrin even refers to the notion that "we tend to trust and like those who agree with us" as "one of social science's most familiar generalizations" (973).

So the expectation is that disliked policies and conditions will lead to negative attitudes toward government: a lack of confidence, an absence of trust, a dearth of support. Similar logic leads to expectations that when government produces policies the people dislike or that lead to unfavorable societal conditions, the nature and level of people's political participation (including their tendency to engage in violent political behavior) and perhaps even their willingness to obey the government's laws and rules will be affected (see Tyler 1990). When people are displeased with current policies, the argument goes, they are more likely to grumble about the government, to take steps to signal their displeasure to the powers that be, and to view the actions of such a flawed government as something less than fully legitimate.

THE LIMITATIONS OF POLICY EXPLANATIONS

It certainly makes sense to expect disfavored policies to lead to a disfavored government, and empirical analyses have often revealed support for these expectations. But a fair reading of the research in this area leads to the clear conclusion that policies – substantive issues, if you prefer – are far less consequential to most Americans than scholars typically expect. In this section we detail the limited explanatory powers of policy when it comes to many of the dependent variables mentioned above.

The concept of policy space has been tremendously influential. Citations in the political science literature to the policy-space concepts of Downs now easily outstrip citations to the psychological concepts found in Campbell et al. and Downs is assigned in more American Politics graduate seminars than Campbell et al. (see Dow and Munger 1990). But the widespread usage of policy-space concepts should not be taken to imply universal acceptance. Serious reservations abound regarding both the theory behind policy space and the evidence of its influence. Some skeptics have difficulty visualizing voters as possessing the requisite ability and inclination to estimate the relative distance in policy space between their own positions and those of the candidates seeking various offices. Instead, vote choice may be the result of psychological attachments to groups and parties. These attachments may exist for less-than-rational reasons and may even predate the ability of most voters to think rationally about complex issues. As is well known, children adopt a party identification long before they understand the policy implications of that identification. People later adopt policies to fit into their existing party identification (see Campbell et al. 1960: ch. 7). And even when these psychological attachments are not determinative, it may be that candidate image, style, slogans, and presentation are more important than issue positions. As Popkin (1991: 78–9) points out repeatedly, personal information drives out policy information. People are enamored with the candidates' personalities far more than with their policies. Thus, while people can turn against their long-term attachments, their reasons for doing so are often not based on policy concerns (see Campbell et al. 1960: ch. 19).

Stokes (1963) has taken these arguments even further and stresses the importance of "valence issues," those that do not distinguish the parties all that much. Both parties, presumably, want lower crime rates, improved economic conditions, and fewer births to teenage mothers. According to Stokes, voters are left to make their best guesses about which candidates are most likely to accomplish these goals. The issue, therefore, is not so much which party is closer to a voter's ideal position on policy space but, rather, which candidate inspires confidence. Stokes believes that Downs has pointed analysts in a particularly unpromising direction and that the explanation for vote choice is generally not the voter's policy utility and (often inaccurate) perceptions of the candidates' policy locations.

Whether the alleged deciding factor is party identification, candidate image, or a valence issue, the basic notion uniting most of the critiques of policy spatial theory is simply that voters tend to decide on the basis of things other than the perceived location of candidates on policy space. The underlying conceit is that issue voting demands too much of voters by requiring that they have issue positions of their own *and* an understanding of the issue positions of the competing candidates. This last point is particularly difficult. As Delli Carpini and Keeter (1996: 76) playfully note after examining fifty years of survey items, only two issue stands of public officials have ever been correctly identified by at least three out of four respondents: Clinton's "don't ask, don't tell" approach to gays in the military and George H. W. Bush's 1989 revelation that he hates broccoli. As a result of their policy uncertainties, voters are more likely to fall back on the shortcuts provided by party identification or countless other heuristic devices (see Popkin 1991).

Perhaps for these reasons, empirical tests of the hypothesis that voters are attracted to candidates with whom they share policy predilections have been disappointing. Scholars have been hard pressed to demonstrate empirically that the perceived distance in policy space between a voter and competing candidates is a key predictor of which candidate the voter will support. The demands of policy voting are great. Voters must feel strongly about an issue, know their own established position on the issue, and know the respective candidates' positions on the issue. Often the candidates go out of their way to obfuscate their positions,[3] thereby making it difficult for even well-meaning voters. Faced with these challenges, voters may simply project their own policy preferences onto their preferred candidate, thus reversing the expected causal sequence (see Niemi and Weisberg 1976: 161–75; Page and Jones 1979). This tendency of voters to attribute desired policy positions to candidates they like rather than to like candidates who have desirable policy positions is incredibly damning to those who stress the causal importance of policies. It suggests that voters merely make up policy positions for candidates, and often the attributed policy positions bear little resemblance to candidates' actual positions.

Are policy positions merely created out of thin air in an effort by voters to justify choices they made on the basis of nonpolicy reasons? No. While sorting out the direction of the causal arrow is methodologically challenging, Page and Jones (1979) engaged in a careful effort to do so. In the two presidential elections they studied (1972 and 1976), they found that policy positions did influence candidate preference. Policy matters. But in both elections they found that the link from candidate preference to policy positions was stronger than the link from policy positions to candidate preference. In these two elections, at least, projection was more prevalent than issue voting. And if this is the case in presidential elections, imagine the amount of projection in lower-level races where candidates' policy positions are harder to determine. Defenders of the importance of policy are fond of noting that voters generally share more policy preferences with the candidates for whom they voted than with those for whom they did not. But work like that of Page and Jones shows that such protestations badly miss the mark. Just as is the case with children and party identification, policy substance often comes well after a vote choice has been made and is less substance than rationalization.

If people *are* issue-involved, chances are their concerns are limited to a very small number of issues. Evidence for this conclusion is found in the scholarly work on issue publics. First articulated by Converse (1964) and elaborated perhaps most successfully by Krosnick (1990; see also Key 1966; RePass 1971), the idea is attractive – so

---

[3] See Page and Brody (1972); Alvarez and Franklin (1994); Hinich and Munger (1994: 235).

attractive that we draw heavily on it later in the book. Voters are not interested in most policies addressed by the government, but some voters are interested in one, perhaps two, policy areas. Though they do not care about much, they may care about government actions in a particular area and they may even be willing to vote on the basis of the candidates' policy stances concerning this issue area. Farmers may follow farm policies, Jews may be particularly interested in U.S. policy toward Israel, and the economically downtrodden may be attuned to welfare and related policies. In this fashion, if policy positions play a role at all, the relevant issue varies from person to person, and most issues are irrelevant to these issue specialists.[4]

In light of the extremely limited concern most people have for most policies, it is not surprising that even those who are the most eager for policy space to predict voting behavior do not often try to test the relationship. Enelow and Hinich (1984), for example, use feeling thermometers for various political figures to predict voting behavior. The idea is that the more warmly a respondent feels toward a political figure, the more likely that respondent is to vote for the political figure. The problem with this procedure, of course, is that there is absolutely no reason to assume the thermometer ratings have anything to do with policy positions. Instead, voters may like certain political figures because of where they were born, what foods they like, or how they part their hair.[5] Concerning the task of predicting vote choice, the verdict must be that policy space is something less than successful. Perceived policy distance may influence vote choice under certain highly restrictive conditions but it is not usually the central concern for most voters.[6]

---

[4] Of course, a slice of the population is deeply involved in policies of all kinds, but this slice is surprisingly small. As far as political information is concerned, people tend not to be information specialists. Delli Carpini and Keeter (1996) found that knowledge in one issue area correlates strongly and positively with knowledge in other areas (see also Zaller 1986; Bennett 1990). People either know a lot about a variety of policies or they know little.

[5] Fiorina (1996) does provide some tests of his institution-balancing model, but his results have been subjected to vigorous challenge (see Alvarez and Schousen 1993; Born 1994; Frymer 1994).

[6] Even those who see policy space as a key element of vote choice do not agree on exactly how it works. Reacting to the occasionally inaccurate predictions yielded by Downsian notions, Rabinowitz and Macdonald (1989) suggest that the absolute distance from voter to target is not as important as being on the same side of the political debate. They refer to this as the directional theory: Voters will vote for a candidate more distant from their own preferences if that is the only way they can vote for a

A similar, fairly dismal assessment can be rendered concerning the ability of policy space to predict whether and how people participate in politics. To be fair, the theoretical basis for hypotheses concerning participation is less clear. What, exactly, is the expected result of a person believing the government's policies depart from his or her own policy preferences? Would such a belief inspire involvement in an effort to change the situation or would it encourage despair and alienation from the system?[7] The absence of a clear answer to these questions is no doubt part of the reason standard investigations of political participation pay virtually no attention to the possibility that the divergence between a person's own policy positions and current perceived governmental policy will be a key determinant of who participates and who does not.[8]

Downs is in a similar boat. His famous treatment of voting abstention (1957: ch. 14) is almost entirely devoted to the costs of voting. He *does* raise the possibility that abstention could be caused not by the perceived location of governmental policies but by the perceived differences between the options being presented by the parties. Specifically, he hypothesizes that the benefits of voting will increase if voters perceive substantial policy differences between the two parties, but he provides no empirical tests. Other than this, even most proponents of policy space as an important independent variable do not claim it has much clout when it comes to standard political participation such as voting, working for campaigns, or contributing money to political movements.[9]

It may be, however, that policy factors are more useful when it comes to less traditional modes of participation. A distaste for current governmental policies (and for the policies being promoted by the two established parties making up the government) could lead not so much to alterations in the tendency to be involved in voting or campaigning for the established parties and their candidates but, rather, to an embrace of less traditional, even illegal, political

candidate who shares their view of the direction needed to move on that issue (see Merrill and Grofman 1999 for an attempt to synthesize the directional and proximity views).

[7] Perhaps this relationship is curvilinear with modest policy discrepancies encouraging participation but gigantic discrepancies resulting in an abandonment of hope.

[8] Rosenstone and Hansen (1993); Verba, Schlozman, and Brady (1995).

[9] For treatments of the relevance of policy spatial theory for political participation, see Hinich and Ordeshook (1970); Ordeshook (1970); McKelvey (1975); Aldrich (1995: 178–80).

participation – or at least of an alternative party. Was support for H. Ross Perot in the presidential races of 1992 and 1996 driven by the fact that his policy positions were more attractive to voters? Do people who are grossly displeased with current government policies protest with greater frequency than their less displeased colleagues? It seems possible that those willing to take to the streets or to turn their backs on the traditional parties would be those most discontented with current policies. However, tests of these ideas have been neither plentiful nor conclusive.[10] Though such hypotheses may eventually prove true (it would seem supporters of Ralph Nader in 2000 were probably more displeased with governmental policies than supporters of Al Gore and George W. Bush), empirical evidence connecting policy space to participation of any kind is mostly lacking.

Our primary interest in this book, however, is to find out what people want out of government. As we have just seen, a widespread expectation is that people are primarily concerned with obtaining their preferred policies and pleasant societal conditions. Popkin (1991: 99) is up-front about this, saying that people "generally care about ends not means; they judge government by results and are . . . indifferent about the methods by which the results were obtained." As has been the case with the other policy-based hypotheses, though, the notion that policy perceptions or outcomes explain attitudes toward government has not fared well on those few occasions when it has been empirically tested. Miller (1974: 952), for example, investigated "the impact that reactions to political issues and public policy have on the formation of political cynicism." His empirical work (done with survey data from the 1960s) produced a string of disappointments. On Vietnam, the most salient issue of the day, "the most immediate observation . . . is that the original prediction that the most cynical would be those favoring withdrawal is partly false" (953). On race, over the very years that governmental policy began actively promoting integration, "individuals in favor of forced integration [became discontented] at a faster rate" (957). Admittedly, Miller is unable to test the hypothesis properly since he does not employ measures of what people perceive government policies to be and only makes assumptions about those perceptions. But the point remains that there is little evidence for the commonsensical notion that citizens who agree with governmental policies will trust

---

[10]But see Muller (1972) and Sears and Maconahay (1973) for some interesting speculation concerning the related concept of violent political behavior.

government and citizens who are "disappointed" with these policies will be cynical toward government.

More typically, scholars have tested whether favorable societal conditions, such as a booming economy, cause people to be satisfied with government. Though surges in support for government sometimes seem to occur during strong economic times, systematic analyses invariably question the role of economic conditions. Lawrence (1997) finds no consistent effect. Putnam, Pharr, and Dalton (2000: 24) conclude that "a growing body of work generally discounts [macro-economic conditions] as the primary explanation for the decline in public confidence in political institutions." Overall, evidence for a connection between satisfaction with outcomes or conditions and satisfaction with government can be classified as only weak. Like so many others, Pharr (2000: 199) is forced to conclude that "policy performance . . . explains little when it comes to public trust." It is easy to understand why della Porta (2000: 202) asked, "[W]hy do policy outputs in general, and economic performance and expectations in particular, play such a minor role in shaping confidence in democratic institutions?"

MORE LIMITATIONS OF POLICY EXPLANATIONS

To this point, we have demonstrated the limitations of policy explanations by relying upon previous research, but the same message is also apparent in data originally collected for this project. To illustrate, we draw readers' attention to two assertions frequently made by ordinary Americans. The first is that the two major political parties are virtual carbon copies of each other, and the second is that the government is out of touch with the people. If people are concerned only with policy ends, neither of these assertions makes any sense.

Americans frequently complain that the two political parties are identical.[11] Interestingly, when people are asked to place the parties on policy space they actually see the parties as being quite distinct.

[11] See Pomper (1972: 419); Margolis (1977); and Wattenberg (1981: 943–4). While the percentage of people who claim there is no difference between the two major parties has diminished since the 1970s, the extent of the decline is not large. The American National Election Study (NES) survey has periodically asked respondents whether they "think there are any important differences in what the Republicans and Democrats stand for." In the 1970s, an average of 48 percent responded that there was no difference, compared with an average of 38 percent in the 1980s and 41 percent in the 1990s.

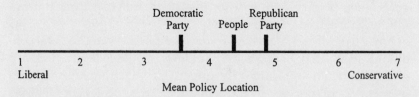

Figure 1.2. Policy space location of the people and their perceptions of the two major parties.

We administered a lengthy survey on policy and process attitudes to a national sample of 1,266 voting-age Americans in the late spring of 1998.[12] In that survey we asked people to locate themselves and the two parties on the ideological (or policy) spectrum. The mean placement provided by respondents is depicted in Figure 1.2. In spite of the prevalence of the belief that "there is not a dime's worth of difference between the parties" or that "they are no more different than Tweedle Dee and Tweedle Dum," people typically attribute much more than a dime's worth of difference to the policy positions of the two parties. While the mean self-placement of respondents was just a little to the conservative side of the center (4.4 on a scale running from 1 to 7, with higher numbers indicating more conservative policy positions, lower numbers indicating more liberal positions, and 4.0 representing the midpoint), the common perception of the policies advocated by the Democratic party is that they are to the left of the people (3.6), while Republican policy positions are located to the right of the people (4.9).[13] The obvious question becomes, how can people see one party as being to their left on policy space and the other party as being to their right and still insist that there is no appreciable difference between the two parties? A total reliance on policy space renders it difficult to understand the situation.

Similar to the claim that the parties are identical, the notion that the government is out of touch has become a touchstone phrase for many Americans. Just a few months before conducting the national

---

[12] See Appendix A for information on the national survey.

[13] For a report of similar results produced by another survey, see Carman and Wlezien (1999). We found, using NES data, that the average placement of the two major parties on a seven-point ideology scale was 3.10 for the Democrats and 4.84 for the Republicans in the 1970s, 3.33 for the Democrats and 4.99 for the Republicans in the 1980s, and 3.28 for the Democrats and 5.02 for the Republicans in the 1990s.

survey, we convened eight focus group sessions at locations across the United States.[14] Several participants in these groups complained about an out-of-touch government. Consider the following comments from two different focus group participants: "[T]he vast majority of Congress's members have no idea really what the people's wishes are" and "I don't think [elected officials] have any idea about what anyone wants." Virtually identical sentiments were recorded in the focus groups done by the Kettering Foundation (see Mathews 1994: 11–48) and can also be heard frequently on most street corners and in most bars. If more systematic evidence is desired, nearly 70 percent of the respondents in our survey disagreed (some strongly) with the statement that the current political system does "a good job of representing the interests of all Americans." The feeling that the political system is unresponsive to the desires of the people is rampant.[15]

The curious thing is that people claim to be moderate in their policy affinities *and* they perceive governmental policies as being essentially moderate, too. To provide the complete picture, in Figure 1.3 we present not just the mean location (as was done in Fig. 1.2) but the entire distribution of people's policy self-placement (the solid line) and their perceived placement of federal government policies (the dotted line). The similarity of the two distributions is striking. Americans are clearly moderates, with 71 percent preferring policies of the middle (e.g., 3, 4, or 5). This is no surprise. More noteworthy is the fact that Americans are almost as likely to see governmental policies as centrist, with 70 percent placing government policies at 3, 4, or 5. The people's desired policies are only slightly more conservative (a mean of 4.4) than the policies they believe they are getting from the federal government (a mean of 4.0). A difference of only 0.4 on a seven-point scale separates preferences from perceived realities (for more on this point, see Monroe 1979).

Of course, these aggregate data may well mask important individual-level differences. As we argued earlier, some people care deeply about policies and pay attention to what the government does in a variety of policy areas. Similarly, some people are not policy moderates, and these ideologues may be inclined to view government policies as far removed from their own policy preferences. Liberals could

---

[14] See Appendix A for information on the focus groups.
[15] See also Wright (1976); Kettering Foundation (1991); Craig (1993); and Phillips (1995).

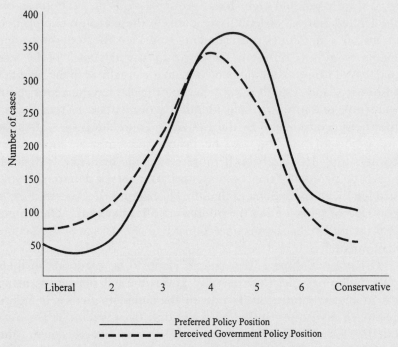

——————— Preferred Policy Position
— — — — — Perceived Government Policy Position

Figure 1.3. Policy space distribution of the people and their perception of actual governmental policies.

think government policies much too conservative, whereas conservatives could think government policies much too liberal. Moderates might also exhibit individual-level differences that are lost in our aggregate analysis. To test whether we have missed something, we divided people into three groups according to their self-placement on policy space: liberals (who placed themselves at 1 or 2), moderates (3, 4, or 5), and conservatives (6 or 7).

Table 1.1 shows the mean self-placement of liberals, moderates, and conservatives as well as their perceptions of government policies. Ideologues clearly see a much larger gap between their own preferred policies and the policies government produces (a gap of 2.75 for liberals and 2.97 for conservatives) than do moderates (a gap of only 0.01). While these results demonstrate that there are individual-level differences between some people's own self-placement and perceived government policy positions, there are two aspects of these results that deserve mention. First, and somewhat surprisingly, liberals, moderates, and conservatives alike perceive

Table 1.1. *Policy preferences and perceived government policies among liberals, moderates, and conservatives*

	Preferred policy position	Perceived government policy position	Difference	N
Liberals	1.46	4.21	2.75	98
Moderates	4.18	4.17	0.01	797
Conservatives	6.49	3.52	2.97	237

Source: Democratic Processes Survey, Gallup Organization, 1998.

government policies as moderate. Liberals and conservatives, who perceive a fairly large differences between their own policy positions and the government's, still place government policy positions well within the moderate range (4.21 for liberals and 3.52 for conservatives). Second, as mentioned above, the vast majority of Americans (over 70 percent) consider themselves moderate, and these moderates view government policies as right in sync with their own preferences (a minuscule difference of only 0.01). So, while liberals and conservatives believe government policies are too moderate given their own proclivities, they make up less than 30 percent of the population.[16] For the vast majority of Americans, government policies match their own preferences.

How, then, can the people be so convinced that the government is wildly out of touch with their interests, desires, and concerns? If the public's perception is that federal policies do not diverge much from the policies they desire, what are people thinking when they insist that the government is "out of touch"? Once again, policy positions on their own are unable satisfactorily to account for an important feature of the American political scene.

---

[16] Liberals and conservatives are not more likely, even given their perception that government policies are far removed from their own preferences, to believe government does not represent all Americans or to feel dissatisfied with government policies. Survey respondents were asked the extent to which they agreed or disagreed (on a four-point scale) with the following statements: "The current political system does a good job of representing the interests of all Americans, rich or poor, white or black, male or female" and "You are generally satisfied with the public policies the government has produced lately." Liberals, moderates, and conservatives gave similar responses to these two questions: means of 2.1, 2.2, and 2.2, respectively, for the representation question, and means of 2.6, 2.6, and 2.3, respectively, for the policy satisfaction question.

WHY IS POLICY SPACE ALONE INADEQUATE?

Perhaps those familiar with American politics will not be too surprised by the inadequacies of policy positions in explaining various political phenomena. After all, using policies to make judgments takes a substantial amount of work, and an impressive and growing corpus of literature points to the conclusion that individual Americans may not be up to the demands of the classical policy-driven democratic citizen. Delli Carpini and Keeter's (1996) investigation into what Americans know about politics concludes that "political knowledge levels are, in many instances, depressingly low" (269). These poorly informed citizens, in turn, "hold fewer, less stable, and less consistent opinions. They are more susceptible to political propaganda and less receptive to relevant new information" (265). Most pertinent to the current discussion, "they are less likely to connect . . . their policy views to evaluations of public officials and political parties in instrumentally rational ways . . . and . . . they are less likely to tie their actions effectively to the issue stands and political orientations they profess to hold" (265). Consequently, Delli Carpini and Keeter found that "for the substantial portion of citizens who are poorly informed . . . voting was poorly connected to their views on issues" (258).

The inability of people's issue stances to explain more of their attitudes and behavior is probably due to the fact that people's issue stances are often not so much stances as dances. Converse (1964) demonstrated long ago that issue positions change alarmingly over time. Zaller (1992) has elaborated on this theme more recently, presenting evidence that, rather than holding preformed attitudes on issues, people construct "opinion statements" on the fly as they confront each new issue, making use of whatever idea is at the top of their heads.

And, of course, there is always the danger that standard research techniques overstate the role of issues. Most of what we know about how issues affect people's political attitudes and behaviors comes from survey research. As John Brehm (1993) has carefully pointed out, survey nonresponse rates have been growing rapidly and are approaching 50 percent. Not surprisingly, those who answer political surveys are not identical to the 50 percent who do not. One major difference is that "refusals are less informed about politics than respondents" (62). Brehm also shows that nonrespondents are less interested in politics, so it does not take a particularly large inferential leap to conclude that survey respondents are probably more likely than typical Americans to care about policies. Brehm additionally recognizes that even his estimates of the discrepancies caused by nonresponse are probably conservative because his baseline (Current Population Studies) has some survey characteristics and therefore some nonresponse problems of its own. In short, traditional survey methodology overrepresents issue concern and still concludes that concern is anemic.

Further support for the malleability of people's policy positions comes from Sniderman, Hagendoorn, and Prior (2000). Continuing an interesting line of work that attempts to determine how easy it is to talk respondents out of their original answers, they conclude that "the portion of the public that can be induced to change their mind on major issues remains impressive" (6; see also Sniderman and Piazza 1993 and Gibson 1998). Even more disconcerting are their findings that "content free" counterarguments (such as "Considering the complications that can develop, do you want to change your mind?") are just as effective at inducing changes as real arguments and that opinion switching is more common if the interviewer paid the respondent an empty compliment before asking the respondent if he or she wanted to change answers. Sniderman et al. conclude quite sensibly that "a substantial fraction of the public is only weakly attached to the positions they take, or possibly not attached at all" (33).

More evidence of the sensitivity of stated opinions to contextual factors is found in a fascinating experiment conducted by Amy Gangl (2000). Details are provided below, but for now the relevant point is that her experimental subjects read about a policy dispute in Congress. Some subjects read an account that stressed divisiveness, while other subjects read an account of a more agreeable congressional exchange. In their posttest evaluations of Congress, the initial policy positions of the subjects were irrelevant to the reactions of those reading the agreeable account, but for those who read about a serious congressional fight, their initial policy preferences had a significant effect on how they evaluated Congress. Pointed conflict, in other words, made it more likely that people cared about the outcome. Gangl's research demonstrates the remarkable degree to which people's policy preferences can be ignited or doused merely by the manner in which issues are handled. If no conflict is present, people's initial policy preferences will lie dormant and may even atrophy. The presence of conflict, however, can heighten the role of initial policy preferences – if the issue is one for which people care enough to have a preference in the first place.

Though open to question, one interpretation of the modern American polity is that, compared with times past, there are now fewer issue disputes on matters about which the people really care. Remember, it is necessary only to go back to the 1950s to find a time in which the stated policy of one of the major parties (the Republicans) was to abolish the Social Security program. Today, neither party makes serious proposals to abolish Social Security, and the only arguments offered concern how the cost of living adjustment (COLA) should be calculated and whether participants should have the option of investing a small portion of their individual holdings in the stock market. These are not unimportant matters and some people have become exercised, at least about the latter, but in the larger scheme of things these disputes pale in comparison to whether or not a mandatory pension plan for the elderly should exist. When the political debate is reduced to the mechanics of COLA calculation, we should not be surprised that many citizens do not have an initial policy preference on many issues addressed in the halls of power.

This narrowing of debate and differences is found in many other issue areas and may, perversely, encourage politicians to be inappropriately strident and petty. Ex-Representative Fred Grandy, reflecting on the political implications of the 1997 bipartisan balanced budget agreement, stated that "coupled with the end of the Cold War . . . party defining issues are getting harder to find . . . it means going into local and personal issues" (quoted in "A Balanced-Budget Deal Won . . ." 1997: 1831). Russell Hardin (2000: 43–44) contends:

The former left-right antagonism has been reduced to a very short spread from those who prefer more generous welfare programs to those who prefer somewhat less generous programs, and the difference between the two positions represents a very small fraction of national income. Radical reorganization of the economy to achieve some degree of equality or fairness is now virtually off the agenda. . . . The odd result is that politics may be noisier and seemingly more intense and even bitter, but it is less important.

Of course, policy differences still exist. But the point is that many of these differences are sufficiently nuanced that a large share of the American public does not regard them as important. Maybe they should, but they do not. The constituency for major policy changes in the United States does not exist. Ask Ralph Nader and Patrick

Buchanan. When people claim to want political change, they are not typically speaking of policy change (as we demonstrate in Chapter 2). The result is that the policy positions of the two major parties frequently seem quite similar. Democratic President Bill Clinton passed a largely Republican version of welfare reform and Republican President George W. Bush's first policy package was a largely Democratic education plan (with a tepid and half-heartedly supported voucher component added for cover). Policy differences obviously remain on the scene, but our point is that the people believe that most of them concern only details and that, therefore, much political conflict is actually contrived.[17] As a result, they have difficulty seeing the point, let alone care about the outcome. People despise pointless political conflict and they believe pointless political conflict is rampant in American politics today.

But perhaps even as people dismiss the relevance, importance, and meaning of most governmental policies, they retain a general predisposition toward the liberal or the conservative side of the political spectrum. After all, such an inclination does not demand an awareness of details. Maybe so, but, attributing great meaning to overarching ideological positions is not without danger. People are not particularly comfortable with an ideological spectrum even though it tends to fascinate elite observers. The terms liberal and conservative, or even the terms left and right, are not deeply understood by most people.[18] These are phrases the public uses only with great prodding, and most do not understand them well even after prodding. Further, people are not good at placing politicians on a liberal-conservative scale and frequently do not tie together issue positions that elites expect to be tied together under the rubric of liberal or of conservative. People do not like to be labeled, and their lack of constraint across issues suggests their dislike is understandable and even well founded. People often think in neither policy nor ideological terms.

So, attempts to salvage issue voting (or even issue thinking) by moving from stances on individual issues to stances on collections of issue positions generally come to naught. Rather than wrestle with the intricacies of individual issues in a technologically complex society or rely on incomplete and inaccurate labels developed long

---

[17] For a critique of the view that the parties are becoming more similar in policy positions, see Gerring (1998).

[18] See Converse (1964); Levitin and Miller (1979); Conover and Feldman (1981).

ago to encapsulate collections of particular policy positions, most people look to something other than the issues in their effort to get a grip on the political scene. And it is nearly time for us to describe what that "something other" is.

CONCLUSION

Most Americans are not political elites, and, thus, policies and policy positions are not politically determinative. This can be seen in their voting behavior, as E. J. Dionne, Jr. (2000: 27), notes in his summation of the presidential elections of 2000: "The exit polls made abundantly clear that a large and critical portion of Bush's support came from voters who are closer to Gore on the issues." A startling number of Bush voters also viewed Gore as more competent to deal with the issues. And the lack of influence of policy matters certainly applies to approval of government itself. Many people who have no particular problem with the policies produced by the government are tremendously dissatisfied with that government.

Interpretations of American politics that rely exclusively on policy space are doomed to failure. A focus group participant named Linda complained that people who run for office "have to believe so strongly in one thing . . . they have to have something that drives them to run for office . . . so sometimes you get the wrong kind of people in government." This sentiment nicely illustrates the attitude toward policy positions of an important segment of the people. They believe, with Linda, that candidates and parties have their "own agenda" and thus must not be "doing it for service to the people." People like Linda neither conceive of politics in policy terms nor think politicians should. They believe candidates with strong issue positions are unlikely to be "the right kind of person." The notion of searching and voting for a candidate with the most desirable policy positions is quite foreign to this way of thinking about politics. People are often confused (and therefore frustrated) by the proposals emanating from the candidates running for office. At the extreme, they even conclude that people with strong policy convictions should not be in government. Policies certainly are not irrelevant to American politics, but people are less concerned with the substance of public policy than analysts seem to realize. When policy preferences do come into play, they are just as likely to be endogenous as exogenous.

If not policy, then what? We believe people are more affected by the *processes* of government than by the policies government enacts.

This is especially true of their attitudes toward government. Dissatisfaction usually stems from perceptions of how government goes about its business, not what the government does. Processes, we argue, are not merely means to policy ends but, instead, are often ends in themselves. Indeed, with most policies being of such casual importance to them, the people's sensitivity to process makes sense. In Part II we address the kinds of processes Americans want, but first we turn in Chapters 2 and 3 to evidence supporting our contention that process preferences in general are important shapers of American political attitudes and therefore of the American polity.

2

Process Space: An Introduction

While policy space has been instrumental in political observers' ability to visualize and to theorize about important issues in American
politics, it is unable to provide complete and adequate answers to
several basic questions. Why might this be? The implication of previous critiques (notably, Stokes 1963) has been that the logic behind
spatial thought is incorrect. If citizens act because of habit, psychological attachments, candidate image, or a vague sense of who might
better handle valence issues, then portraying politics in spatial terms
is unhelpful and misleading. Habits, psychological attachments, and
images cannot easily be placed on a spectrum running across a meaningful space. What would the poles of such a spectrum be labeled?
Analysts, according to this line of thought, would be better off projecting from respondents' previous attachments and behavior rather
than forcing people into some type of space.

Though policy space may not provide answers to many of the core
questions of American politics, throwing out spatial theory because
of the failings of *policy* space would be tantamount to throwing out
the baby with the bathwater. The problem is not spatial theory itself,
which, after all, is only a way of contrasting preferences and perceptions; the problem is the sole reliance on *policies*. If, as we argued in
Chapter 1, most Americans are not deeply concerned about policies,
the next step is to locate features of the political system about which
people *are* deeply concerned. Once this is done, the basic spatial
logic, which we still find appealing, can be employed.

PROCESS RATHER THAN POLICY?

It is our belief that Americans are attuned to the way government
works more than to what it produces, to the processes more than the

policies. This appears a foolish claim at first blush. After all, processes would seem to be complex and nearly incomprehensible to ordinary people who are much more likely to be concerned with results than process, with ends than means. Ask people whether they would rather have their preferred governmental policies regardless of how those policies are produced or their preferred processes regardless of the resultant policies and surely they would opt for desirable policies, right? Probably. But the more important point is that when we move this scenario from the realm of the abstract to the realm of the real world, process concerns become central and comprehensible to ordinary people. Academic observers are fond of asserting that process is complicated, and it is, but as we explain in Part II, people are concerned only with one basic feature of process and mostly ignore process details. Process is not complicated to the American people, and they believe they understand it.

For most of our careers, we never seriously questioned the supremacy of policy preferences. We assumed people were confused by governmental processes while retaining at least a few clear policy desires. But research we undertook in the early 1990s on the reasons for public dissatisfaction with Congress led us to challenge this particular bit of conventional wisdom (Hibbing and Theiss-Morse 1995). In focus groups conducted for that book we were taken aback by the tendency of ordinary people to focus on governmental processes rather than policies. It was, it turned out, the policies that they found to be complicated and the processes they thought to be simple. Who knew what to do about the big issues of that time – drug abuse, teenage violence, the deficit, international trade, and tragedies in Bosnia and Somalia? Government processes, on the other hand, they could understand – and they did not like them.

Consider the following sampling of comments generated by asking focus group participants in the early 1990s what they liked or disliked about government:

Roger: It seems the Democrats and Republicans are always fighting. I mean they want the same thing, I hope anyway. They should concentrate on the problems and work together to solve them.

Naomi: There are too many lobbyists in Washington and as far as I am concerned they should be outlawed because they are not representing the entire country.

Bill: I think maybe some of them [elected officials] might have good intentions, but when they get in there it's like a corrupt system. They have to start going alone against the whole works, you know. The system is corrupt.

Bob: I think there has to be major communication between the Democrats and Republicans and the Senate and the House, you know, everybody.

Molly: The vast majority of Congress's members have no idea really what the people's wishes are.

Steve: They [politicians] are in touch with the extremes. Those are the people they listen to... [because] the majority doesn't scream and shout.

What ties these responses together is the lack of any real policy content. People were eager to express their thoughts on political parties, interest groups, and elected officials but rarely did we hear sentiments suggesting that policies were too liberal or too conservative; that Social Security reform had been bungled; that military spending was not high enough; or that nationalized health insurance was needed. When policy matters did come up, the lack of specificity was notable.[1] People clearly believed that middle America was not getting its way and this bothered them. This constitutes a policy position of sorts, but it is quite different from the kind of policy beliefs necessary for meaningful placement of people in policy space. And the participants in our focus groups were not unique. Sociologist Nina Eliasoph (1998) observed and interviewed members of volunteer organizations. She concluded that when it came to specifics, her volunteers "did not have fixed preferences at all" (82) even though, as active members of groups, they should have been more attuned to policy than ordinary citizens.

Consistent with the comments of Steve (above), most people believe their views are in agreement with a majority of real Americans, but they have concluded that this consensus yields little influence because special interests and their cronies in the political parties and in government have commandeered the entire process (see also Fiorina 1996). Our sense is that people do not see the process as having been redirected to the left or the right (though, as Table 1.1 shows, there is the tendency for liberals to think policies

[1] When survey instruments ask people about policies, as they usually do, respondents feel obligated to give a position even when they may not have one. In this sense, while recognizing the liabilities of focus group research, we prefer the approach of merely asking people to discuss what they like and dislike about government and observing whether they mention policy factors.

are not liberal enough and conservatives to think policies are not conservative enough). In fact, they have little idea which special interests are left of center and which are right of center. The upshot of this mind-set is the deeply felt belief that the welfare of ordinary people is not government's prime concern. People have little idea what they would tell elected officials to do about policies if they had the opportunity, but that is not the point. They just want the system to understand and to care about them and not about special interests. They want a different process even if it is accompanied by no policy change at all.[2]

People usually do not know what would change, say, drug and education policies for the better, but they do know that special interests, entrenched political parties, and careerist politicians have a stranglehold on the political process.[3] This sentiment is straightforward and manageable. It requires no mastery of the nuances of parliamentary procedure. In fact, it requires remarkably little information at all, it does not pick sides, and the scapegoat (special interests) is vague enough that few people, save perhaps the occasional professional lobbyist, are likely to be offended. In fact, loathing special interests constitutes a unifying belief in modern America. It allows people to talk about politics without a shred of specific evidence and, like the weather, pulls people together against a common, seemingly uncontrollable, enemy.

The inclination of people to view politics in process rather than policy terms therefore makes perfect sense. Policy information takes effort for people to acquire, and, as we saw in Chapter 1, people do not view most policies on the government's agenda as particularly relevant. Popular media outlets provide only superficial issue coverage, preferring instead to turn every policy dispute into a crass contest for political advantage.[4] If they want to discuss an issue knowledgeably, people must make a concerted effort to locate quality information sources and learn the intricacies surrounding the issue. Few have the motivation and perhaps time to do so, especially since a simplistic process orientation allows them to lambast the government, probably to the approval of all those within hearing distance.

[2] Our sentiments here are in general accord with the important work of Margaret Levi (1997, 1998).

[3] Evidence and arguments compiled by Stephen Craig (1993, 1996) are supportive of this claim.

[4] See Fallows (1996); Capella and Jamieson (1997); and Kerbel (1999).

DELINEATING PROCESS SPACE

While recognizing that the remarks of focus group participants are only suggestive, we were intrigued enough about the potential importance of process attitudes to construct a more systematic research design bearing on the topic. We intended that this research would help us to learn more about the importance and nature of people's process attitudes. In the course of conceiving and designing this project, we naturally looked to previous research for guidance. We were surprised to discover that there is little research on how the people want their democratic processes to work. Philosophers, since the birth of democracy in Athens 2,500 years ago, have been voicing their opinions on the proper workings of government. On this central matter we know the views of these philosophers, but we do not know much about the views of the common people. Investigators have not been eager to solicit ordinary Americans' preferences for governmental processes, opting instead to quiz survey respondents on which candidates, parties, and policies they prefer. Granted, extant survey research helps us to know the people's views of selected reform proposals. Respondents are occasionally asked their opinion on whether the current government is honest, trustworthy, competent, and "on the right track." People have revealed their level of approval for specific governmental institutions and for democracy in general, but never have they been asked in detail their beliefs about how they want government to work, to go about its business, to be structured. It is one thing for citizens to be allowed to gripe vaguely about current processes; it is quite another to ask them to specify a preferred process toward which they want the government to move. It became our goal to determine the people's preferred governmental processes.

Our first pass was intentionally coarse. We asked our 1,266 survey respondents to place themselves on what we call process space. Just as the concepts "liberal" and "conservative" can serve as poles in policy space, poles in process space are needed to anchor the spectrum. On one end of the process spectrum we placed direct democrats – individuals who believe the best process is one that permits the people themselves to make decisions, unperturbed by effete political institutions and elected officials. This could be accomplished by adopting the type of government exemplified by an old-style New England town meeting or by mass popular decisions rendered through some kind of initiative process or by the use of coaxial cables and electronic democracy. Other options include people's courts, now up and active in about forty states, or selective groups cobbled together via one of a wide range of procedures usually employing random sampling (see Dahl 1989; Fishkin 1991). Despite the important differences of these approaches, they all are based on the notion that traditional representative institutions must be replaced or at least supplemented by arrangements in which public opinion translates more directly into public policy. The belief is that only through such a process will the nobility of the common person be able to shape public policy to the benefit of the policy (Rousseau 1946 (1762)), the person (Mill 1975 (1861)), and the legitimacy of the system (Wahlke 1971). Institutions and elected officials can only get in the way of the general will. The answer, then? Direct democracy.

The other pole represents the belief that policy decisions should be made by officials who have been elected to political institutions and not by the people themselves. Edmund Burke's (1949 (1774)) description of the elected official as a trustee fits this pole well. Advocates of such a position hope that the officials serving in governmental institutions would exercise their own discretion as they formulate and enact public policy. These "institutional democrats" do not mind at all if elected representatives aggregate, rearticulate, and reshape public opinion before it becomes law. Burke believed that "the mature judgment, the enlightened conscience" of elected officials should not be sacrificed to public opinion. An institutional democrat agrees with Burke (1949 (1774): 115) that "government and legislation are matters of reason and judgment, and not of inclination; and what sort of reason is that in which the determination precedes the discussion, in which one set of men deliberates and another decides, and where those who form the conclusion are perhaps three hundred miles distant from those who hear the arguments?"

According to this logic, institutions should be active in transforming the public's sketchy, ill-formed, and factually malnourished ideas into coherent public policy. If in the process these institutions become highly professionalized, with a complex array of rules, committees, staffers, and infrastructures, so be it. If political parties and interest groups become specialized and multifaceted in order to keep pace with the formal governmental institutions, so be it. If within the formal institutions themselves, lengthy debate, elaborate reports, and painful compromises between opposing interests are necessary to arrive at some sort of solution, however little this solution might resemble the public's initial preferences, so be it. We need unashamedly transformative institutions, according to institutional democrats. People should have influence in determining the composition of the membership of institutions (else the government would not be democratic), but once that membership has been established, officials in the institutions should be free to do what they think is best.

Between these extremes, of course, resides a variety of options. Just as we recognized a range of positions on the policy spectrum, so can we recognize a range of positions in process space. Most people support a mix of institutional and popular influence on policy outcomes, and, of course, between the two poles is where most people are located. Since few are likely to hold the pristine Hamiltonian position that public policy should be made with total disregard for public opinion, just as few people are likely to hold the contrary view that all institutions of representative government should be removed to let raw public opinion reign unencumbered. Individuals between the two poles recognize the need for governmental institutions but want these institutions to exercise a lighter touch than would be desired by an extreme institutional democrat. This notion of porous institutions is nicely captured by Burke's instructed delegate model of representative government. This model requires the existence of elected officials (unlike the "direct democrat" model) but holds that these officials should be extremely sensitive to the wishes of ordinary people (unlike the "institutional democrat" pole).

Process space so conceived is anything but new. Suksi (1993: 18) goes so far as to give his opinion of where various political theorists would fit on a somewhat similar spectrum, with Hobbes closest to the institutional democrat pole (Suksi calls this pole "the state") and Rousseau closest to the direct democrat pole (he calls this pole "the people"). If the American founders had been included, presumably Hamilton would be keeping company with Hobbes just as Jefferson would be with Rousseau. And the location of elected officials on process space has been recorded as well. In their classic book, *The Legislative System*, John Walhke and his colleagues surveyed state legislators in four states about whether they acted as delegates (doing whatever constituents want them to do) or trustees (doing what they as representatives think best regardless of the views of constituents). Not surprisingly, only a scattering of representatives said they attempted to fill the delegate role. The vast majority went with a role closer to the "institutional democrat" end of the spectrum (Wahlke et al. 1962; see also Rosenthal 1998: 9).

But what is of primary interest, particularly in a system such as that of the United States, is the process preferences not of theorists and not of elected officials but of ordinary people who are able to alter processes. Surprisingly, this information has never been collected in any systematic fashion. So we return to the question: What kind of government do people claim to want? One in which they call the shots directly? One in which elected officials are free to do what they want? Or something in between? Failure of previous research to get a read on people's answers to these questions is especially mystifying in light of the importance of process matters to the people.

To fill this gap, we asked our survey respondents to place themselves on the spectrum described above. The specific question was:

Some people say what we need in this country is for ordinary people like you and me to decide for ourselves what needs to be done and how. Others say ordinary people should instead allow elected officials to make all political decisions. Still others say a combination would be best. Imagine a 7-point scale with "1" being ordinary people making all decisions on their own and "7" being elected officials making all the decisions on their own, while "2," "3," "4," "5," or "6" indicate opinions in-between the two extremes. Which number from 1 to 7 best represents how you think government should work?

Just as a person's overall position on policy space is an amalgam of positions on a variety of policy issues, so a person's overall position on process space is likely to be a similar composite of individual process issues. Instead of issues such as welfare, crime, and the environment, the specific issues for process space are whether decisions should be made by the federal government or by state and local governments, whether members of Congress should be delegates or trustees, and whether key policy decisions should be made directly by the people through initiatives and referenda. We get to people's preferences on these more specific items in subsequent chapters, but for now we concentrate on where people place themselves in global process space. In addition, parallel to questions posed about the policy spectrum (see Chapter 1), we also asked respondents to provide their perceptions of the location on the process spectrum of the current functioning of American government and of the processes desired by the Democratic and Republican parties.

PROCESS EXPECTATIONS

What do we expect to find when we ask Americans about how they want their government to work? It seems obvious that many people believe current processes are too heavily influenced by institutions and elected officials. At the same time, it is our sense that few Americans actually want direct democracy even though public discourse often gives the impression that people want as much political power, and as many populist reforms, as they can get.[5]

In the focus group sessions conducted in late 1997, we found that people were anything but wild-eyed direct democrats. In fact, when we suggested the possibility of ordinary people making key political decisions on their own, the idea was invariably met with a cold shoulder (specific remarks are presented in Chapter 4). Although clearly desirous of weakening elected officials and political institutions, few people responded enthusiastically when presented with the stark reality of going all the way to a process in which they would make political decisions on their own. People may be dissatisfied with the dominance of institutions and elected officials in the political process, but this does not mean they have a desire for ordinary people to take over the process. In fact, our sense was that the last thing people want is to have to assume more responsibility in the political arena. As a result of their desire to weaken the power of institutions but not strengthen the power of ordinary people, we predict that people's location in process space typically will be firmly between the poles of direct and institutional democracy.

In many respects the more interesting expectations involve not the processes people prefer but the location of their own desires relative to the processes they see being championed by the two political parties as well as the processes people believe to be on display in government itself. With regard to the processes people perceive the two political parties to be advocating, we believe the pattern in process space will be quite different from that found in policy space (Fig. 1.2). Recall that in policy space, people were in the center and saw one party to the left of them and one party to the right. To be specific, 64 percent of all respondents believed their own policy preferences were bracketed by those of the political parties, with the result

---

[5] See Magleby (1984); Cronin (1989); Morone (1990); Citrin (1996); Brinkley (1997a, b); Polsby (1997); Schedler (1997); and Bowler, Donovan, and Tolbert (1998).

being that in policy space the people perceived the two parties to be fairly distinct from each other.

But we expect that *process* space will be able to solve the puzzle of why so many Americans complain about the similarities of the major parties. While they may see the parties as fairly distinct in the policies they advocate, we believe people see the parties as similar in the processes they favor. After all, people see both parties intimately involved in the campaign finance mess. They believe both run nasty, negative campaigns, make promises they have no intention of keeping, and are heavily invested in special interests and the cocktail-party circuit. In short, people believe both parties are at the heart of the overly institutional democracy currently afflicting the country. Accordingly, we predict people will place the parties close together on process space and well to the right (that is, toward institutional democracy) of the people's preferred processes.

Perhaps even more important, we believe the public's perception is that actual governmental processes (as opposed to those favored by each of the parties) are also well toward the right side of process space. Most Americans, we predict, believe that governmental processes are inappropriately dominated by elected officials and, therefore, by the institutions these officials inhabit. In light of pervasive public comments along these lines, we are not going out on much of a limb in this prediction. Still, if we are correct about where people place actual governmental processes, relative to their own preferences, process space will be in a position to solve another of the puzzles of American politics described in Chapter 1: Why people think the government is out of touch even though government is seen as providing policies closely approximating those that people desire. But for this explanation to fit, the data would need to indicate that people's process preferences and their perceptions of the processes government actually provides are markedly different, a situation that clearly did not apply in policy space (see Fig. 1.3).

THE DISTANCE BETWEEN PROCESS DESIRES AND PROCESS REALITY

Figure 2.1 presents the mean self-placement of our 1,266 respondents on the seven-point process space spectrum. As predicted, people tend to prefer a process virtually equidistant from pure direct democracy and pure institutional democracy. In fact, the people could hardly be more middle-of-the-road, averaging 4.01 on the 1 to

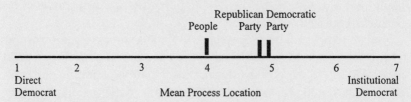

Figure 2.1. Process space location of the people and their perceptions of the parties.

7 scale with 4.00 representing the exact midpoint. Despite all the rhetoric about public desires to empower the people, the figure reveals no compelling tendency of people to hug the direct democrat pole. They want a balance of influence between elected officials and ordinary people with neither dominating the other.

But Figure 2.1 also contains people's mean perceptions of the styles of government favored by each of the two major political parties, and it is at this point that the results become more revealing. As expected, people see very little difference between the process positions of the two parties. People place the Democratic party at 4.94 and the Republican party at 4.85, a difference of only 0.09. Contrast this with the perceived difference between the parties in policy space (1.30). People perceive the Republicans and Democrats as supporting different policies but the same processes. Thus, we think it likely that when people complain about the similarities of the parties they are not thinking of the *policies* of the parties but rather of the *processes* promoted by the parties. People see both parties steeped in an aloof and isolated process, motivated only by inside-the-Beltway minutia, money, and malarkey and not by the valid concerns of real people. If eyes never stray from policy space, it is difficult to understand how the perception that the parties are identical could take root, but once process space is introduced, the situation makes perfect sense.

When attention turns to perceptions of how the *government* actually works rather than the parties' preferred processes, the results are equally supportive of our predictions. Figure 2.2 is essentially the companion to Figure 1.3, only this time the key variable is process and not policy. As in Figure 1.3, we present the full distribution (not just the location of the mean) for people's preferences (the solid line) and also for their perceptions of government (the dotted line).

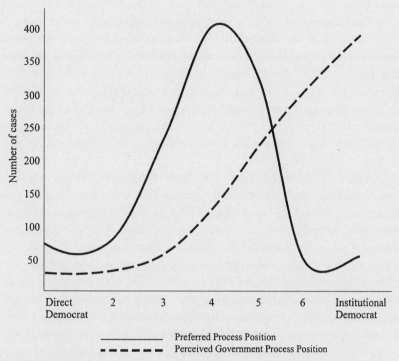

Figure 2.2. Process space distribution of the people and their perceptions of actual governmental processes.

The full distribution allows us to underscore the point made earlier about the desire of Americans for a balanced process. Of the 1,253 usable responses, 975 (78 percent) register a preference of 3, 4, or 5 on the 1 to 7 scale. Only 119 brave souls want elected officials to have largely unfettered decision-making authority once elected (that is, locate their preferences at 6 or 7). More surprising perhaps, only a few more (170) want ordinary people to be in charge (that is, state a preference for 1 or 2). People would seem to be anything but the unadulterated democrats political elites often paint them to be. They do not want institutions to go away, but they do not want these institutions to be unchecked. They embrace direct, popular rule no more than detached, distant institutions.

But the more important question is, regardless of their personal preferences, where do people place current governmental processes? Who do they think has the power? The answer is contained in the dotted line of Figure 2.2. In Figure 1.3 we discovered that people both desired and felt they were receiving centrist policies. But Figure 2.2 shows that, although they also desire centrist processes, they definitely do not believe they are getting them. Instead, many people are convinced current government processes are badly out of whack – and out of whack in a specific direction. Better than 55 percent believe current processes to be dominated by elected officials and institutions (in other words, give current processes a 6 or 7 in process space), while only 5 percent believe people exercise a great deal of influence (in other words, give current processes a 1 or 2).

A comparison of the solid and dotted lines in Figure 2.2 supports the conclusion that many people believe they are not getting the governmental processes they want. These results invite the interpretation that people's beliefs about an out-of-touch government (see Chapter 1) have little to do with policies and much to do with processes. The allegedly unresponsive elements of the government center around the way decisions are made and not the specific content of those decisions. Moreover, the results also suggest that process may trump policy since governmental policies generally match public preferences and governmental processes generally do not, yet the people's summary judgment is that government is out of touch.

DISTINGUISHING PROCESS SPACE

People seem to attach great importance to the processes of government, and when they are asked to do so, people can locate themselves (and other political entities) in process space. Moreover, they deal with process space in ways that square with reasonable expectations and in ways that provide solutions to existing puzzles surrounding American politics. Still, many observers undoubtedly will remain skeptical.

Some might be inclined to claim that process space is nothing more than another component of policy space. People have positions on welfare policy, crime policy, environmental policy, foreign policy, and what might be called "process" policy. What, after all, is so different about taking a position on military aid to Kosovo and on whether legislators should have their terms limited? Preferences still exist, positions are still discerned (or not), and efforts to convert preferences to reality still occur. If this logic were convincing, process positions could be swallowed up by the larger concept of policy space and processes would be just a certain kind of policy. Perhaps, as a leading scholar once suggested to us, "a preference is a preference" (Krehbiel 1997, personal communication).

Some critics may be inclined to go even further, by maintaining that process preferences are merely by-products of policy satisfaction or dissatisfaction. If people like the outcome, they like the process; if people do not like the outcome, they project their dissatisfaction onto the process that produced it. This, at least, is the claim of McGraw, Willey, and Anderson (1999). Reacting to earlier work of ours claiming the importance of process, they write that it is "premature" to accord "causal antecedent status to procedural perceptions" (6). Interestingly, however, recent work by Mark Hetherington (1999) provides evidence that it is policy positions and not process preferences that are endogenous. He finds that policy stands are often the product of people's perceptions of the capabilities of governmental processes. As such, Hetherington's findings constitute, in many respects, a complete reversal of the more traditional notion that policy positions are best seen as supreme and exogenous (for supportive findings, see Chanley, Rudolph, and Rahn 2001).

Be this as it may, the process skeptics raise important concerns, and, given historical biases in favor of policy matters, it is incumbent upon us to provide additional evidence of the relevance and usefulness of Americans' process preferences. In the course of doing so, we also suggest why process space is so different from policy space; for example, we explain why it seems to defy the rules of policy space so carefully delineated by Downs. And we provide additional evidence of the ability of process space to help us make sense of American politics.

The Relationship of Process and Policy Spaces

Process attitudes behave as they should in survey results and are frequently volunteered in focus group sessions. People have strongly held preferences and perceptions about process, and satisfaction with process has effects on people's attitudes independent of policy outcomes (see Chapter 3). But this does not mean process attitudes are necessarily unrelated to policy attitudes. In fact, the possibility that a certain set of process preferences correlates with a certain set of policy preferences is intriguing and deserving of additional attention. In which direction should a correlation between policy and process be expected to run? It is not immediately clear, for example, that the desire for decisions to be made by institutions and elected officials is necessarily connected to a particular policy ideology. If it is, how is it? It often seems as though most of the recent agitation for reducing the influence of governmental institutions is coming from the conservative side of the policy spectrum. Movements for legislative term limits have drawn most of their support from political conservatives. The same can be said of pressure for more initiatives and referenda. A clear populist sentiment imbues the words of well-known conservatives such as Pat Buchanan and Rush Limbaugh.

But left-wing populists are common, too. In fact, a century ago the populist movement was dominated by what we would now call liberals. Government, these populists believed, had been captured by powerful business interests and the only way to solve real problems was to give the government back to the people. "Congress was accused of being more responsive to corporate lobbyists, foreign as well as domestic, than to ordinary citizens" (Kazin 1995: 270; see also Morone 1990: 107). Civil service reform, trust busting, primaries, initiatives, public review of court decisions, recalls, referenda, and the direct election of U.S. senators were all favorite themes of this group (Morone 1990: 112).

Even today, conservatives have not cornered the market on the desire to empower people at the expense of governmental institutions. Pat Buchanan may rail about the need to attack the governmental institutions that pay more attention to the United Nations and international trade agreements than to the needs of patriotic, working-class Americans, but liberals such as Molly Ivins (1992, 1998) and Jim Hightower (1997) do, too. The enemy for them is no more likely to be the corporate downsizer than "the federal bureaucrat, overeducated and amoral, [who] scoffs at the God-fearing nuclear family, in its modest home, a crucifix on the wall and a flagpole in the yard" (Kazin 1995: 1).

Moreover, many conservatives are aghast at the prospect of giving ordinary people more say in key political decisions. George Will, for example, embraces a totally different kind of conservatism than Buchanan and Limbaugh. In his book *Restoration* he admiringly quotes Edmund Burke's warning to his own constituents of Bristol that he would not be going to Parliament to serve "local interests" and to reflect "local prejudices" (1992: 101). Will castigates the many members of the modern U.S. Congress (even holding up fellow conservative Newt Gingrich as an exemplar of the problem) for slavishly attempting to meet with all constituents, calculate their interests, and unfailingly act on those interests. He sees this as a complete misunderstanding of the proper role of a representative. Will believes far too many modern representatives are "hyperresponsive and oversolicitous" (114) and he is eager to secure for government more "constitutional space . . . more social distance" (231). In short, the last thing Will wants is for the people to be given additional influence in the political process. George Will and Pat Buchanan may share several individual positions in policy space and can both be reasonably placed to the right of center on the overarching policy space continuum, but their differences in process space are so dramatic that they do not deserve to be lumped together under an identical rubric. Rather, they deserve to occupy unique locations in a more developed spatial presentation.

A parallel argument applies on the left side of the policy spectrum. As has already been noted, Molly Ivins is an unabashed champion of the "little" person. She does not trust government to protect working people, seeing Congress, agencies, even the courts as mere puppets whose strings are being pulled by big business – out to make a buck at the expense of real America. She fumes with equanimity against big business and big government. Elected officials, particularly members of Congress, are favorite targets of hers. Ivins (1998: 6b) refers to Congress as "bought and paid for by corporate special interests." The clear message of her writings is that elected officials and institutions should not be as influential as they are. Contrast Ivins's views with those of another policy liberal: Ted Kennedy. For decades, he unsettled the business community by using his position in the U.S. Senate to push for a higher minimum wage, government-controlled health care, and consumer protection. As such, instead of despairing that government can only make problems worse, Kennedy's instinct is to look to governmental institutions, not the people themselves, for ways of improving the situation. His career in office has been based on the idea that the institutions of government can be used to do good, to help provide people with protections and opportunities they would otherwise not be accorded. Though both are policy liberals who wish to assist ordinary people, Ivins is more likely to see political institutions and officials as a source of the problem, and Kennedy is more likely to see them as a potential solution. Similar in policy views, they are so very different in their process views.

Thus, conflating policy and process preferences to a single spectrum is bound to be misleading. We prefer to use the two dimensions

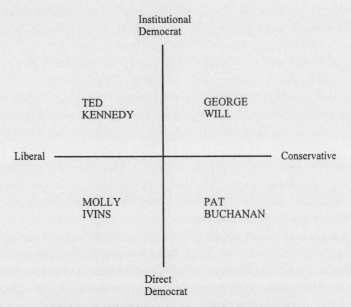

Figure 2.3. Combining policy and process space.

to create four quadrants, which we do in Figure 2.3. The horizontal axis of this figure represents policy space, from left to right. The vertical axis represents process space, with the direct democrat pole positioned on the bottom and the institutional democrat pole occupying the top. To help give the figure some grounding, we have labeled each of the four quadrants with the public figures we have used to illustrate the four different beliefs.

Policy liberals can be process "populists" (we use this term loosely to refer to those who want to give the people more power) or process "institutionists" (for want of a better term). The same is true of policy conservatives. Knowing a person's position on policy space may not be of much help in predicting that person's position on process space. There would seem to be no sound theoretical reasons for expecting a strong correlation. Do policy conservatives or policy liberals tend to be process populists? If conservatives are more likely to be populists, the correlation should be negative (given the way we have coded the variables). If liberals tend to be populists (remember, our survey was done in 1998) a positive correlation should be observed.

As it turns out, Rush Limbaugh notwithstanding, liberal policy beliefs are slightly more likely than conservative policy beliefs to go

Table 2.1. *The relationship between policy preferences and process preferences*

	Policy liberals (%)	Policy moderates (%)	Policy conservatives (%)
Institutional democrats	30	31	40
Process moderates	32	41	30
Direct democrats	38	29	30
Total	100	101	100

Source: Democratic Processes Survey, Gallup Organization, 1998.

along with populist attitudes. The actual correlation is a positive 0.09, perhaps indicating a continuation of liberals' post-Vietnam disillusionment with government (see Nie, Verba, and Petrocik 1976: 125–8). In any event, the George Will version of what might be called classical conservatism is more prevalent than Pat Buchanan's "power to the people" conservatism. And Molly Ivins's "everybody is out to get the common person" approach to liberalism receives more support than Ted Kennedy's strategy of getting the government to help the downtrodden.

Table 2.1, which presents the column percentages of a crosstabulation table, makes it possible to see the mix of procedural preferences held by policy conservatives (self-placement at 5, 6, or 7 on the ideological scale), policy moderates (self-placement at the midpoint of 4), and policy liberals (self-placement at 1, 2, or 3). The process categories are institutional democrat (self-placement at 5, 6, or 7 on the process scale), process moderate (self-placement at the midpoint of 4), and direct democrat (self-placement at 1, 2, or 3). The conclusion is, of course, identical to that generated by the positive correlation coefficient mentioned earlier: Policy conservatives prefer the institutional democrat portion of the process spectrum, whereas policy liberals prefer the direct democrat portion of the spectrum.

Still, the real news is not the positive relationship between policy liberalism and process populism but the weakness of that relationship. The explanatory power of policy space on process space (or vice versa) is less than 1 percent ($0.09 \times 0.09 = 0.0081$). In light of these findings and the questionable theoretical basis for expecting a relationship in the first place, it is virtually impossible to claim that process space is merely a part of some larger policy construct. What people want government to do and how people want government to do it are, more often than not, simply two different things. If anything, it might make sense to expect that those who want government to do little would prefer weak institutions, but we now know there is no empirical support for this expectation. To the extent there is any relationship at all, it runs the opposite direction.

Process Space Has Different Laws Than Policy Space

Even though the relationship between policy positions and process positions is anemic, it may still be possible to handle process space in the same general fashion as policy space, to expect the same overall forces to operate. In other words, whether orthogonal to or highly correlated with policy preferences, we could still treat process preferences in the same way as policy preferences. We could array parties and voters and make predictions about the consequences of varying distances between preferences and perceptions. The problem with such an approach is that there are fundamental differences between the laws governing policy space and those governing process space.

In presenting process space in the same general format as policy space, we have no doubt conveyed the impression that they work the same in a Newtonian sense. If so, we must disabuse readers of this notion. Process space does not conform to the fundamental principles set forth by Downs for policy space. The difference is evident in Figure 2.2, where we discovered that in process space people perceive both the Democratic and Republican parties to be far to the right of the people's own preferences. According to simple spatial logic, so ably articulated by Downs, the parties should go where the voters are. If the name of the game for parties is to minimize the distance between their perceived position and the position desired by the largest group of people, what is keeping both parties from embracing the processes people want? Skillful efforts may be successful at explaining why the parties do not completely converge on *policy* space (see Aldrich 1983; Rapaport, Abramowitz, and McGlennon 1986), but nothing in Downs anticipates a situation in which the parties will be both far from median preferences *and* on the same side of those preferences. The parties should quickly leapfrog each other toward the more populist positions desired by the people. The apparent inability of process space to engage in this self-equilibration constitutes a dramatic departure from the workings of traditional spatial theory.

What could possibly explain this completely un-Downsian outcome?[6] Why do we not see the parties doing more to adopt the processes the people want? The answer to this question is complex. First, parties may not be convinced their position on process space is particularly relevant to what they want; that is, to win elections. On one level, this possibility is obviously untrue. Politicians know the danger of giving the impression that something other than the people's desires might be considered in their decision. Edmund Burke may be the last elected official who told his constituents that he intended to make decisions for them without soliciting their every whim (and that was in the early 1780s!). It should be noted that Burke was not representing those constituents after the next election due in part to their displeasure with his cavalier attitude toward their desires, primarily on the Catholic and Irish questions that were so salient at the time. Politicians today fall all over themselves letting the people know their philosophy of governing is to do whatever the people want, even if under the cover of anonymity they readily admit they are predominantly trustees rather than delegates (Wahlke et al. 1962). They know political hay can be made by expressing enthusiasm for anything the people desire. The parties know this, too.

On another level, though, the parties may not fully understand that process concerns are as vital to the people as they are. Political elites are policy wonks – they like thinking about, learning about, and working with policies. Political scientists have certainly held to a policy-oriented view of the political world, and politicians and party officials may hold that same policy-dominated orientation. It is likely, therefore, that the major parties and elected officials think first and foremost about policy stands when they strategize about how to win an election. Process concerns do not readily come to mind to political elites who are steeped in policy.

A second possibility is that the parties are philosophically convinced that elected officials and institutions should have more influence than ordinary people and that, since the parties have principles, they refuse to give the people what they seem to want on this matter. In other words, the parties know they could reap rewards by adopting a populist line, but they believe populist reforms would harm government and they are willing to take their electoral losses for the

---

[6] Our thanks to Steve Ansolabehere for pushing us on this question.

sake of the system. While elected officials are probably more likely than ordinary people to be institutional democrats (although we have no data to know this for sure), are they likely to risk losing elections to hold to a principled institutional democrat stand? We are not as cynical as many people about the motivation of political parties and elected officials, but we still find this explanation to be patently absurd. Recent history suggests the parties are willing to do quite a lot to win elections. The notion that scruples keep parties from reaping the electoral rewards of shifting process positions is difficult to defend.

A third explanation is much more believable than the first two and helps to delineate the basic distinguishing feature of process and policy space: The parties do not move on process space because they cannot move. Actually, they *can* move but it is difficult. Shifting positions on process space is much more challenging for parties and candidates than shifting positions on policy space. Why? For starters, many aspects of process have been written into constitutions. In fact, the lion's share of most constitutions is devoted to a specification of process and structure, not policy. Questions such as who is eligible for office, how office holders will be elected or selected, what rules will govern their decision making once they are chosen, and so on are usually answered in constitutions. Efforts to specify policy in constitutions often lead to trouble. Consider the U.S. Constitution. Its clearest statements on policy have been subsequently reversed: permitting slavery, forbidding an income tax, and prohibiting the manufacture, sale, and transport of alcoholic beverages come quickly to mind. It makes much more sense for a constitution to set up the processes by which policies are made and to leave the making of policy in the hands of that process – and that is what constitutions tend to do.[7] But this means that, since it is difficult to change constitutions, it is difficult to change process. Supermajorities are often required, and frequently consecutive supermajorities.

The movement to limit the terms of legislators is a perfect illustration of the difficulty of altering process. The Supreme Court ruled unconstitutional state laws limiting terms of federal lawmakers (even though the idea was favored by a consistent 70 percent of the

---

[7] It is interesting to note that many state constitutions in the United States specify policies as well as processes. Changing policies in these states then becomes more difficult.

American population). Efforts to get around this court ruling by permitting candidates at the specified term limit to run but only as write-in candidates were similarly thrown out by the courts. And efforts to get around *that* court ruling by allowing representatives to be on the ballot but with a "scarlet phrase" indicating that they did not abide by the voters' wishes with regard to term limits were, predictably, thrown out by the courts. While some states have been successful in limiting the terms of state legislators, it appears that the only option now available to advocates of federal term limits is to amend the Constitution. The lack of movement on this front is testimony to the difficulty of amending the Constitution; in other words, to the difficulty of changing process.

Of course, not all process is covered in the Constitution and some changes are possible. The houses of Congress can change their own internal rules, and important changes have, on occasion, been undertaken (e.g., the many changes made by the new Republican majority in the House of Representatives in early 1995). But the fact remains that process is supposed to have some stability. After all, process is really another way of saying institutions – and institutional structure is by definition sticky.[8] It is hard to conceive of a policy-making institution changing as rapidly as the policy itself. Such a transitory creature could hardly be called an institution.

Astute observers could readily point out that the parties and their members can make changes in process, even given the obstacles, if they truly want the changes. This brings us to the final, and most important, reason the parties and their members do not grab the electoral and other advantages that would undoubtedly accompany a full-fledged, "let's help the people be heard" platform: The people *perceive* them to be unwilling to pursue this platform. To put it differently, process space is fundamentally different from policy space because people believe elected officials have a vested interest in process space, an interest that only elected officials share. Most members of Congress are wealthier than average Americans and therefore would personally benefit from, say, tax cuts and investment incentives, but they are not the only ones who benefit. And many policy decisions do not directly benefit elected officials (such as welfare policy), save for the potential political advantage gained by supporting or opposing the policy. Contrast this with process

---

[8] See Baumgartner and Jones (1993) and the many works associated with so-called new institutionalism.

decisions. Rightly or wrongly, the public believes politicians have it made. They believe politicians singularly benefit from current processes, which allow them to be pampered and to enjoy a cushy lifestyle at the expense of the taxpayers. The public does not believe politicians would be serious about giving up the authority that allows them to perpetuate that lifestyle.

Thus, the people believe welfare reform, tax reform, or even reform of the health care system may be possibilities (depending on the activity of special interests), but they see no likelihood of serious reduction in the congressional pension plan, staff support, congressional salaries, or the intimate contacts of elected officials with special interests. As an ordinary citizen named Norman Lynch put it, "I will happily give up my [Social Security benefits] as soon as Congress gives up its million-dollar retirement fund and goes on Social Security like the rest of us, drops its health and medical insurance and goes on Medicare, and stops fleecing America of billions" (*Houston Chronicle*, 1998: 25A). In the eyes of the people, changes in the process will not occur, since elected officials have the power to stop anything that would jeopardize their pampered positions. So the public believes politicians' cozy relationship with special interests, their junkets, and their perquisites (the core of people's frustrations with the process) will remain ad infinitum. The public's suspicions on these points are not entirely misplaced. The amount of posturing in Congress on term limits probably exceeded that occurring on the typical policy issue by a factor of ten. It was an opportunity to voice support for a wildly popular concept, knowing the chances of it seeing the light of day were slim to none.

Immediately upon assuming office, elected officials become the beneficiaries of the process and, in the public's eyes, quickly lose any desire to change the process in a fashion pleasing to the public. Elected officials may represent the people's views in policy space, but in process space the people are resolved to the fact that it is going to be "us against them."[9] Parties and their candidates could fill their platforms and campaigns with promises to work toward empowering the people by way of a national initiative, term limits, and a more democratic structure for the courts and the bureaucracy. The

[9] Thus, it is perfectly reasonable for people to believe the system is producing generally satisfactory outcomes but to be bitterly dissatisfied with the system and the elected officials in it, perhaps due to such factors as the perceived influence of special interests and, relatedly, the motivation of decision makers, which leads to divisive politics. More on these points below in this book and in Fiorina (1999).

problem is that people would not believe the promise makers were serious about enacting changes that would go against their own self-interest.

Downs's discussion of policy space assumes the ability of parties and candidates to move on the spectrum. To be sure, he recognizes limitations on this movement, but a key part of the policy space concept is the ability of political actors to shift positions. Such shifts could occur on military spending, on abortion policy, or on the entire package of policy positions. What makes process space something other than just another type of policy – just another concept that can be modeled the same way as policies – is the fact that people view the parties' existing process positions as highly immovable. And in terms of understanding public attitudes and behavior, actual party positions are nothing; perceived positions are everything.

The public yearns for changes in the processes employed in the modern American polity. Yet the prevailing explanation for what moves actors in the political system (offered by Downsian spatial models) will not do when it comes to understanding process. Rather, we must accept the differences between policy space and process space and set to work detailing the consequences that flow from a public that, more often than not, wants to change process more than policy. If we are correct, the public's emphasis on process and desire for procedural alterations will unavoidably lead to frustration and disapproval since the public is convinced that the people best positioned to change the process are those who already benefit from it. Dissatisfaction based on policy unhappiness will come and go; dissatisfaction based on process unhappiness is much more likely to stay.[10]

[10] For these reasons, we also fear that the rationalizing feature of the movement from individual to aggregate policy positions (described so effectively by Page and Shapiro 1992) may not apply to process issues. Page and Shapiro discarded all process questions in their analysis, so we can only speculate, and we will. While their evidence shows that aggregate policy opinion tends to respond in rational ways to disturbances (e.g., increased support for regulation after an environmental disaster), aggregate process opinion does not have this same desirable attribute. Durr, Gilmour, and Wolbrecht (1997), for example, discover that support for Congress in the aggregate responds perversely to the procedures on display. The more Congress is in the news and the more it is checking executive power, the less people approve of it. On process issues it seems the public's reaction to new information, even at the aggregate level, is anything but rational. Importantly, though, it becomes rational if the public wants to minimize political conflict, and this is exactly the possibility we broach in Part II.

CONCLUSION

Process space is *not* a mere derivative of policy space. In fact, distinguishing process preferences helps us to categorize people and positions in the modern polity. It in no way duplicates distinctions introduced by policy space. Moreover, it cannot accurately be thought of as just another issue on which distinctions can be made. Process is unlike any policy issue largely because the public, with some justification, perceives there to be so little movement, and so little motivation for officials and parties to move, on it. Given its importance and independence from policy positions, the potential exists for process attitudes to lead, among other things, to serious dissatisfaction with the political system, to nonparticipation in the system, to a desire for reform, and to noncompliance with the outputs of the system. Whether or not these consequences of process dissatisfaction actually materialize under suitable controls is the topic of the next chapter. If they do, this would be still further evidence of the value of studying the process attitudes of the American public.

3

Using Process Space to Explain Features of American Politics

To this point, we have argued that process concerns are distinct from policy concerns, and we have shown that making the distinction between the two allows us to understand aspects of American politics in a way that policy space alone does not. We have not yet shown, however, that process preferences and perceptions have a significant impact on people's political attitudes and behaviors. That is precisely what we hope to accomplish in this chapter. We concentrate on four possible consequences. The central and most obvious is the likelihood that, regardless of the policies being produced, people who are convinced that governmental procedures do not match their own preferred procedures are more likely to be unhappy with the government. The other three can be seen as spinning off dissatisfaction with government. Specifically, dissatisfaction with process could lead people to advocate various approaches to reforming governmental processes, to vote for candidates who make procedural reform a major part of the campaign, and even to be less likely to comply with the outputs of the ostensibly flawed process.[1]

Were we living in an unchangeable, autocratic police state, these potential consequences would not be important, but the United States is a democracy in which the people have a voice and in which a significant level of voluntary compliance with the law is necessary. If people are denying the system its needed support, are being seduced by unworkable reforms, or are ignoring statutes because they question the legitimacy of the procedures used to make them, the polity is weakened and the government will be less able to perform necessary tasks.

[1] For more on these consequences, see, for example, Tyler (1990); Nye and Zelikow (1997: 277); Orren (1997: 79); Scholz and Lubell (1998).

Of course, dissatisfaction with policies could lead to these same, potentially serious, consequences, and we think it likely does. But past research has not taken seriously enough the distinction between process and policy. In Chapters 1 and 2, we made such a distinction and now we use it to determine the *separate* influence of process and policy dissatisfaction on these four important dependent variables. By including unique terms for process and for policy dissatisfaction, we will be in a position to determine whether and when process is important.

This emphasis on process is at odds with the prevailing view in the discipline. As previously mentioned, political scientists have long been interested in the impact of policy concerns on people's political behaviors and on public policy outputs. Political scientists have held up issue voting (people selecting a candidate on the basis of relative proximity to the voter on the issues) as the centerpiece of classic representative democracy, and as such they have given policy or issue positions an inordinate amount of attention. But we take issue with those who believe the only reason to study public opinion is its influence on public policy.[2] Public opinion does not always pertain to policies and can lead to dissatisfaction with government and to a variety of other related and crucial behaviors including noncompliance with laws. It is important to know what people think should be done on the issue of abortion, for example, but it is also important to know whether they have confidence in the institutions making abortion policy and to know their preferences for how abortion policy should be made. Much public opinion is not directed toward policies themselves.

POLICY OUTCOMES AND OUTPUTS

But if we are to be at all convincing that people care about political means as well as ends, we must be careful to control for their satisfaction with policy ends. Two main categories of policy satisfaction

[2]This view is most prevalent among rational choice scholars but is also common elsewhere in the discipline. For example, consider the following passage: "Why should we care about [public opinion]? In a representative democracy there is some prospect – no sure thing – that public opinion matters for the formation of public policy. Take that away and the study of public opinion becomes as interesting as cataloguing buttons. Representation, that is, is the justification for the study of public opinion, the only one that matters" (Stimson 1995: 180). Psychologists have been far more accepting than political scientists of the argument that process matters.

exist. The first deals with outcomes, the actual conditions of society that are sometimes thought to be at least partially the result of governmental policies. Included are such factors as the status of the United States abroad or, most commonly, the state of the economy. The second way of conceptualizing satisfaction with policies involves determining the policies a person wants and then the policies that same person believes the government is providing. The larger the gap between the two, the greater that person's policy dissatisfaction.

Scholars often contend that dissatisfaction with government is largely a reflection of whether the economy is prospering, peace is at hand, and other aspects of life seem to be satisfactory. This is called the policy-*outcome*-based view. Decades ago, Robert Lane (1965: 877) suggested a relationship between economic conditions and overall trust in government. In a similar vein, Luttbeg and Gant (1995: 214) believe that "nothing short of an unprecedented era of national economic prosperity seems likely to cause a dramatic upturn in public confidence," but since many "social, economic, and technical" problems "defy easy solution . . . a major rebound in political trust [is unlikely]." Nye (1997: 8), in his discussion of why trust in government tends to be so low, explains that "people may be properly unhappy with poor social outcomes." Scholars have also used policy outcomes to explain why particular groups are more or less likely to be satisfied with government and to give institutional support.[3] Clearly, the processes of government are not the main issue in such a view, since the idea is that people would put up with virtually *any* government structure if it would help them obtain the favorable conditions they desire. Popkin (1991: 99), drawing on Fiorina (1981) and others, most directly makes this point when he says that people "judge government by the results and are generally ignorant of or indifferent about the methods by which the results are achieved." If Popkin is right, it is results that matter, not how the results are reached.

But the empirical evidence does not usually support this model, leaving open the possibility that process really does matter. At the

[3] Regarding government dissatisfaction among groups, see Dawson (1973: 102) on skilled workers, Wilson (1975: 126–9) on middle-income citizens, and Miller (1974) on African-Americans. On variations in institutional support, see Mueller (1973) and Kernell (1978) on presidential popularity; Davidson, Kovenock, and O'Leary (1968), Patterson and Caldeira (1990), and Durr, Gilmour, and Wolbrecht (1997) on congressional approval; and Caldeira (1986) and Caldeira and Gibson (1992) on approval of the Supreme Court.

aggregate level, confidence in government dropped most dramatically in the late 1960s (see Lipset and Schneider 1987) when the economy was doing quite well and shortly after Lane (1965: 877) declared that the new "age of affluence" would lead to "a rapprochement between men and their government and a decline of political alienation." Lawrence (1997: 111–13) correctly observes that "it is by no means clear that economic performance has actually played a decisive role in generating this decline in trust. . . . [T]he major rise in dissatisfaction with government actually predates the period of slow productivity growth, increasing inequality, globalization, and technological change." Moreover, the end of the unpopular war in Vietnam did *not* result in an increase in trust. And victory in the Cold War and the incredibly strong economy from late 1992 to mid-1997 brought some of the worst marks for dissatisfaction with government since the beginning of systematic public opinion data. As Seelye (1998: A15) notes with surprise, "most Americans still deeply distrust the Federal Government despite the end of the cold war, the robust economy and the highest level of satisfaction in their own lives in 30 years." And in late 2001, attitudes toward government improved markedly just as the economy was going into recession and the country was in a state of war. Analysis at the individual level is equally ambiguous, as research finds no or only a modest relationship between policy outcomes and institutional approval.[4] While outcomes (conditions) are clearly relevant to public attitudes toward government, they leave much unexplained.

Rather than focus on the perceived condition of the nation, the policy-*output*-based view is concerned with the match between the policy desires of citizens and the perceived policy decisions of the government. If, for example, an ideologically conservative individual believes the government is producing ideologically liberal policies (regardless of the overall condition of the country), he or she will likely be more dissatisfied with government than an otherwise identical ideological liberal. As was the case with the outcome-based view, the output-based view does not expect people to be particularly concerned with the process itself, but only with the policies that emerge from that process.

The gap between policy preferences and the perceived policy offerings of various parties, institutions, and governments has been a workhorse variable of political research. Scholars have argued that

[4] See Caldeira (1986: 1219); Patterson and Caldeira (1990); and Mueller (1973).

it influences the policy choices of institutions and parties as well as individual citizens' party identification, vote choice, modes of political participation, desire for divided government, and general support of the government.[5] In their famous exchange on the meaning of public mistrust, for example, Citrin (1974) and Miller (1974) disagree on many things, but Citrin makes it clear that he "accepts Miller's main conclusion that policy-related discontent is a source of political cynicism" (974). But, as was the case with policy outcomes, policy outputs have limited explanatory power. The support for this statement was provided in Chapter 1, where we found weak relationships between policy output satisfaction and most variables except for vote choice, which had a stronger relationship. And even for vote choice, indications are that a substantial portion of the correlation is due to people projecting favorable policy positions onto candidates they already prefer. Thus the door is left wide open for process to play a role. We agree with March and Olsen's (1984: 742) assessment of the situation: The discipline's "theoretical presumption [is] that the main point of a decision-making process is a decision. For many purposes, that presumption may be misleading. The processes of politics may be more central than their outcomes."

THE CONSEQUENCES OF PROCESS FRUSTRATIONS

The core question of this chapter can be posed directly. Once satisfaction with policy outcomes and policy outputs is controlled, does the gap between people's desired and perceived processes cause them to disapprove of their government, to want to reform their government, to vote for nontraditional candidates, and even to believe they need not comply with the laws passed by their government? Before describing our tests of these hypotheses, we should make clear we do not anticipate process dissatisfaction will affect either political participation or vote choice between the two major parties. Such effects may be present, but the justification for expecting them is not as clear as for the four hypotheses we test. Process dissatisfaction could make people more likely to get involved in politics (in the hopes of bringing about change) but could also make them less likely

[5] On these various effects of the policy gap, see Downs (1957); Muller (1972); Sears and Maconahay (1973); Citrin (1974); Miller (1974); Enelow and Hinich (1984); Rabinowitz and Macdonald (1989); Fiorina (1996); and D. King (1997).

to get involved (if they see the process as so flawed that there is no point). With regard to choosing a Democrat or a Republican, Figure 2.1 suggests that many people do not see a great deal of difference in the process dispositions of the two parties. Where are the process disaffected to go then? Since most voters identify process problems with both major parties (and presumably with most of those parties' candidates), it is difficult for voters to use process perceptions to discriminate between Democrats and Republicans.

While we do not believe procedural perceptions are a primary source of voting behavior in most elections, there are times when their potential power is evident. We would suggest, for example, that the major reason for H. Ross Perot's strong showing in 1992 and, to a lesser extent, in 1996 was his position in process space. Perot's policy positions, after all, were something of a mish-mash (prochoice, anti–free trade, entitlement hawk) and many voters had concerns about his personality. But his process claims (pry government out of the hands of elites, get under the hood and just fix it, electronic town meetings, kick all the incumbents out) were very popular. The Republican surge in 1994 is also partially traceable to public dissatisfaction with the way the Democratic majority in Congress was conducting business – a theme skillfully exploited by then Republican Leader Newt Gingrich (see Hibbing and Tiritilli 2000).

To sum up our expectations, imagine an individual who believes special interests are dominating the political process to such an extent that they prevent elected officials from being able and willing to understand the plight of ordinary Americans. This is not by any stretch of the imagination the kind of political process the person wants. The person is upset, but what kind of specific repercussions can we legitimately expect as a result? Are the person's process frustrations likely to increase or decrease political participation? We are not sure. It may depend on the intensity of the frustration. Is the person more likely to vote for a Republican rather than a Democrat or perhaps a challenger rather than an incumbent? Probably not. Most people judge both parties equally culpable in terms of cozying up to special interests and ignoring common people. And winning challengers, the people believe, all too quickly begin acting like the incumbents they defeated. But we believe this person's process frustrations will enhance tendencies to think less of the government itself, to vote for a nontraditional, process-oriented candidate like H. Ross Perot, to support various methods of reforming the process, and to be less willing to comply with laws that are produced by the flawed process. It is to these four hypotheses we now turn, beginning with disapproval of government.

EXPLAINING DISAPPROVAL OF GOVERNMENT

We first test the hypothesis that, other things being equal, people who see the government operating the way they want it to operate will be more likely to approve of government than will those who see the governmental process as flawed. The U.S. government is multi-faceted, however, and not all parts are likely to bear the brunt of process dissatisfaction. We expect process frustrations to be most strongly related to broad assessments of the government, such as the federal government as a whole or the overall political system, and to approval of the branch of government whose processes are highly visible to the public, namely, Congress (see Hibbing and Theiss-Morse 1995). Process frustrations seem less likely to be significantly related to attitudes toward individual actors within the political system, especially actors for whom people have a substantial amount of additional information. We therefore do not think process concerns will significantly explain presidential approval. And it is also unlikely that people will equate process frustrations with parts of the government that keep their procedures hidden from the public eye and that people believe are not in cahoots with special interests. The Supreme Court does its work behind closed doors and away from blatant lobbying. People are therefore unlikely to draw much on their process frustrations when assessing the Supreme Court.

To test these hypotheses properly, we need to control other likely causes of approval. Fortunately, a battery of demographic and political variables has become standard and is incorporated here (see Appendix A for a description of the variables used in these analyses).[6] In addition to these traditional explanatory variables, we include perceptions of policy outcomes, policy outputs, and governmental processes. Respondents' satisfaction with policy outcomes is measured by standard questions on whether their own financial situation and that of the nation had improved, stayed the same, or

---

[6] See Finifter (1970); Citrin (1974); Miller (1974); Wright (1976); Hibbing and Theiss-Morse (1995); and A. King (1997).

declined during the previous year. While these questions do not
cover everything having to do with outcome satisfaction, they
measure a central element of overall conditions: perceptions of the
economy. To measure the extent to which respondents believe they
are receiving preferred policies, we compute the absolute value of
the gap between policy preferences and perceived policy realities
using the overarching ideology scale. The gap could range from 6,
representing a person claiming to be extremely liberal but who sees
federal policies as being extremely conservative (or vice versa), to 0,
representing a person who believes government policy outputs perfectly match his or her preferences. We constructed a parallel process
gap measure using the process space continuum, thus providing
an indication of the extent to which each person sees preferred
processes and actual processes as being the same (0) or different
(up to 6).

When approval of the various parts of government is regressed on
the independent variables described above, we anticipate the following results. Expectations for the effects of demographic controls,
such as age, gender, income, and race, on governmental approval
are not readily apparent. Those who are elderly, female, uneducated,
poor, or nonwhite could be the most upset with existing power structures and, therefore, with the government. On the other hand, these
are the very people who are most in need of governmental assistance
or protection of some sort and, therefore, could be the most approving of government. Previous research, perhaps because of these conflicting expectations, has produced decidedly mixed results, and we
predict generally weak and insignificant effects for these five demographic variables.

Moving from demographic to political variables, hypotheses
become somewhat clearer. We might expect those with more political knowledge and external political efficacy to be more approving
of the various parts of government than their less knowledgeable and
efficacious counterparts. An understanding of the political process
should lead people to be more sympathetic to government, just as a
sense that one person can make a difference should also lead to
more sympathy. Previous research, however, while detecting that the
inefficacious are more disapproving of government, has somewhat
surprisingly found little hard evidence to support the contention that
politically knowledgeable respondents are more likely to approve of
government. Occasionally, knowledge even inspires a greater dislike
of government. It seems that knowledge leads people to hold high

expectations and to be critical when government fails to live up to those expectations.[7]

Identification with a political party likely affects approval depending on the part of government under consideration. Approval of the federal government will probably be higher for Democrats than for Republicans and Independents, since Democrats have traditionally been more progovernment than Republicans. Approval of specific parts of the government may depend, however, on which party controls Congress or the presidency at the time. Since the survey was administered in 1998, we expect Republicans to be most approving of the then-Republican-controlled Congress and Democrats to be most approving of the sitting president at the time, Bill Clinton. We expect identification with a major party to be unrelated to approval of the Supreme Court. The Court is often viewed as above politics and therefore it is unlikely to garner more support from partisans than nonpartisans.

But the key variables in our theory involve policies and processes. Those people who are generally pleased with outcomes (an improving financial situation) should, of course, be more approving of government, as should those pleased with governmental policies (that is, those believing their own overall policy preferences are reflected in recent governmental actions). But, as stated above, since we maintain that people are often motivated not just by policies but also by their perceptions of how these policies were made, we hypothesize that even after controlling policy satisfaction, the more people believe their process preferences are embodied in the actual workings of government, the more they will approve of the overall political system, the federal government, and Congress. Thus, we anticipate a negative sign for both the policy gap and the process gap variables (the greater the distance between preferences and perceptions, the lower the approval of the government).

We see from Table 3.1 that, as expected, the demographic variables are not particularly useful in specifying the kind of person likely to be dissatisfied with the various parts of the government. Male and female, black and white, rich and poor – all are roughly similar in their attitudes toward government. The demographic variables related to approval of government are sex (women were more approving of President Bill Clinton), education (the better educated were less approving of President Clinton and more approving of the

[7] See Hibbing and Theiss-Morse (1995) and Kimball and Patterson (1997).

Table 3.1. *Explaining public approval of the political system, the federal government, and the institutions of government*

Variable	Political system	Federal government	Congress	President	Supreme Court
Age	−0.02	−0.02	−0.05	−0.10*	−0.10**
Income	−0.01	−0.02	−0.01	−0.003	−0.01
Race	0.02	0.02	−0.03	0.04	−0.02
Gender	−0.01	0.002	0.01	0.04*	−0.02
Education	0.03	0.01	0.02	−0.09**	0.06*
Efficacy	0.09**	0.08**	0.09**	0.02	0.07**
Political knowledge	0.03	0.03	−0.06*	0.02	0.03
Democrat	0.07**	0.06**	0.06**	0.15**	0.04**
Republican	0.05**	0.00	0.05**	−0.12**	0.01
Personal financial condition	0.04	0.04*	0.02	0.07*	0.02
Country's financial condition	0.06**	0.09**	0.04*	0.14**	0.03
Perceived policy gap	−0.14**	−0.16**	−0.11**	−0.18**	−0.06*
Perceived process gap	−0.07*	−0.10**	−0.08**	−0.06	−0.07*
Constant	0.43**	0.44**	0.50**	0.48**	0.55**
F	12.60**	16.81**	8.59**	27.94**	5.87**
Adj. R^2	0.15	0.20	0.10	0.29	0.07
N	846	848	846	852	832

Note: *$p < 0.05$; **$p < 0.01$.
Source: Democratic Processes Survey, Gallup Organization, 1998.

Supreme Court), and age (the elderly were less approving of President Clinton and of the Supreme Court). More substantial effects begin to appear with the political variables. Those who feel politically efficacious are more likely to approve of the various parts of the government (excluding the president). The politically knowledgeable are less approving of Congress. And as expected, major party identifiers are more likely than Independents to approve of the political system and to use their partisan leanings to evaluate President Bill Clinton. Unsurprisingly, Republicans are more approving than Independents of the Republican-controlled Congress, but so are Democrats. In fact, Democrats stand out in their approval of all aspects of government, even the theoretically nonpartisan Supreme Court.

Still, the real questions of interest pertain to the policy and process variables. With all the control variables entered, are those who are pleased with policy more likely to approve of government than those who are displeased? Yes. One of the policy outcome variables – sociotropic financial conditions – is related to approval of all parts of government except the Supreme Court, whereas the other – personal financial condition – is related only to presidential approval and approval of the federal government. The sociotropic formulation is clearly the more powerful, as previous research leads us to expect (see Kinder and Kiewiet 1979). Moving to the policy output hypothesis, the policy gap variable has the expected negative sign and is highly significant. This indicates that the farther people perceive governmental policies to be from their own preferences, the less satisfied they are with all parts of government. So, both the policy outcome and policy output hypotheses work as expected.

But is this the end of the story? Do people only care about policies or do they also want these policies to be produced in a fashion they find acceptable? If people are concerned only with policy, the coefficients for the process gap variable should be small and insignificant. But if, as we expect, people want both acceptable policies and an acceptable process, the coefficient for the process gap should be negative and significant when considering the overall political system, the federal government, and Congress. Table 3.1 offers a clear verdict. Process matters. Even with all the other controls included, particularly those for policy outcomes and policy outputs, a close match between a person's process preferences and the perceived workings of government increases approval of government. Process concerns even matter when people evaluate the Supreme Court. As anticipated, process is unrelated to presidential approval, the only aspect of government for which it is not significant. Apparently, people's approval of government is driven by more than just policy concerns. It is also driven by perceptions of the extent to which processes match what people desire processes to be.[8]

[8]To offer a better feel for the magnitude of "process" effects on approval, we collapsed the federal government dependent variable (column 2 in Table 3.1) to approve or disapprove and employed probit to estimate the change in the probability that a person would approve of the federal government owing to shifts in the process gap (with all other independent variables held constant at the mean). Compared with someone maximally distant from perceived governmental processes, an individual believing governmental processes to be exactly the desired mix of institutional and popular input is predicted to be 0.11 more likely to approve of the federal government ($p = 0.63$ rather than 0.52). Interestingly, although in Table 3.1 we see that the OLS coefficient for policy gap is larger than the process coefficient, when probit is employed with the collapsed dependent variable, altering the policy gap in the same fashion would predict a change in probability of only 0.09 – less than was

EXPLAINING PEOPLE'S REACTIONS
TO ROSS PEROT

We mentioned above that we did not expect people's process frustrations to be related to their approval of individual actors within government. It is highly unlikely that people typically base their vote choice or their party choice on process concerns, since they believe both major parties are part of an evil process (see Chapter 2). Process positions cannot distinguish between Democratic and Republican candidates or between the two parties. On the other hand, support for third parties and their candidates could well be based on process frustrations *if* the third-party candidates make process pleas to the public. This is precisely what H. Ross Perot did in both the 1992 and 1996 presidential elections. While Perot took issue stands in his bid for the presidency – such as balancing the budget, limiting immigration, and keeping the United States out of the North American Free Trade Association – he also portrayed himself as the candidate who would shake things up and stop "business as usual" in the nation's capital. Perot emphasized government efficiency and came out very strongly against the nefarious influence of special interests. People liked that Perot was not a conventional politician (61.5 percent in a 1992 Harris poll) and that he would "bring about a needed overhaul in *the way things are done* in Washington" (58 percent in a 1992 Harris poll; emphasis added). Many pundits argued that Perot's support came from angry Americans who were disgusted with politics as usual (see, e.g., Germond and Witcover 1994).[9]

We begin by analyzing people's approval of Perot's ideas and then consider whether they voted for him. We asked people, "Regardless of what you thought of Ross Perot as a person, did you strongly

the case with process. In other words, with the collapsed dependent variable, the process gap is more important than the policy gap. On the whole, however, the probit results are remarkably similar to those generated by OLS. The signs are always the same and those that meet traditional significance levels in one always do so in the other (full results available from the authors).

[9] Whether Perot's support was based on policy or process concerns remains an open question. Alvarez and Nagler (1995) find that the economy was the primary determinant of vote choice in 1992, not people's anger toward the processes of government. "Voters were angry, but they were angry about the state of the economy – not the state of the government" (Alvarez and Nagler 1995: 738). But they measure anger toward government using support for term limits, which is a very indirect way to get at process frustration, and they concede that "Perot's appeal seemed to have little systematic component" (739).

Table 3.2. *Explaining public approval of Ross Perot's message*

Variable	b	s.e.	p
Age	−0.09	0.04	0.05
Income	0.04	0.04	0.26
Race	−0.07	0.02	<0.01
Gender	−0.04	0.02	0.02
Education	0.02	0.03	0.65
Efficacy	−0.03	0.02	0.24
Political knowledge	−0.03	0.04	0.37
Democrat	−0.04	0.02	0.05
Republican	0.03	0.02	0.18
Personal financial condition	−0.003	0.03	0.90
Country's financial condition	0.01	0.03	0.67
Perceived policy gap	−0.06	0.04	0.11
Perceived process gap	0.13	0.04	<0.01
Constant	0.62	0.04	<0.01
F	4.62		<0.01
Adj. R^2	0.05		
N	815		

Note: The question respondents were asked was "Regardless what you thought of Ross Perot as a person, did you strongly approve approve, disapprove or strongly disapprove of what Ross Perot had to say when he ran for president?"
Source: Democratic Processes Survey, Gallup Organization, 1998.

approve, approve, disapprove, or strongly disapprove of what Ross Perot had to say when he ran for president?" In 1998, fully 68 percent of respondents said they either approved or strongly approved of Perot's message, leaving only 32 percent claiming they disapproved or strongly disapproved. People liked what Ross Perot had to say. But did they approve of his message because of his policy stands or because of his process stands? We ran an OLS regression with approval of Perot's message as the dependent variable and the standard independent variables included in Table 3.1. Table 3.2 shows that people did not resonate with Ross Perot because of policy concerns. None of the policy outcome or policy output variables is

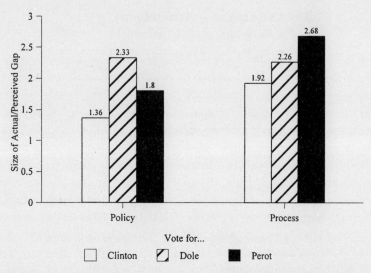

Figure 3.1. Policy and process effects on 1996 presidential vote choice.

significant. The strongest variable in the equation is process gap. In other words, the more people saw government processes as being far removed from their own desired processes, the more they approved of Ross Perot's message. Younger people, whites, and males were also more approving of his message, whereas Democrats were less approving.

But were they willing to vote for him? Was process frustration related to vote choice in the 1996 presidential election? Figure 3.1 shows that the more frustrated people were with government processes (not policies), the more likely they were to cast a vote for Ross Perot. People who perceived a larger *policy* gap between actual policies and those they wanted were more likely to vote for Robert Dole (the candidate of the nonincumbent major party). Just as we expected, Perot voters were process-frustrated, not policy-frustrated. Process concerns can matter in elections, but we contend that they matter most when candidates are nontraditional and make process relevant in campaigns, which Ross Perot did in both 1992 and 1996. Given Americans' substantial level of process dissatisfaction and modest level of policy dissatisfaction, third parties' best chance is a process-, not policy-, based campaign. It is not a coincidence that Perot stressed process and received 19 percent of the vote, whereas eight years later Nader stressed policy and received 2.5 percent.

EXPLAINING THE DESIRE TO
REFORM GOVERNMENT

If the impact of people's process concerns were limited to approval of government or to the relatively rare third-party candidate who focuses on process, the importance of those concerns could be questioned. But we believe there is reason to expect process attitudes and perceptions to influence other spheres as well. For example, locations in process space could reasonably be expected to influence support for reforming government – an area with the potential to be anything but benign. People who believe governmental processes are far removed from desired processes are likely to be more enthusiastic about changing those processes than would those who believe government policies are dissimilar to their desired policies. This is almost tautological.

To what extent do Americans support reforming the political system? A great deal, according to our data. We asked people whether they strongly approved, approved, disapproved, or strongly disapproved of five reforms: banning political parties, forming a new political party, devolving power from the federal government to the states, increasing the number of ballot initiatives, and limiting campaign spending. Figure 3.2 shows the percentage of people who approved or strongly approved of each of these proposed reforms. Banning

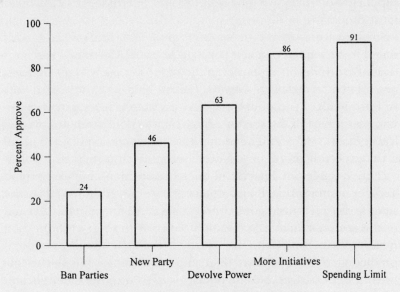

Figure 3.2. Support for specific reforms.

political parties had the least support of the five reforms, garnering only 24 percent approval. The most approved reform was campaign finance reform (91 percent), followed closely by increased use of ballot initiatives (86 percent), while forming a new political party (46 percent) and devolving power to the states (63 percent) received lesser but substantial support. The desire to reform the political system is not limited to a few fringe elements in the United States. Many people would like to see things done differently.

The next question is whether this support for reforms is primarily due to frustration with policy or frustration with process. To test the impact of process and policy concerns on support for reforms, we conducted a regression analysis with the same independent variables as those listed in Table 3.1. The dependent variables in this case, though, are approval of the various reforms. We expect the gap in process space to be strongly and positively related to support for reforms, even with other forces controlled. Table 3.3 shows that our expectations are borne out by the data.

Looking first at the demographic and political control variables, a clear pattern does not emerge as to who is most supportive of reforms. The less efficacious tend to be more supportive of some reforms – banning political parties, campaign finance limits, and more ballot initiatives – but not of others – forming a new political party or devolving power to the states. And whereas younger people tend to be more supportive of forming a new political party, it is older people who are most supportive of devolving power to the states. Partisans are naturally more averse than Independents to the idea that political parties ought to be banned or a new party started, and Republicans are more supportive of devolving power to the states, but party identification is not related to campaign finance reform or to the increased use of ballot initiatives (no doubt the lack of variance in these dependent variables is part of the reason). All in all, the demographic and political control variables do not demonstrate that certain types of people are consistently more supportive of reforms.

The variables of interest, though, concern policy and process. Table 3.3 shows that policy outcomes are generally *not* related to support for reforms. People who are dissatisfied with their personal or the nation's financial condition tend not to support more of the reforms than those who are satisfied. Policy outputs do better at predicting reform support than policy outcomes, but the gap between policy desires and the policies passed by government is not a significant predictor of support for campaign finance reform or increasing the use of ballot initiatives.

Table 3.3. *Explaining public support for reforming the political system*

Variable	Ban political parties	Campaign financing limits	More ballot initiatives	New political party	Devolve power to states
Age	−0.02	0.01	−0.04	−0.12**	0.16**
Income	0.01	0.08**	−0.01	−0.06	0.10**
Race	0.06**	−0.01	0.02	0.01	0.005
Gender	0.01	0.03*	−0.003	0.001	−0.02
Education	−0.10**	0.10**	0.02	−0.02	0.01
Efficacy	−0.05**	−0.05**	−0.07**	−0.03	0.02
Political knowledge	−0.05	0.07*	−0.05	−0.03	0.01
Democrat	−0.03*	−0.01	0.00	−0.05**	−0.01
Republican	−0.05**	−0.02	0.01	−0.05*	0.06**
Personal financial condition	−0.02	0.003	0.01	−0.02	−0.07**
Country's financial condition	0.02	−0.02	0.01	−0.01	−0.03
Perceived policy gap	0.05*	0.01	0.01	0.10**	0.09**
Perceived process gap	0.12**	0.04	0.17**	0.10**	0.15**
Constant	0.44**	0.60**	0.64**	0.59**	0.42**
F	9.08**	5.29**	7.14**	6.66**	9.73**
Adj. R^2	0.11	0.06	0.09	0.08	0.12
N	848	850	853	838	843

Source: Democratic Processes Survey, Gallup Organization, 1998.

The variable with the greatest impact on support for reforms is the gap between process desires and perceptions of current government practices. It may not be particularly surprising that when people perceive the government to be out of step with their process preferences, they are more likely to want the system reformed, but it is still an important consequence of process frustration. And it applies for all the reforms we raised with respondents except campaign finance reform. People who are frustrated with current processes want to see the system changed in virtually any way possible. According to many of those who are frustrated with processes, any change is better than the status quo.

EXPLAINING COMPLIANCE WITH THE LAW

Finally and perhaps most important, we examine the extent to which the process gap, along with the other independent variables in the

Table 3.4. *Explaining compliance with the law*

Variable	b	s.e.	p
Age	0.06	0.02	0.01
Income	0.04	0.02	0.06
Race	−0.01	0.01	0.32
Gender	0.06	0.01	<0.01
Education	0.03	0.02	0.15
Efficacy	0.01	0.01	0.28
Political knowledge	0.07	0.02	<0.01
Democrat	0.01	0.01	0.31
Republican	0.02	0.01	0.23
Personal financial condition	0.02	0.02	0.25
Country's financial condition	−0.02	0.01	0.30
Perceived policy gap	−0.02	0.02	0.25
Perceived process gap	−0.06	0.02	<0.01
Constant	0.48	0.02	<0.01
F	9.20		<0.01
Adj. R^2	0.11		
N	828		

Note: $^*p < 0.05$; $^{**}p < 0.01$.
Source: Democratic Processes Survey, Gallup Organization, 1998.

model, is able to account for variations in the willingness of people to comply with the law. In many respects, civil society is built on popular compliance with legislation produced by legitimate institutions. If people perceive the procedures followed by these institutions to be deficient, however, they may be less predisposed to comply (see Tyler 1990). To test this notion, we utilized a survey item that asked respondents whether "people should obey the law even if it goes against what they think is right." The response options were strongly agree, agree, disagree, and strongly disagree. Over a quarter of all respondents disagreed or strongly disagreed with the statement. Did they tend to be the process-frustrated?

When compliance is regressed on the same battery of independent variables used in this chapter, the results indicate that the noncompliant tend to be young, male, and less politically knowledgeable (see Table 3.4). Most important, they also are those who see current governmental procedures as being different from what they want

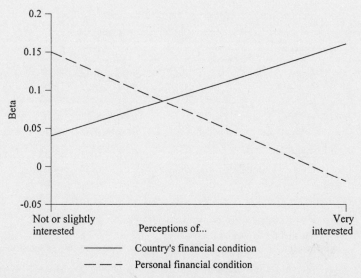

Figure 3.3. Effect of financial perceptions on approval of federal government by political interest.

those procedures to be. On the other hand, those who believe governmental policies are not what they want them to be are *not* consistently more likely to display cavalier attitudes toward complying with the law. This ability of process (and inability of policy) to explain why some people are nonplused about complying with the law is one of our most important findings. Once again, the results suggest that knowing people's perceptions of how policies are made is at least as important to understanding their orientations to government as knowing people's level of agreement with those policies.

HIGH INTEREST AND LOW INTEREST

Of course, not all people are likely to stress the same factors in the formation of their political attitudes. Using approval of the federal government (perhaps the most traditional dependent variable in this chapter) to illustrate, it is easy to show that those people with a substantial amount of interest in politics make determinations in ways different from others. Consider financial perceptions. Figure 3.3 presents the coefficients for the effect of personal financial condition and the country's financial condition on approval of government (controlling all the factors included in Tables 3.1–3.4), depending upon whether respondents were "not at all" or only "slightly" interested in politics or instead were "very" interested in politics.

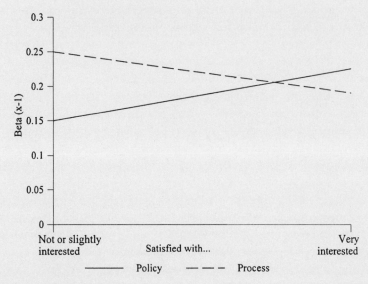

Figure 3.4. Effect of policy and process satisfaction on approval of federal government by political interest.

Among the politically uninterested, personal conditions matter and the country's conditions do not. Approval of government is driven by a personal retrospective approach and not a sociotropic one. But (assuming for the sake of simplicity that the trend in effects is linear) even before the midpoint of interest is reached, the lines cross, and among those who are very interested in politics, the country's financial condition is the economic perception that matters. Whether or not a politically interested person's finances have improved or not has no bearing whatsoever on approval of the government. The relationship is not statistically significant and the coefficient is not even properly signed. The uninterested are fixated on themselves; the interested are keyed into the country's status.

More pertinent to the theme of this book is the interaction of political interest with process and policy perceptions. We repeated the procedures leading to Figure 3.3, only this time the coefficients singled out are the policy gap and process gap variables. Policy and process concerns have statistically and substantively significant impacts on governmental approval for both the politically uninterested and the politically interested, but Figure 3.4 indicates a revealing pattern. Just as we expected, policy concerns are more important among the politically interested and process concerns are more important among the less interested. In fact (again, assuming linearity), the lines cross fairly close to the "very interested" side of the figure, suggesting that it is only among political activists, the highly interested, that perceptions of policy matter more than perceptions of how that policy was made. While the evidence in Figure 3.4 is more illustrative than conclusive, it is perfectly consistent with our view of American politics. Policy is the prime concern of the people who write about and discuss politics as well as the people with whom these pundits interact. As a result, disseminated views of what Americans want out of politics have been far too heavily influenced by these interested, issue-oriented politicos. Our book is intended to describe the political preferences of the long-ignored rest of the country. They may not have college degrees (74 percent of American adults do not), read the *New York Times* (99 percent of American adults do not), know the name of the Chief Justice of the United States (94 percent of American adults do not), or be politically interested, but this does not mean they never become exercised about politics. It is just that the source of their displeasure is more likely to be how the government works rather than what it does.

CONCLUSION

Process matters in people's attitudes toward the government. People's policy concerns are important, but we cannot fully understand people's attitudes toward government without taking into account how they think government ought to work and how they think government works in practice. We found that policy frustrations were more predictive of people's approval of various parts of the government than were process frustrations. People who believe the nation's economic condition is getting worse are much more disapproving of almost all parts of the government than those who believe it is getting better. Similarly, people who see a large gap between the policy outputs of the government and their own policy desires are much more likely to be dissatisfied with all parts of the government. Policy frustrations have definite consequences for people's reactions to the government and also for some types of voting behavior.

Process concerns, for their part, matter precisely where we would expect. First, as far as government approval is concerned, they matter where people can see processes in action or where discussion of processes by political elites is loud and public. Thus, people's reactions to processes significantly affect their approval of Congress, the institution that the people believe most publicly displays those processes most reprehensible to them: bickering, compromise, inefficiency, selling out to special interests. Process concerns also affect approval of the political system as a whole, the federal government, and the Supreme Court. Only presidential approval is unaffected by people's dissatisfaction with process.

Second, process can matter in elections if voters see one candidate offering real procedural alternatives. This situation seems unlikely to apply when both candidates are drawn from the established parties, parties the people believe to be hopelessly complicit in the existing process. But Ross Perot demonstrated the kind of traction that is possible when a third-party candidate focuses on process. It is evident from our analysis that his appeal was strongest among those dissatisfied not with governmental policies but with governmental processes. In most elections people are not in a position to vent their process frustrations because of the limited candidate choices they are provided, so process does not affect election outcomes. But process dissatisfaction is a potent resource for third parties inclined to take advantage of it.

Third, processes matter in ways that have more serious direct consequences for the political system. Democratic governments depend on people obeying the laws, and fewer resources need to be expended if people do so voluntarily. What increases the likelihood of compliance? Our research, and that of others (see Tyler 1990), shows that compliance is primarily a function of people's perceptions of process. The more people believe they are getting the government processes they desire, the more they believe even objectionable laws need to be obeyed. Somewhat surprisingly, people are not more casual about the need to obey the law when they dislike the *policy* outputs of the government. Policy frustration is not significantly related to compliance, but process frustration is. This result is not wholly unexpected, as theorists have recognized previously the importance of process relative to policy. Dye (1966: 30), for example, writes that "the legitimacy of the democratic form of government has never really depended upon the policy outcomes which it is expected to produce." But such observations have never resulted in an appropriate amount of research interest (the major exception is Tyler 1990). Our results suggest that procedural justice should be considered further.

Finally, processes matter when people think about reforming the political system. Frustration with policy outcomes or policy outputs does not systematically prompt people to want to change how the political system works. They may well want to change who is in office, but they are less likely to conclude that the whole system – or even parts of it – needs to be revamped. Instead, when people believe governmental processes are broken, then change, almost any change, becomes an attractive option. The desired changes may even appear slightly irrational on the surface, for example, simultaneously wanting to ban political parties *and* have a new political party form. When people are unhappy with processes, they often believe something – anything – must be done.[10]

Reforming the political system is not necessarily a bad thing. Sometimes the system needs to be changed. But what *is* cause for alarm is that the people may be so estranged from current processes that they are willing to grasp at any alternative to the procedural status quo, even alternatives that would give the people less voice than they have now. Thus, procedural dissatisfaction may contribute not just to a desire to reform democratic government but perhaps a willingness to entertain reforms that many consider to be something less than democratic. We take a closer look at the processes people say they want, including those that suggest some undemocratic tendencies among the American people, in Part II.

[10] It is important to note that reverse causation of the sort that severely afflicts issue voting is much more difficult in the formulations presented in this chapter. While it is easy to imagine voters assuming a favored candidate must be "correct" on the issues, it is not so easy to imagine that someone who does not believe it is necessary for people to comply with a law they dislike is more likely as a result to perceive governmental processes as quite distant from the processes preferred by that individual. The absence of viable instrumental variables makes it impossible to conclude for certain that no reverse causation is occurring, but the theoretical justification for expecting it is lacking for many of the relationships addressed here.

The Processes People Want

W E HAVE TRIED TO PROVE in Part I that process in general is important to the people. In Part II, we identify the particular process people most desire. Process can be incredibly complicated, and therefore beyond the ken of many people, but we do not claim people have detailed – or even accurate – knowledge of political processes. We do not believe many people have preferences on the minimum number of legislators that should be required to invoke cloture in Senate debate, or on whether multiple committee referral of bills should be permissible in the House. People are amazingly ignorant of political process at such levels, and why shouldn't they be? But just because they lack detailed knowledge about process does not mean people do not care about process. They do.

As we mentioned earlier, the picture painted in Part I concerning people's process preferences was somewhat misleading. People placed themselves squarely in the middle of a broad process spectrum. What does this mean? In the next three chapters we lay out the evidence that helps to answer this question. Put simply, people do not want to make political decisions themselves, but they want those who do make the decisions to be unable to make them on the basis of selfish motivations. People are amazingly attuned, hypersensitive even, to the possibility that decision makers will attempt to improve themselves at the expense of everyone else. They are therefore left with a dilemma. People want to turn political matters over to somebody else because they do not want to be involved themselves, but they do not want to turn decision making over to someone who is likely to act in a selfish, rather than other-regarding, manner. The findings we report in the next few chapters suggest that the people would most prefer decisions to be made by what we call empathetic, non-self-interested decision makers. Elites are not what the people fear; self-serving elites are. The people are surprisingly smitten with the notion of elite experts making choices – provided those experts have nothing to gain from selecting one option over another.

Claiming to know what the people want (even though they often seem to be saying something different) is presumptuous at best. Data do not exist on what the people *really* want, and we are fully aware that we are unable to prove our claims about popular desires for the political process. But we believe the evidence is at least consistent with our description, and we ask readers – particularly those who have been trained to believe the people want badly to get more involved in and to reconnect with politics – to keep an open mind to the possibility that the people might just want to turn politics over to someone else if only they could trust that someone else to act in the interest of the people as a whole. In other words, they might just want a stealth democracy rather than the direct democracy certain scholars believe people want or the special-interest quasi-democracy the people believe they have.

In Part II, we present evidence of people's attitudes toward existing processes and their preferences for alternatives. We begin in Chapter 4 by investigating people's more specific procedural attitudes, especially their reactions to a variety of possible reforms and their evaluations of various parts of the political system. We then move in Chapter 5 to the people's evaluations of the political capabilities of political elites as well as the capabilities of the American people. We find, perhaps surprisingly, that people do not think terribly well of American people generally and their capacity to govern specifically. We conclude in Chapter 6 by drawing attention to people's preference for a democracy that is not particularly democratic (but can be made to be if needed) but which renders it impossible for decision makers to act on the basis of selfish motivations. This is the key chapter, as it lays out people's desire for stealth democracy.

4

Attitudes toward Specific Processes

We know Americans are not pleased with political elites, but neither do they want to shoulder the burden of participating actively in politics themselves. When we asked our survey respondents to place themselves on a spectrum running from direct democracy to institutional democracy, they put themselves right in the middle. They want to take decision-making power away from elected officials and give more of it to the American people, but they do not want to get rid of elected officials completely. The problem is that this simplistic process spectrum, which we employed in Part I, is misleading because each pole contains something the people do not like (see Fig. 2.1). The right-hand pole is attractive to them because ordinary people do not have to be involved, but, on the downside, existing political institutions and elites, with all the accompanying special-interest-induced selfishness, are left to make the decisions. The left-hand pole removes all that diabolical, selfish elite influence but comes with a high cost of its own: Ordinary people are forced to become much more deeply involved in politics than they wish.

Imagine, instead, that this spectrum is disaggregated into two separate components as shown in Figure 4.1. Here, one spectrum runs from selfish political elites dominating every political decision to selfish political elites having no influence at all (notice there is no indication of whom or what would take the place of selfish political elites). The other spectrum runs from all political decisions being made by ordinary people themselves to ordinary people exercising no influence at all (once again, without concern for what *would* make the decisions in such a situation).

We predict that if people placed themselves on these two spectra, they would be well to the left on both; that is, they would prefer

Figure 4.1. Preferred decision making by political elites and by ordinary people.

selfish political elites to have little influence on political decisions just as they would prefer ordinary people to have little influence on political decisions. No doubt they would be more opposed on average to current political elite influence than to influence by ordinary people, since the intensity of distaste for current political elites and their partners, the special interests, is difficult to overestimate. But, as we show below, people are far more opposed to ordinary people being involved in political decisions than analysts typically believe. The only reason it appears the people want to get more involved in politics is that survey items (including ours) generally force them to make a tradeoff between elected elite control and popular control. If people want to limit the power of self-serving elites and special interests, they can only register that desire by saying they want the people more involved.[1]

In this chapter and the next, we tease apart people's attitudes toward political elites and institutions and toward the American people. We draw heavily on the focus group discussions as well as the survey results to determine the processes people seem to like and dislike. The focus group comments demonstrate that people have concerns even about reform proposals that are wildly popular in survey responses.

---

[1] And efforts to place people on each of the spectra in Figure 4.1 would be unwise because people cannot be expected to know how much they want to weaken a source of power without knowing what is replacing it.

WHICH WAY SHOULD THE PEOPLE
BE EMPOWERED?

Just *how* do people want to proceed with moving power away from existing institutions? Though it is clear that this is what they hope to accomplish,[2] this goal could be pursued in several different ways. For example, some may want to expand the use of policy initiatives that appear on the ballot. Twenty-six states and the District of Columbia permit initiatives and referenda, and some states, such as California and Oregon, use ballot initiatives regularly. Others may not want to wait for an election and instead prefer a teledemocracy in which the Internet or coaxial cables hooked up to television sets allow people to vote regularly on issues of the day. Others may prefer more of a deliberative tone to their democracy as exemplified by New England town meetings, with opportunities for all citizens of a small community to come together to debate and to decide on local matters. In many academic circles, these deliberative, communitarian approaches to decision making have become quite popular.[3]

Still others may not be comfortable with this level of direct democracy and may instead prefer to make changes in representative

[2] Better than two out of three people (807 of 1,180) in our national survey said the influence of existing political institutions should be less than it was at the time the question was asked. Only 14 percent said current processes were perfectly consistent with their preferences, and just 18 percent preferred a process in which elected officials would have *more* input. This imbalance is a far cry from policy space. There, more people were perfectly content with the tenor of policies (21 percent), and among those who were not, those wanting policies to be more liberal (45 percent) very nearly balanced out those wanting them to be more conservative (55 percent). So, unlike policy space, in process space there is strong agreement (more than two thirds of the people) as to the overall direction in which processes should move: away from existing institutions and elites.

[3] On ballot initiatives, see Magleby (1984), Cronin (1989), and Bowler, Donovan, and Tolbert (1998); on teledemocracy, see Grossman (1995); on deliberative, communitarian approaches, see, for example, Sandel (1982, 1984), Avineri and de-Shalit (1992), Etzioni (1996), and Tolchin (1999). For a good, if alarming, account of the overall growth in elite interest in "instant" democracy, see Weberg (2000). To illustrate the level of interest in alternative mechanisms for getting the people more directly involved in the governing process, the following papers were presented at the 1999 meeting of the American Political Science Association: "Defending and Protecting Initiative and Referendum in the United States," "Expanding and Improving Democracy through the Internet," "Philadelphia II: A National Citizen Initiative Theory and Process," and "Rejuvenating the New England Town Meeting via Electronics."

Table 4.1. *People's support for initiatives, term limits,
and devolution (%)*

	Use ballot initiative more	Term limits for members of Congress	Shift power to state and local governments
Strongly agree	16	19	11
Agree	68	49	52
Disagree	15	29	34
Strongly disagree	1	4	3
Strongly agree and agree	84	68	63

Source: Democratic Processes Survey, Gallup Organization, 1998.

institutions. For example, many individuals would like to devolve power from the federal government to state governments (see Hetherington and Nugent 2001; Uslaner 2001), believing that decision making on the state level allows people to be closer to the government and to exert more influence on what governments do. And still others may content themselves with changes in federal processes and arrangements, such as limiting the terms of members of Congress, reducing staff presence, cutting the power of committees and parties and, for that matter, limiting the power of anything that comes between the people and their designated elected officials.

The goal of increasing the influence of ordinary people relative to existing political institutions can be pursued in a variety of ways. How do the people feel about each of these various alternatives? Is one more popular than the others? We do not have information on popular support for each of the many important procedural variants, but the survey and focus group data do allow us to address the public's assessment of several distinct strategies.

Table 4.1 presents public reaction to three methods of shifting power away from existing elites: increased use of ballot initiatives, term limits for members of Congress, and devolving power from the federal government to state and local governments. On the basis of the survey, increased use of ballot measures appears to be extremely popular, with nearly 84 percent agreeing or strongly agreeing. Interestingly, focus group participants were substantially more guarded about the prospects of increasing the number of ballot propositions.

Though some were supportive, others adopted a view consistent with the following exchanges:

Linda M.: There's things I can read in there [on the ballot] and I can read it, and I can read it, and I'm still not sure. Maybe the language when they're trying to describe a bill or a . . . or when you go to vote it's like you think you should be voting yes, but no, you really want to vote on the way it's worded. I think sometimes maybe there might be an education – I'm not saying I'm stupid, but there might be an education gap in what people understand or what they read and what they're trying to understand.

Glen: Sometimes when you go vote on some of these bond issues and it's sort of like, "what're you trying to say?" I mean, you see this big long thing that's sort of like does this mean we build a school, do we build a street, or we don't build. . . . Some lawyer writes this big long thing up.

Cathy: This sounds good this way and it sounds good this way. I don't know. I end up leaving it blank because I don't really know what I want.

Andrea: I wouldn't trust everyone. . . . You see some of the decisions that people make just in terms of their own personal lives and you say, "hmmm, not a good choice." . . .

Alfredo: . . . The people that are not very intelligent relating to what's going on in politics would be swayed by a couple of dollars. . . . It just wouldn't work. . . .

Chris: . . . We are not all educated enough in every field to vote. I mean I wouldn't feel educated to vote on a good site for nuclear waste material, something like that. That's why we elect people to make those decisions.

These comments were volunteered in response to the moderator question, "Some people think we should move toward a direct democracy where the people vote directly on important political decisions and we wouldn't even need to have elected officials anymore. What do you think of this idea?" It seems likely that many of the survey respondents would have voiced similar reservations if given the opportunity. The people may want more initiatives and referenda, but this desire is tempered by worries over their own ability and the ability of the American people to understand the issues involved.

Although our survey did not contain numerous questions dealing specifically with instituting a direct democracy in the United States in a more concerted and regularized fashion than the occasional ballot proposition, focus group participants spoke at length on the topic. For the most part, they did not relish the prospects of being responsible for following and voting on all issues, and they had little faith that their fellow Americans could handle the task, either.

Moderator: One argument that's been made . . . is that we could have a direct democracy. . . . Every individual would be voting directly on policies. . . . What do you think of that idea?

Missy: Well a lot of people don't get involved though so maybe it wouldn't work, you know.

Bob: I think something like that would make people get involved because the electoral system to me represents a whole lot of power in the states that have a whole lot of people.

Linda: And so you're saying that what a direct democracy would give us is rule by California and New York?

Bob: Well I . . . I don't know. I really don't know.

Moderator: Any other thoughts about direct democracy?

Colin: So if we get 51 percent we can pass any law we want?

Linda: You said it.

Missy: That's just it though. What would happen if the 51 percent vote and the other 49 percent they don't like that vote and we have this big . . .

Linda: So you wouldn't like direct democracy?

Missy: Well I don't know. . . . There's a lot of crazy people in this world.

Linda: Yeah, shave your head.

Missy: Exactly.

Linda: Shave your head before you go to kindergarten.

Missy: And like he said, you know, somebody from a state that's bigger than ours. . . . And there's a lot more weirdos in California and New York [laughter].

Reactions to the prospects of coming together in groups to discuss issues with fellow citizens were not any more favorable than reactions to the nondeliberative style of direct democracy, as is indicated in the following exchange.

Moderator: What are your thoughts if we had a direct democracy such that every person would be making directly the decisions that affect us. . . . It would be like . . . a New England town meeting. . . . What do you think of that?

Cathy: It would be chaos.

Liz: No.

John: There would be a lot of violence.

Jim: I agree. I think it would be chaos because, you know, a lot of us don't take time to find out about issues. . . . That may work in a town, you know. A small town. I'm talking about 300–400 people where everybody thinks the same. You couldn't do it in [a large city]. And it wouldn't work for [his state]. And it wouldn't work as a national government.

Glen: We can't even get it to work in our family.

Linda: It sounds neat but I don't think it's feasible.

Cathy: It's not going to be effective.

Liz: Well, and I think the public, too, a lot of times is very short-sighted. . . . They want an immediate solution.

Linda: Right there, yup.

Liz: And they aren't looking 10–20 years down the road. . . . And problems change. And so elected officials are at least in a position where they can find out more about. . . . They have to look at the long term.

A participant in another session had this to say.

Carol: If you get this little kind of town meeting and these people are trying to vote against gay rights, do you really think the gay man standing there is saying, "oh, you know what, I disagree with this?" I don't think so. I think he'd be quiet for fear of retribution. And I don't . . . also people that go to these meetings are the ones who really want this. What about the apathetic people. . . .

Or consider this exchange in which a person originally supported more direct styles of democracy but then quickly reversed her position.

Pam: I like the townspeople thing where it's more responsibility, you know, more accountability, more conscientiousness, where we've got, we as a people have to make the time. We've got to get involved because we're losing, we're, you know, we've lost the sense of family values. . . . Ideally I like the townspeople thing, to get involved, somehow set it up so we're truly represented.

John: I'm fearful of the town, no offense to . . . you, but that kind of scares me in the sense that I think we need leadership. . . . With leadership, that's going to somehow even that out because the interests of [the minority] will be somehow more weighed.

Paul: I agree there needs to be some representatives. I mean there are things that they are privy to . . .

Pam: Yes, I was going to say yeah.

Paul: There are things they're privy to that I don't have time to be privy to. I, I, you know, none of us have the time during the day to, to get into the issues as much as they do. . . . I don't think we could go about making decisions completely.

Pam: Because we'd end up with hanging parties.

More enthusiasm is apparent for reforms that would continue with the general approach of turning many decisions over to elected officials while moving those officials further from special interests. For example, many advocates think that limiting the number of terms members of Congress can serve would weaken the connection between members of Congress and special interests (but see Will 1992). According to our survey (and several others), term limits are supported by just over two-thirds of the public. Given this level of support in the national sample, it is not surprising that when term limits for legislators did come up, focus group participants tended to be enthusiastic about them. Cary said: "I favor term limitations, regardless of how good a person is in office. I say a constant turnover is good. Then you get a more variety of candidates." The surprising thing, perhaps, is that term limits did not come up that often, even when people were asked for reform ideas. People still prefer limiting terms, but the issue is not as salient as it was in the early 1990s.

Shifting power from the federal government to state and local governments is favored by nearly as many people as term limits (63 percent of respondents in the national sample). Focus group participants were also supportive, though not without concerns. The following exchange is illustrative.

Dave: It [state government] is closer to home. That's one advantage. I mean you've got people you're a little closer to, and you can reach a little easier to promote things, you might say on a state-wide basis rather than having to be in Washington, where you're dealing with your senators and representatives, but I guess there's some advantages to that.
Linda: Well, you have to have some things done nationally – like defense. I mean we can't have 50 different little defenses, can we? So there has to be . . . each one has a role to play. . . .
Moderator: So you think leave it as it is?
Roger: A bit more involvement by the state. I think there's more things that the state government could do. . . . [The federal government has] so much involvement in the state level governments that it takes up time and energy and money and everything too. It's stupid.

More ambivalence, as well as lessons in history, civics, and theology, is contained in the remarks emanating from another focus group.

Moderator: Would you like to see power switched from the national government to state and local governments?
Erin: No.
Missy: No.
Erin: In some areas, yes.
Bob: Well the problem with that is once the feds submit their guidelines to you, you know, or once you agree to take that money, then they put all kinds of strings on you.
Missy: I like the government where it is. I wouldn't want to see it changed. Maybe a few things, but, you know, nothing major like that. No.

Adrienne: Do you think that if it did change, this state, it would be kind of cliquey? Because you'd know, I think that maybe it would be a little scary because the people that were appointed they might, especially if you live in like a smaller area, they might want to like only look out for . . .

Linda: Cliquey?

Adrienne: Yeah. Well it's all cliquey, but I mean I think it would be even more so because of . . . I just, I just, I don't know. I don't know what I'm saying

Erin: Does that mean that each state would have their own laws?

Beth: Yeah, so that . . .

Colin: They do. They do right now.

Erin: True, but I mean the federal government doesn't oversee those laws.

Colin: No, they don't. States are above the federal government. We've got to understand where we came from. Before we left England, before we separated from England there was a long period of time when we didn't have a Constitution. We didn't have the, the 1787 Convention.

Linda: 1981 to 1987, 1787.

Colin: The idea's first. First comes God. Then man was created by God. Man got together for his own good and created a state, in this case the original 13, the brief version. And those 13 states got together and said, "For our own good let's create a federal government." So the states are above the federal government. The federal government is supposed to serve and facilitate the states.

In sum, the people's process preferences are not as populist as they initially appeared. True, their desire to reduce the level of discretion of elected officials is undiminished. We asked people to agree or disagree with the following statement: "Members of Congress should do what they think is best regardless of what the people in their district want." This notion of a pure Burkean trustee model of government is clearly not what the people want, as four out of every five respondents (80 percent) either disagreed or strongly disagreed with the statement. But when attention is turned to the precise arrangements for redistributing power, people quickly identify problems with the frequently mentioned alternatives, such as teledemocracy and New England–style town meetings. So the overall public sentiment is beginning to come into focus. A direct democracy? No. An institutionally dominant indirect democracy? No. Weakening existing political elites? Yes.

ATTITUDES TOWARD MORE SPECIFIC REFORM PROPOSALS

With these general attitudes in mind, we can proceed to an analysis of the public's reactions to more focused modifications of current arrangements. What specific aspects do they want changed? Taking note of attitudes toward specific reforms will clarify the trouble spots people see in the current political system. Table 4.2 presents a sampling of the public's view of specific reform ideas.

In the table we see, for example, that the public definitely supports limiting campaign expenditures. People are often somewhat reluctant to strongly agree or strongly disagree with survey items, but with regard to campaign finance, more than one-third *strongly* agrees that "limits should be placed on how much money can be spent in political campaigns." Another 58 percent agrees, leaving only a smattering of dissent. The people want campaign spending to be limited. *Buckley v. Valeo* be damned.

The only other proposal that approaches this level of support is less a formal proposal than a wish that the media "quit focusing on all the negative news." Three out of four respondents signed on to this sentiment. Three out of five respondents believe the media do not let government know the people's concerns. The other reforms in Table 4.2, it should be noted, would entail somewhat more disruption to the current system and, perhaps for this reason, are accorded less support. For example, a majority (55 percent) does *not* favor banning interest groups from contacting members of Congress; only 46 percent long for a new national party to run candidates for office; and just 21 percent of American adults would like to see political parties banned from politics. The lack of enthusiasm for a new party is particularly surprising in light of public dissatisfaction with the current party system. Still, the real news from this table may be the significant minorities who do lend support to these proposals, some of which are quite radical. Specifically, one out of five respondents would like to banish political parties and nearly half would like to ban interest groups from ever contacting members of Congress. So much for the First Amendment right of petition to the Congress! This desire to rein in interest groups is hardly surprising given the widespread view that interest groups have too much control in the political system.

Nothing in the focus group remarks necessitates major qualification to these conclusions. Participants were eager to see the campaign finance mess cleaned up (one noted sarcastically that politicians listen only to people who pay $200 a plate to attend a fund-raising dinner) and were quite critical of the media, including what they saw as unnecessary negativity and prying into the lives of

Table 4.2. *Public evaluations of reforming the linkage mechanisms (%)*

	Limit campaign spending	Ban interest groups from contacting MCs	Special interests have too much control	Ban political parties	Need a new national party	Media should quit focusing on the negative	Media does well letting government know the people's concerns
Strongly agree	36	9	19	3	5	22	2
Agree	58	36	58	18	41	55	37
Disagree	7	50	22	70	49	21	49
Strongly disagree	0	4	1	10	5	2	12
Strongly agree and agree	92	45	77	21	46	77	39

Source: Democratic Processes Survey, Gallup Organization, 1998.

politicians. Neither were participants reluctant to place some of the blame for the problems of the political system on the political parties.

Moderator: If you could devise an ideal government . . . what would it look like?

John: Something that does away with . . . maybe adding a third political party. Something that kind of does away with the whole, you know, the bipartisan, Democrat and Republicans. And I think government [would be] much more effective if there wasn't that constant . . . Not that there wouldn't be with three parties, but I think it might even out more. So there'd be less time wasted, less energy wasted on just the constant fighting between parties.

Linda: And even in between their own parties they sometimes can't come to a good answer, and they can't come to a . . . you know, they bicker between, you know, their own party. It's like, wait a minute, are you with me, are you against me, you know, it just doesn't seem like it's . . . [drifts off].

But the level of animosity toward the media and toward political parties cannot measure up to that directed at interest groups, or, to use the public's preferred phrase, special interests. We reproduce just one of many focus group dialogues about special interests.

Bessie: Interest groups control government. The groups with the most amount of money, the most political clout, they say when.

Robert: I agree with that. I think interest groups . . . have too much control of what our elected officials say in our government. If you have enough money, and you can give them enough money for their campaigns, then they're going to get you to sway your vote. . . . I don't understand why some interest groups are allowed to give millions and millions of dollars and other groups can't afford to do that so they are, they can't represent the people they're trying to represent. And Congress people are basically just like, "Well this guy gave me ten million dollars, so no matter what I think, I've got to vote this way." They're bought, you know, bought by the interest group.

Many, many people see special interests at the core of the political system's problems.

PUBLIC APPROVAL OF GOVERNMENTAL INSTITUTIONS

We now move from linkage mechanisms to the institutions of government themselves. As has been documented previously (Hibbing and Theiss-Morse 1995), people have quite different views of the various institutions and levels of government. It seems likely that disparate institutional processes have much to do with the public's willingness to confer more approval on some institutions than others.

Table 4.3. *Approval of the political system and its parts (%)*

	Supreme Court	President Clinton	The Congress
Strongly approve	4	9	1
Approve	68	52	51
Disapprove	24	24	42
Strongly disapprove	4	14	7
Strongly approve and approve	72	61	52

	State government	Federal government	Political system overall
Strongly approve	3	1	1
Approve	67	53	56
Disapprove	26	40	37
Strongly disapprove	4	6	6
Strongly approve and approve	70	54	57

Source: Democratic Processes Survey, Gallup Organization, 1998.

Specifically, the Supreme Court has consistently been the most favored institution of government, and Congress the least (with the presidency bouncing erratically, but usually being more popular than Congress and less popular than the Court). One explanation for the sizable gap in the popularity of the Court and of Congress is that congressional procedures are very open. Congressional debates and compromises are frequently conducted in full view. Disagreements are often public and vocal. The Court, on the other hand, conceals disagreements masterfully. Debates and compromises among the justices are not exposed to the public. Disagreements are private or contained in written, scholarly prose. Certainly, it would be hard to explain the Court's relative popularity by claiming that its policy outputs are more consistent with people's policy preferences. After all, the Court has issued tremendously controversial and often unpopular decisions in the past few decades (school prayer, criminal rights, flag burning, and presidential election vote counts, to name just a few). So process seems the likely culprit.

Our recent results provide additional context for the public's feelings about political institutions. In Table 4.3, we present the public's level of approval for the three institutions of the federal government

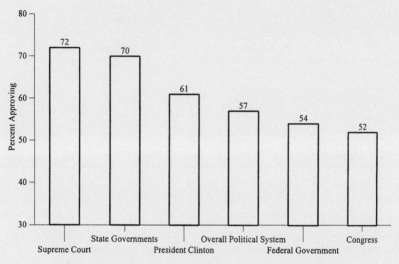

Figure 4.2. Approval of the political system and its parts.

and for the federal government as a whole, for state government, and for "the political system overall." These results are con-
densed and presented in graphic form in Figure 4.2.

The Supreme Court continues to reign as the most popular part
of government (72 percent either approving or strongly approving),
with "state government" not too far behind (70 percent). President
Clinton's approval rating was 61 percent. Remember, our survey
was conducted in April and May of 1998, well after allegations of
"inappropriate intimate contact" between the President and Monica
Lewinsky first surfaced in late January of 1998, but well before the
Starr Report was referred to Congress for the subsequent impeachment of the President and trial in the Senate (in September of 1998).
Of course, most observers were surprised that Clinton's popularity
was undiminished by the crisis and, in fact, went up by five to ten
percentage points.

The "overall political system" was approved of by 57 percent of
the population, even during this unsettling period of time, while the
federal government received slightly less approval (54 percent, to be
exact). Congress, once again, brings up the rear with just 52 percent
of the American public expressing approval at the time the survey
was conducted. While the pattern across institutions is interesting,
revealing, and supportive of previous work, it should be noted that
the level of approval of all these referents is quite high. A majority

of the population even approved of Congress. We now know that, in contrast to Clinton's popularity, Congress's was preparing to take a substantial hit from the impeachment proceedings. But starting in the summer of 1996 and continuing until the fall of 1998 (and then resuming after the impeachment brouhaha subsided), Congress enjoyed a period of popularity. It is likely that the cause of this popularity was the partisan cooperation in connection with the balanced budget agreement, the strong economy, and the lack of a desire on the part of congressional leadership to become enmeshed in controversy (Hess 1998). Once again, we see the importance of public perceptions of institutional processes. When Congress is relatively nonconflictual (such as after September 11, 2001), its popularity soars; when partisan or other infighting is visible (impeachment), its popularity drops (see Durr, Gilmour, and Wolbrecht 1997).

The larger point is that media and even scholarly accounts may at times overstate the public's displeasure with government. The popularity of the Court and state governments frequently can counterbalance the relative unpopularity of the Congress and the federal government, allowing a majority of the people to offer approval of the overall political system. Americans may not be fond of parts of the political system, but they are generally well disposed to the entire package.

WHO HAS TOO MUCH POWER?

While people may approve of the American political system, they do not think power is appropriately distributed. We asked our respondents whether they perceived various parts of government to have "too much power," "about the right amount of power," or "not enough power." The answers, though not all that surprising, are instructive. They are presented in Table 4.4. Focusing on the percent believing an entity has "too much power," we can see that the people's sentiments are clear. The main bogeyman continues to be interest groups. Two-thirds of American adults believe interest groups have too much power. The federal government is next, with 61 percent of the people believing it has too much power. Parties, as noted earlier, do a little better. A majority, but a smaller one (59 percent), see too much power residing in political parties. State government is in a different league from the other parts of government. Just 29 percent of the people believe state government has too much power, not that much more than believe it has "not enough power"

Table 4.4. *Which parts of government have too much power? (%)*

	Political parties	Interest groups	Federal government	State governments
Too much power	59	67	61	29
About right	36	22	34	55
Not enough power	5	11	5	17

Source: Democratic Processes Survey, Gallup Organization, 1998.

(17 percent). The majority of people (55 percent) believe state government is right where it ought to be in terms of power.

Whose power should be increased? It comes as no surprise, given our results in Chapter 2, that respondents believe ordinary people have too little power in the current system (78 percent) and only a handful (1 percent) believe they have too much power. In the minds of the American people, a fair distribution of power would look very different from the current distribution. The people would like to see the power of special interests, the federal government, and political parties greatly diminished, though they are not so keen on increasing the power of state government. State government power is fine where it is, the people believe.

PUBLIC ATTITUDES TOWARD THE OVERALL POLITICAL SYSTEM

We mentioned just a few paragraphs ago that at the time of the survey, approval of the overall political system was quite high (though not as high as it would get after September 11, 2001), thanks largely to the popularity of state government and the Supreme Court, but the concept of global or systemic approval is a tricky one. Therefore, it may behoove us to look more carefully at the public's overall likes and dislikes with regard to the political system. We have a few questions in the survey that fill this bill and they are presented in Table 4.5.

Nearly 60 percent of Americans approve of the overall political system. This finding makes it less surprising to discover that 62 percent agree that "our basic governmental structures are the best in the world and should not be changed in a major fashion." This is in many ways a remarkable level of approval for an enterprise –

Table 4.5. *Public views of the overall political system (%)*

	Our government is the best in the world; no major changes needed	American government used to get the job done but not anymore	Current political system does good job representing the interests of all Americans	Generally satisfied with recent public policies
Strongly agree	9	8	1	1
Agree	53	52	30	55
Disagree	35	38	53	39
Strongly disagree	3	3	15	6
Strongly agree and agree	62	60	31	56

Source: Democratic Processes Survey, Gallup Organization, 1998.

politics – that is despised by most people. But before we conclude the American public is happy as a clam with its governmental system, we should take note of several facts. The first is the people's expansive notion of "major change." Indeed, Americans are perfectly capable of saying they want "no major change" in the political system while simultaneously advocating the banning of political parties as well as the prohibition of interest groups from advocating their interests. Many observers would consider these "major" changes, to say the least, but the people seem to view "major" as replacing a democratic system with an authoritarian one or replacing a capitalist system with a socialist one.

More to the point, responses to other general survey questions suggest there may be a fly in the ointment. For example, if a longitudinal perspective is forced upon the people, most of them are of the opinion that the political system in the United States is performing worse today than it has in the past. Fully 60 percent of the respondents agreed (some strongly) that the "American government used to be able to get the job done, but it can't seem to any more."[4] Further, in terms of its performance in representing the interests of "all Americans, rich or poor, white or black, male or female," people

[4] Saying the U.S. government is worse than it used to be is a safer response than saying it compares unfavorably with other political systems around the world. It can be made without fear of being labeled unpatriotic.

Table 4.6. *The public's beliefs about the need for governmental complexity (%)*

	Congress needs committees	President needs staffers
Strongly agree	6	8
Agree	66	63
Disagree	24	26
Strongly disagree	3	4
Strongly agree and agree	72	71

Source: Democratic Processes Survey, Gallup Organization, 1998.

believe the government comes up well short. Only 31 percent believed the statement accurately reflects reality. Relatedly, when we asked respondents whether public officials cared a lot about what "people like you think," only 28 percent (not shown in Table 4.5) said yes. On the positive side, a solid majority of Americans (56 percent) are "generally satisfied with the public policies the government has produced lately," as could have been expected on the basis of the findings in Chapter 1.

BELIEFS ABOUT THE COMPLEXITY OF GOVERNMENT

We conclude the empirical portion of this chapter by presenting responses to two survey items dealing with the American public's desire for governmental organization and infrastructure. They are presented in Table 4.6.

Most of the public concedes that "Congress needs to have committees to get its work done" and that "the President needs a lot of staffers to get his work done." But it is noteworthy that a sizable minority disagrees. Better than one out of four people (27 percent) believe it is unnecessary for Congress to have committees, and slightly more (30 percent) do not believe the president needs much staff help. For this many people to think the president, sitting atop a sprawling government in today's complex world, needs only minimal staff assistance in order to do his job is somewhat astounding. Combine these results with those mentioned earlier, indicating that 21 percent of the public wants to ban political parties and 45 percent wants to ban interest groups from making any kind of petition to the Congress, and it would appear a substantial minority of Americans has a truly novel, perhaps even bizarre, outlook on government. No committees, no staffers, no parties, and interest groups that are forbidden to express interests.

CONCLUSION

People want to decrease the power of governmental institutions, linkage mechanisms (especially special interests), and elected officials, and they seem to want to increase the power of ordinary people (although we suggest below that this latter finding is misleading). They clearly do not want to do away with governmental institutions. The people have no desire for direct democracy, but if the options are for decisions to be made by elected officials or by the people, they are eager to give more power to the people since they are convinced that current governmental arrangements give far too much power to biased elected officials. In fact, people are so eager to weaken the influence of current political elites that they favor a variety of paths to get there. Expanded use of ballot initiatives and referenda is extremely popular with the public. Advocates often portray term limits and shifting power from the federal government to the state governments as reforms that would weaken existing elites. Both proposals are supported by two out of every three American adults.

In terms of specific alterations and reactions to the current system, people's primary concern is with interest groups. They believe special interests have hijacked the political process. The squeaky wheel gets the grease and the people see the special interests as squeaky wheels. It matters little to them whether these special interests are on the left or the right; the important point is that they are different from ordinary people and they usually get their way, or so it seems. From the people's perspective, ordinary Americans are in the middle, surrounded on all sides by shrill, demanding, and unrepresentative interest groups.

Thus, when asked whether the political system does a good job representing the interests of all Americans, people respond with a resounding "no". This is not because they are worried that minority views are going unrepresented. Quite the contrary. Most people are convinced that minority views dominate the system and that clear-thinking, salt-of-the-earth, ordinary Americans are ignored (more on this later). They think that without so many staffers and committees and long-serving politicians in far-off seats of government, the system would be less likely to heed the wishes of special interests. Four out of five American adults think "special interests have too much power."

But do the people really want to empower themselves at the expense of political institutions? Initially, this may seem a silly question. Everyone wants more power, right? As we have seen, this is not right. The people could increase their power even more by striving for a direct democracy, but they have no desire for this. Indeed, the people often wish they could be exposed to less about politics and political decisions. No, the apparent desire to create a political system in which special interests have less influence than they do now is based on something other than a power grab on the part of the people; instead, it has to do with perceptions of the strengths, talents, motives, and capabilities of ordinary people as opposed to politicians. In the next chapter, by paying careful attention to the public's perceptions of people and of elected officials, we explain what is behind the public's desire to shift power away from existing political institutions.

5

Public Assessments of People and Politicians

Does the federal government have too much power, about the right amount of power, or not enough power? A meager 5 percent, according to our national survey, believe that it has "not enough power." Do the American people have too much power, about the right amount of power, or not enough power? Some 78 percent say "not enough power." An overwhelming majority of American adults would like to see power moved away from elected officials and interest groups whom they perceive to be so influential. The primary purpose of this chapter is to dig a little deeper into why the people want to weaken existing institutions of government presumably by granting more power to ordinary people. What is it about the American people or about existing political institutions and elected officials that causes so many individuals to want to transfer political power from institutions to ordinary people? To answer this question, we rely heavily on focus group comments, but we begin this chapter by presenting the results of several survey questions relevant to the task at hand.

EMOTIONAL REACTIONS TO PEOPLE AND TO GOVERNMENT

If further evidence is needed of people's unfavorable reaction to government and relatively favorable reaction to ordinary American people, it can be found in a small battery of survey items on emotions. We asked respondents to tell us whether or not certain aspects of the political system made them feel proud and then asked whether those same aspects made them feel angry. Previous research has

Table 5.1. *Emotional reactions to the American people, state government, and the federal government (%)*

	Proud of the American people	Proud of state government	Proud of the federal government
Yes	77	56	41
No	27	44	59
	Angry with the American people	Angry with state government	Angry with the federal government
Yes	52	52	71
No	48	48	29

Source: Democratic Processes Survey, Gallup Organization, 1998.

indicated that emotions play an important role in politics independent from cognitions.[1]

This may be, but people's aversion to government, at least to the federal government, is negative enough and their fondness of the American people positive enough that these "emotional" questions generate responses similar to the more cognitive items discussed earlier. This conclusion is evident from Table 5.1, where we present the percentage of people who admit to having felt proud of the American people, their state government, and the federal government. These results are followed by parallel items for anger rather than pride.

As might have been expected, when it comes to a positive emotion (pride), fewer people (just 41 percent) have felt it toward the federal government than either state government or the American people. When we turn to the negative emotion (anger), the federal government is easily the target most commonly mentioned (71 percent). The American people, on the other hand, are the most frequently identified target for the positive emotion (with state government ensconced firmly in the middle) and are in a virtual dead-heat with state government for the least-mentioned object of anger. Interestingly, though, more than half of all respondents have at one time or another felt anger with the American public, so respondents seem to be adopting a realistic attitude. Of course, the American people

[1] See, for example, Kuklinski et al. (1991); Marcus et al. (1995); Hibbing and Theiss-Morse (1998).

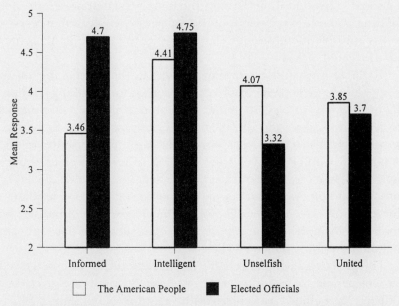

Figure 5.1. Perceived traits of the American people and elected officials.

on occasion make people angry, but they are much more likely to make people proud. The federal government, on the other hand, has made three out of four people angry but only 41 percent proud. So people's preferences for weakening existing federal institutions are based on emotional as well as cognitive reactions.

HOW DO THE AMERICAN PEOPLE COMPARE WITH ELECTED OFFICIALS?

But what traits do people associate with ordinary people? What is it about people that makes so many respondents want to transfer political power to them? Are they seen as intelligent, magnanimous, well informed, and consensual? More to the point, how do these perceived traits compare with those of elected officials, the group the public wishes to weaken by strengthening ordinary people? Preliminary answers to these questions are provided in Figure 5.1.

Respondents were asked to place the American people and then elected officials on four seven-point scales: extremely uninformed (0) to extremely informed (6); extremely selfish (0) to extremely unselfish (6); extremely divided (0) to extremely united (6); and extremely unintelligent (0) to extremely intelligent (6). A reasonable hypothesis, in light of the people's stated preference for shifting power into the hands of the American people, is that respondents attribute more positive characteristics to the people than they do to elected officials.

To bring this into operational terms, we computed the mean response on each of the four characteristics for all usable respondents (low N was 1,245) so that we can compare people's assessments of Americans generally and elected officials specifically. Somewhat surprisingly, elected officials come out fairly well relative to the American people. People believe elected officials are much more informed than the American people. In fact, the gap between elected officials and the American people is wider for information level than for any of the other items. They also perceive elected officials to be more intelligent than the American people, although here the gap between the two is much smaller.

The American people, relative to elected officials, are perceived by the people to be united and unselfish. In these areas, elected officials lag behind, particularly with regard to being selfish. When attention is shifted to the raw mean, the American people score the highest on intelligence, next highest on unselfishness, then cohesion, and lowest in level of information. People view Americans as unselfish and intellectually capable but not in possession of much information. They view elected officials as smart and steeped in information but fractious and greedy.

A logical inference from combining these results with the fact that people want to shift power away from elected officials and toward ordinary people is that most would rather put up with uninformed decision makers than with self-serving and divisive decision makers. The implied sentiment is that it is better to have policies that are wrong than policies that are the product of personal greed and bickering. People judge the American public to be quite deficient in political knowledge, but this does nothing to derail the desire to give more power to these poorly informed people.

As a sidebar, it is interesting to determine whether public perceptions about the American people's lack of information are accurate. In our survey, we asked four political knowledge questions: "What job or political office does Al Gore hold?" "What job or political office does Tony Blair hold?" "Who has the final responsibility to decide if a law is constitutional or not: the President, the Congress, the Supreme Court, or don't you know?" And "Which party currently has the most members in the U.S. Senate?"

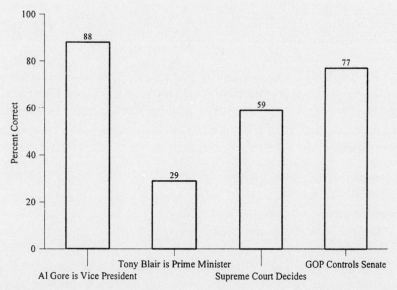

Figure 5.2. The public's level of information on four political knowledge questions.

There is no firm guideline allowing us to conclude that the people are either woefully uninformed or, alternatively, not as bad as respondents judge them to be. No doubt the results in Figure 5.2 will strike some as high and some as low. As of May 1998, some 88 percent were able to identify Al Gore as vice president of the United States, while only 29 percent knew that Tony Blair was the prime minister of Great Britain. The visibility of the vice president and Americans' traditional diffidence toward international matters make these results unsurprising. With regard to the final two items, it is encouraging that solid majorities know the Supreme Court has the final say on the constitutionality of statutes and that the Republicans controlled the Senate at the time of the survey, though the other way of looking at these results is that about one out of four adults is unaware of the majority party in Congress (when guessing between the two major parties would yield 50 percent correct) and 41 percent of the public is unaware of the Supreme Court's most fundamental role in the political system. It would seem at least a third of the people could safely be classified as uninformed.[2]

---

[2] A much more detailed treatment of the level of public knowledge can be found elsewhere. See, especially, Delli Carpini and Keeter (1996) and Morin (1996).

Table 5.2. *Miscellaneous perceptions of the American people (%)*

	The American people could solve country's problems	If American people, not politicians, decided, the country would be better off	People don't have enough time or knowledge to make political decisions
Strongly agree	7	5	7
Agree	56	51	58
Disagree	34	41	33
Strongly disagree	3	4	3
Strongly agree and agree	63	56	65

Source: Democratic Processes Survey, Gallup Organization, 1998.

THE AMBIVALENCE OF PUBLIC PERCEPTIONS OF THE AMERICAN PEOPLE

A key finding of this section on people's perceptions of the political capabilities of the American people is that, even though the desire to increase the clout of ordinary people vis-à-vis existing institutions is widespread, this does not mean there is no ambivalence about shifting power to them. Quite the contrary; ambivalence is rampant and nowhere is this better illustrated than in Table 5.2. Here we see the answers to three survey items. Could the American people, if just given a chance, figure out how to solve the nation's problems? Nearly two-thirds say yes. Given the complexity and intransigence of many of the nation's problems, this is an astounding vote of confidence in the capacities of the American people. It is the "can do" spirit at its best, but the next item suggests greater uncertainty on the part of the people. Here, respondents were faced with a fairly stark choice: "If the American people decided political issues directly instead of relying on politicians, the country would be a lot better off." This question split respondents nearly down the middle. Slightly more than half the respondents, 56 percent, thought the country would be better off if the people decided, but this means nearly half of the respondents believed the country would be better off if politicians and not the American people decided political issues.

Table 5.3. *Public perceptions of the trustworthiness of the American people (%)*

Most people can be trusted	40
Can't be too careful in dealing with people	60
Total	100
Most people try to be fair	48
Most people would take advantage of you if they had the chance	52
Total	100

Source: Democratic Processes Survey, Gallup Organization, 1998.

This ambivalence about the abilities of the American people is even more apparent in the next item where 65 percent of all respondents agreed that "people just don't have enough time or knowledge to make decisions about important political issues." Once again, it is difficult to avoid the conclusion that the desire to shift power toward the people is not based on tremendous confidence in the ability or willingness of those people to render informed and improved political decisions. Something else seems to be driving the desire to shift power closer to the people.

If further evidence is needed about the mixed feelings evoked by the concept "American people," consider the results in Table 5.3. Here the focus of attention is not the people's ability to process information or the time they have available to commit to politics or even their willingness to acquire information, but, rather, the extent to which ordinary people can be trusted. In Figure 5.1 we saw that most respondents believed the American people were relatively unselfish, certainly compared with elected officials. But this is not quite the same as determining the extent to which respondents perceive people as being trustworthy.

Two items in our survey seem appropriate for the task at hand. The first asked, "Generally speaking, would you say that most people can be trusted, or would you say that you can't be too careful in dealing with people?" As can be seen from the table, a majority of respondents opted for the less positive "can't be too careful" position and were not willing to declare that "most people can be trusted." But being careful is good policy regardless of what one thinks of the trustworthiness of other people, and this may explain the result. From this standpoint, the second item might offer a better test. This item read, "Do you think most people would try to take advantage of you if they had a chance, or do you think they would try to be fair?" Even with this language, people express a guarded attitude toward "most people." More people believe "most people would take advantage if they had a chance" than believe that "most people would try to be fair," although the difference is small. It would seem the desire to empower the American people is not based on the belief that ordinary people are trustworthy. They are perhaps more trustworthy than elected officials, but this does not necessarily mean they are trustworthy.

PEOPLE'S COMMENTS ON THE AMERICAN PEOPLE

So, the public wants to give more political power to ordinary people even as the public openly admits that these ordinary people are often poorly informed, not particularly trustworthy, and only marginally capable of solving the nation's problems more proficiently than elected officials. This somewhat paradoxical conclusion begs for a more detailed investigation of the public's perceptions of the capabilities of the American people relative to elected officials. To acquire this more detailed information, we turn to the eight focus group sessions we conducted late in 1997. Of course, selective presentation of quotes could be used to make many different, sometimes conflicting points, and a determined moderator could coax participants toward certain remarks. These remain core problems with the use of focus groups (see Polsby 1993). Nonetheless, focus groups constitute one of the few ways to go beyond the terse questions and closed-ended responses that typically characterize survey research, and we prohibited our moderator from coaching. We believe a fair reading of the transcript from each of the focus groups we conducted across the nation, from southern California to New England, suggests a clearly dominant view of the political capacities of the American people. We begin with people's comments about the strengths and weaknesses of ordinary Americans and then move on to comments about politicians and political institutions.

We were taken aback by the extent to which focus group participants believed that the American people generally do not have the time, motivation, orientation, knowledge, and even intelligence it takes to get up to speed on the political issues of the day, unless those issues might be of vital interest to the person. Previous writing typically has claimed that Americans view elected officials as incapable and ordinary people as both capable and willing (see, e.g., Mathews 1994; Grossman 1995; Kidd 2001). Our results directly challenge these previous claims. While some participants viewed the American people as capable, most seriously questioned their intelligence and information levels. And it was an extremely rare voice that said the American people were willing to shoulder the responsibility of deciding tough political issues. One often-expressed argument for this lack of willingness was that people are too busy to commit the time necessary to engage fully in politics. This sentiment is apparent in the following comments from focus group participants.

Jean: Well, we're not to blame. I would love nothing more than to sit down and read three newspapers in the course of the day. But I feel I'm too busy supporting this big machine that just sucks the money out of my paycheck every week. Realistically, I'm too busy trying to support this big business that I feel should be run like a business, with accountability, a little more balance.

Mike: We have people who don't care. They're like, "What's this issue? Oh, I don't care." You know, whatever. I want somebody who actually cares; I'm going to think about this.

Jackie: And I'm the same way. I don't read the newspaper. I listen to the news in the morning from six to seven, while I'm smoking a cigarette getting ready to get up and go to work. And that's all I know.

Others saw being busy as a major problem but were unwilling to suggest that people would become engaged if given a chance. According to these participants, most Americans are apathetic about politics – apathetic *and* busy.

Ernie: How many of us in here want to make a change by going to the government or how many of us can? . . . I think we're so occupied by trying to keep up in this society that there's not enough people who have the difference to go in there and say "this is what I want to do." . . . There is just not enough people doing what should be done to make a difference.

Tammie: Well people are trying . . . are too busy, you know trying to keep up . . .

Ernie: Yeah, exactly.

Tammie: They don't have time to worry about how the government's run.

Rhonda: People need to be motivated, too. Like every four years they get motivated around election time. They all get into all, you know, issues and stuff. And like they get into their rut. They need to be motivated every,

I don't know how you'd do it, because they would be more interested. Because, you know, you forget it. You put it on the back burner . . .

Mike: You've got so many things going on. Your interest level in government, when you get home from work and your kids are there, is nothing.

Rhonda: Well how would you get people interested? That's something we'd have to look at, too, instead of every four years, like I think, like me.

Some participants disputed the "no time" explanation, viewing it less as a reason and more as an excuse. People, they felt, could spend less time sprawled in front of a television set watching game shows or even the evening news that contains little "real" news, thereby freeing up time to learn about and become involved in politics.

Carol: You know, we say that we don't have time, but nobody goes to city council meetings. I had to go for a class. I had to go so I went. I don't have to go now so I don't go. *Wheel of Fortune* is on. I'm comfortable. It's cold out. So I'm as guilty as anybody.

John: And the other thing is, you know, no offense to you but . . . people in general are like, "I don't have time. I don't have time." But how many of us make time to watch *ER?*

Jackie: We're too apathetic and I think the media is a big problem.

Jill: Turn off the TV.

Robin: Well it's a great electronic baby sitter, you know [and the parents need it because they are] working so damn hard to keep their heads above water, they can't worry about government, OK.

Jill: And when they can they go back to the TV because it is a mental check-out. It's not, I'm not saying that these are bad people, [only] that you don't have to think. It happens to me. If I turn the TV on, I am sucked in for the whole night.

Ron: You've got so many people that are just blind sheep that follow every-thing that the media throws at them. . . . We are a very lazy society that wants everything given to them. . . . They sit in front of the TV night after night being told the same things. . . . You'll watch a two-second segment on the problems with Iraq and then they'll have a 20-minute segment on Fluffy the Dog that got saved by a little kid.

Focus group participants overwhelmingly agreed that Americans are uninformed about politics, a view that clearly reflects the results from the national survey (see Table 5.1). Americans know little about politics, but the explanation for this lack of knowledge varied. Some people, such as Ron above, blamed the media. If the media gave people the information they need, they would be better informed. Others blamed the complexity of the information they received, arguing that if information were presented in a more simplified form, people would be more knowledgeable. And still others simply felt overwhelmed by the volume of information they received.

Wanda: Government should simplify some of the things that they are doing and directions that they are going so that the average American of a certain IQ can feel a little less intimidated and want to be a little more involved so that [people] don't . . . just give up and, you know, not get involved. . . . Keep it simple and I think there would be much more involvement.

Andrea: What I have a problem with is our Voter Information Books. They're about this thick, and you don't understand what they're talking about. . . . Why can't they just put it in plain English?

Linda: I get overwhelmed by the volume. . . . You want to do such and such. Well, you know, most people want to do whatever this issue is, this is a good thing. . . . But . . . you go through all these layers of this person's got to do this with it. And by the time it actually gets to wherever it's going, it may not even be what you first thought it was going to be. . . . It's hard to cut through I guess, all the politics stuff and the apathy and stuff. It's hard to cut through and see this is really the issue to this. And most people throw up their hands and go, "Oh well, the country hasn't fallen apart yet."

John: People are satisfied with their way of life and everything right now.

Linda: There. They've got a job. They got their car. They're living somewhere . . .

John: And they're going to let everybody else take care of . . .

Linda: Exactly.

Glen: And if this isn't going to impact me, I'm not going to . . .

Linda: But most people, as long as they've got, you know, they're going to school, or they're going to work or whatever. Unless it personally impacts them it's like, "well. . . ." They'll ignore it, you know. . . . It is, I think, it's very overwhelming. Just pages and pages of pictures of people and their kids, and their wives, and where they go to church you know and all this stuff. And you are trying to read all of it. And you get done, and I'm still like, "well, now. . . ."

A surprising number saw the problem of an uninformed public as residing not with the media or with the government or with the information people receive – and not even with the busy schedules of ordinary Americans – but rather with the people's intelligence and motivation.

Linda: I don't think most people are informed enough or smart enough to make all the decisions that have to be made. A lot of things have to have a lot of research behind them, and nobody has the time to do that unless it's their job. . . . Many, many, many, many people don't vote at all, unless it's something they really want like when we were voting on the lottery. How many people voted that had never voted in their life? They wanted the lottery so they went to vote. . . . I do believe in elected officials, giving them the time and the ability to serve, and do what they're supposed to do, and research the subjects that come up. I'm not qualified to make any judgments or vote on EPA issues or things like that. I know nothing about it. I could vote on something, but I might be voting for something totally wrong, out of ignorance.

Mike: But, I believe at this point, as a society as a whole, we are more ignorant of our country than we were 200 years ago. . . . Our country was formed on the fact that there are certain people that, right, wrong, or otherwise, are more intelligent. That they know how things work. That they can make decisions. My decision, since I'm not one of them, is to discern who is, who I want out there. . . . People don't care. I mean in polls, people can't tell you, it's amazing, like 40 percent . . . didn't know who the vice-president of the United States was.

Lisa: Don't you think some of that though is because people . . . don't feel what they have makes any difference, so they don't care. They tune themselves out. I think that if one vote counted for one vote on every issue, that people would really be more interested in what's going on.

Mike: I think that's an excuse. Because there were times when I didn't vote. Honestly, it wasn't because I didn't think my opinion counted, it was because that was out of my way. You know, I had something else that I wanted to do that day. . . . You look at the sixties, you know the black community, they would walk and march, you know. . . . We here in this country have given that right up.

Robin: People aren't that bright. [Laughter.] No, seriously. Have you ever worked with the public? There are people, I mean they're just not that bright. . . . There's a problem when we have people graduating high school who can't read. . . . A weakness of the people is that we're not bright enough to get the picture, the big picture, or even the little picture sometimes.

Believing the American public lacks innate intelligence is a far cry from the view that people simply do not have enough time or cannot wade through all of the complex information they receive. Questioning the public's intelligence raises the issue of whether the American people *should* get more involved in politics. Some participants similarly questioned Americans' motivations: The American people are too self-interested and narrow, and therefore perhaps should not be involved in politics.

Jill: I think a huge weakness of our society is that people have the attitude that "you owe me." Government owes me, my neighbor owes me, every, I mean everybody owes me. And they don't feel like they need to do anything for themselves. . . . Kids today . . . think that they really deserve something that they haven't worked for. I mean all the time.

Michelene: I'm real limited, you know. I have tunnel vision because what I care about is what's going on in my world. I care about what's happening in [her hometown]. I don't really care what's happening in Washington, DC. I want my streets safe for my kids. I want the roads safe for us to drive. . . . These are my concerns. You know, maybe that's selfish. . . . I don't care what's happening in New York. I could care less. I care about what's happening here. . . . That's what I care about.

Alfredo: The only people that are going to exercise their voice are the people that are being affected at that particular time.
Jason: That's right.
Alfredo: For example, the Hispanic community doesn't normally vote but then when an issue comes by, such as immigration law, all of a sudden the Hispanic community will rise up and become a voice . . . the American Indian, for example, they would rise up if something happens to their slot machines in their reservations.

Mike: Well . . . are we too big a nation to be governed by a democracy?
Pam: I don't think we're too big. I think we're too greedy and too self-centered, that we're not up to make sacrifices that it would take for us to be truly governed by a democracy.
John: I think our government was set up for the people but I think the attitude, kind of what you are saying, the attitude is now "for me and by me."
Pam: Yeah.
John: We're greedy about our individual aspect of what the government is providing.

This sentiment that the American people are too self-interested and narrow may appear to fly in the face of the survey findings we report in Figure 5.1. Survey respondents were much more likely to view the American people as unselfish compared with elected officials, yet here we see focus group participants strongly stating that the American people are selfish. It is important to note, though, that one-third of survey respondents believe the American people are selfish. The American public may appear less selfish at the aggregate level than elected officials, but there is a large group of people who are unwilling to categorize Americans as unselfish.

Perhaps of even more concern than those who question the intelligence and motivations of people are the individuals who are disillusioned with democratic government because they somehow believe it should provide them with everything they want. When this eventuality fails to materialize, they withdraw from the political process, apparently unable to realize that no system could give every citizen everything he or she wants. Typical of this attitude is the following comment.

Ernie: I know the only kind of political background I had was my senior year of civics really, and when I took [indecipherable] at a junior college. But it was never an interest because of all the things, all the negativity you're always hearing, what you can't get in government. And then the last election was the first time I just said, hey, you know, I'm always bitching about this and this and that. So I registered and voted. You know and I think that out of . . . all the changes that I wanted, I think only one of them happened, you know. . . . I could care less right now. Because it's just like everything you wanted to see changed still hasn't happened. And I think I'm just like any other people, I let other things take my time. And it's like, [elected officials] are keeping in touch because I get in the mail, "Hi I'm representative. . . . This is what's going on. If you want to come here . . ." But I get them [and throw them away] because I have no interest.

Regardless of the reason people give for not being involved in politics, they are quite aware of the dangers of their reluctance to participate. They recognize their own deficiencies and the problems these deficiencies create for the political system. They are even willing to recognize that their apathy directly contributes to special interests having more power in the political system.

Cynthia: We get very apathetic in what has happened, so we lose our power by not voting. . . . If we have someone in Congress that is not really representing us the way that we want to be represented, by not voting, by not speaking up, we let it continue.

Liz: I still have the feeling that . . . special interest groups would not be as strong as they are if the regular, average citizen would just assert themselves more. And take seriously the responsibility of, I need to vote every time there is an election. I need to find out about the candidates. I need to find out about the issues. I need to be involved. I mean.

Linda: I don't think most people take time to read. . . . OK, you open the paper and here's eight different people, and what they're going to do, and what they believe in, and whatever. And I don't think most people sit down and actually take the time to find the issues.

Glen: You have to have confidence that they [elected officials] have enough information, that there was a reason why they did that [voted a certain way on a roll call matter].

Linda: They know those things that somebody at home maybe does not know.

What is notable about many of these comments is that the people are willing to shoulder the blame for their lack of involvement. No passing the buck to some institutional feature they might perceive to be mildly off-putting. The people are forthright in saying the problem is them, not a defect in the political system itself.

Jim: We pretty much have the ideal government. But I think what we have are less than ideal citizens. If people would take the time out to be more involved in the election process . . .
Cathy: You can't force people to do that.
Jim: Well, no you can't, you know.
Eric: I think we have avenues to contact our representatives, though. I don't think that structurally we lack the ability to let our representatives know what we want. We just choose not to do so.
Pam: Right.
Pat: I'm not Generation X, but I definitely am a card-carrying member of the disenfranchised, because I have, in a sense, opted out.

The acknowledged shortcomings of the American people led several participants to muse on the benefits of giving power to designated representatives, as is illustrated by the following discussion.

Alfredo: We have to trust these people that we voted in are going to make the decisions for us, otherwise we wouldn't vote for them. And then if they don't make the decisions that we want them to make, then we vote them out the next time around. So that's not a problem.
Jason: You sit around until your feathers are ruffled. . . . Logging industry? OK, Mr. Whoever, you take care of that situation for me. I'll trust that you'll make the best decision. Tomato industry? OK, tomato industry, go ahead. Car industry? . . . What do we know about these things? The communications industry? What do we know about these things?
Alfredo: Let them do their job.
Jason: That's what they're there for. They're there because . . . they know what they're doing. Do I trust them? No.

PEOPLE'S COMMENTS ON POLITICIANS

This last comment serves as a perfect lead-in to the participants' comments on politicians. Many individuals, like Alfredo, recognize the need for letting these elected officials "do their job" but, like Jason, do not really trust those officials. It is clear they do not have full confidence in the American people, but neither do they have confidence in politicians. It is time to look more deeply at the public's perception of the strengths and, especially, the weaknesses of politicians.

Many of the things the public dislikes about politicians are obvious
and have been noted earlier, but the comments of the focus group
participants provide useful twists on these notions and deserve to be
juxtaposed with public sentiments toward ordinary people.

Disagreements among politicians are an important source of
public dissatisfaction with politicians, no doubt partially because the
media delight in presenting political disagreements as a failure on
someone's part. As Kerbel (1999: 121) puts it, "when disagreement
appears in the news ... it is inevitably portrayed as problematic ...
when friction results, the media dutifully report it as a sign that things
are malfunctioning." But whatever the source of the unfavorable view
of normal political conflict, politicians' perceived proclivity for conflict is a key reason the public evaluates them as they do. Fighting is
equated with an absence of productivity. Ben, a focus group participant, noted that politicians are "always fighting" and that "they sit
in their little offices up there and hold their meetings every day
but nothing happens." Junior responded by observing that "we get
so many promises" and by making it clear that he felt the promises
were seldom kept. Relatedly, most participants believed the primary
source of bickering and the lack of productivity among politicians is
special interest influence. In fact, complaints about the susceptibil-
ity of politicians to special interest influence could fill a book by
themselves. Here we present only four illustrative quotes.

Lisa: I don't like the way they seem so easily influenced by lobbyists. I don't
... there should be a better way that money and influential groups that have
a lot of money shouldn't be, shouldn't be able to influence the decisions
that the law makers make so easily. ...

Maria: They [politicians] think about who's in power, who's the dominant
group. And they do the laws according to who's going to benefit from it.

Kelly: It's the loudest people who get represented. The people who make
the most noise, you know, the squeaky little [unintelligible] instead of
looking at the big picture.

Robert: I think interest groups have too much control of what our elected
officials say in our government. And Congress people are basically just like,
well this guy gave me ten million dollars so no matter what I think, I've got
to vote this way. They're bought, you know, bought by the interest group.

And here, of course, is where the other shoe falls. People believe
politicians are susceptible to special interest influence not just because they are weak but because it is in their financial interest to

befriend special interests. This is how elected officials get trips to Tahiti; this is how they get to stay in office; this is how they receive lavish campaign contributions and gifts. One participant said he had voted for Ross Perot in 1996 because he felt Perot's wealth would allow him to be relatively impervious to the money that special interests dangle in front of politicians. He did not particularly like Perot but he loved Perot's pledge that "the people will be the only people pulling my strings. . . . That concept got my vote, you know." People do not typically distinguish between campaign funds and the personal funds of a politician. When they hear about large contributions to a candidate, the suspicion is that the politician as well as the politician's campaign benefited. Campaign contributions, they believe, enrich politicians.

The result is that, in the public's eye, politicians become enmeshed in a Washington system in which they spend time with special interest leaders, they solicit money from them, and they pander to their whims. As much as they deplore it, ordinary people have no trouble understanding the tendency of politicians to fall prey to this Washington system. Indeed, in an earlier national survey conducted in 1992, we asked respondents if they thought we just happened to get the wrong kind of people in Congress or if the system transformed good people into bad. About half of the respondents believed the system was exclusively to blame, and more still believed it was partially to blame. Many of our focus group participants even conceded that they would do exactly the same thing if they were elected officials. Here is how one participant views political careers.

Ben: They [politicians] come into this corporation thinking they're going to make all these changes, you know. They have the right thing in mind. You know they generally do, I believe. But then as they start seeing all these things around them, and they start, you know, valuing . . . well, that's [when they start wanting to be like a senior member of Congress]. . . . I want to drive that car and get that office and this and that. . . . And you have kind of got to, you know, do these things, cut those corners [to get there].

Whether politicians are seen as "wrong" from the start or "wrong" because of their exposure to the corrupting Washington system, almost all people are dissatisfied with the orientation of politicians. The main problem, people believe, is the fact that the desire of politicians to please special interests takes them into a world that is quite apart from the world of the ordinary people they are supposed to represent. Many people fear that the money chase and the high-rolling special interests prevent elected officials from obtaining a true understanding of the problems of ordinary people, as is apparent in the following comments.

Kelly: The people who are in positions of power, once they get there, they're living in a class of people that are out of touch with what's really going on with the masses that they're supposed to be representing. . . . Even if they started out young and fresh and they had a good attitude in the beginning you absorb what's around you.

Maria: They [politicians] forget about the people that are down here, you know, in the lower class or the poor, you know, and how it's going to affect them.

In sum, the typical assessment of politicians seems to be that they are knowledgeable and informed but that they have been sucked into a situation in which their self-interest and advantageous position in the polity encourage them to enter a different realm. In so doing, they lose touch with ordinary people and instead become overly intimate with special interests. While politicians may have a grasp of the issues, their motivations are all out of whack. The result is that a cabal of elected officials and special interests consistently takes advantage of ordinary people. For people to have warmer feelings toward government, no policy would need to change, but these perceptions of decision-maker motivation would.

CONCLUSION

We have spent less time describing public attitudes toward politicians because the story seems a more familiar one. For some time, the public's antipathy toward politics and politicians has been widely known. Political observers write books to explain "why Americans hate politics" (Dionne 1991) and even refer to the modern era as "antipolitical" (Schedler 1997). Our survey respondents and focus group participants have helped to fill in some of the details, but the general description of the public's largely negative attitudes toward politicians will come as a surprise to few observers.

Our findings with regard to the people's view of themselves deserve more emphasis, as they are anything but consistent with a mountain of previous research and claims. Past work has stressed ordinary people's desire to govern and confidence in their own ability to govern. It also often contends that the high level of frustration people feel with the political system is traceable to the fact that they are not involved in the political system on a routine basis. For example, Cronin (1989) claims that "for about a hundred years Americans have been saying that voting occasionally for public officials is not enough" (1) and that people "would participate if they had a better way to make themselves heard" (5). Miller (1991: 27) writes that "the pretense of American politics is that the people know best." Rauch (1994: 22) believes "the dominant key of political rhetoric today" is that "someone has taken over the government and 'we' must take it back." Grossman (1995: 148) refers to the "continued yearning of Americans to govern themselves." Citrin (1996: 268) sees the current era as being animated by a populist spirit. Greenberg and Page (1997: 5–6) believe Americans prefer democracy over other forms of government, since "ordinary people want to rule themselves." Barber (1984) is determined to make a strong rather than thin democracy by securing rich citizen involvement in governmental activity and decision making. Mathews (1994: 11) writes that people have been "forced out of politics by a hostile takeover." This alleged takeover, we are told, has been accomplished by a "professional political class" (15) consisting of lobbyists, the media, and constantly campaigning politicians and has made the people eager to reconnect with the political system, to debate issues, and to meet frequently with their neighbors about societal problems. In fact, Mathews (1994: ch. 6) believes the main task of reformers should be to find a place for these meetings. Given people's desire to meet and to talk and to be informed about politics, a place to do it is all we need. Kidd (2001: 5) asserts that "today . . . the cry of the people to be let in – to be able to share in the ruling of themselves – continues to be heard."

Not only does past work claim people want to be involved in politics, but it also believes they are far more capable than elected officials. Becker and Slaton (2000: 3), for example, believe that "citizens are . . . well beyond and above narrowly selfish interests, institutional pressures, and the nearsightedness of elites. . . . Deliberative citizenries are far wiser and fairer than any political elite ever could be."

The evidence we have obtained from listening to the people themselves points toward quite a different conclusion. It is true that people are skeptical of the professional political class. We are in total concurrence with conventional wisdom on this point. But the notion that the people are champing at the bit to get back into politics on

a personal level is simply wrong.[3] The truth of the matter is that the
people themselves, not just arrogant members of the political class,
have sizable reservations about empowering ordinary people. People
overwhelmingly admit that they and the American people generally
are largely uninformed about political matters. They also have reservations about the trustworthiness of the American people, with half
of the people not trusting their fellow citizens. People are not at all
certain that the "country would be better off if the American people
rather than politicians decided important political matters." In fact,
just as many people disagree with this statement as agree.

The open-ended comments of ordinary Americans in our focus
group sessions are even more revealing of their true views of the
political moxie and motivations of ordinary people. The overall impression is apparent in the comments we now list seriatim. These
comments hardly suggest popular confidence in the political capabilities and motivations of the American public.

Ron: We are a very lazy society that wants everything given to them.
Maria: A lot of people, they don't want to be informed.
Eric: We have avenues to contact our representatives . . . we just choose
not to.
Jackie: We're too apathetic. . . .
Mike: There were times I didn't vote. Honestly, it wasn't because I didn't
think my opinion counted, it was because that was out of my way. You know,
I had something else that I wanted to do that day.
Robin: People aren't very bright.
Mike: We have people who don't care.
Chuck: I think the biggest problem with our government is not the government, it's the people. . . . We really don't care to take an active role and it
don't bother us, you know, as long as it doesn't directly affect me. Just leave
me alone.
Glen: And if this isn't going to impact me, I'm not going to [get involved in
politics].
Cary: See, we're all concerned about survival, what we have to do 8 hours
a day in order to make . . . meet bills, and therefore, regardless of what's
taking place across town that really irritates you, you say, "well that's across
the town." Let me do my 8 hours and do my thing rather than really getting
involved.
Jill: I think a huge weakness of our society is that people have the attitude
that "you owe me." . . . And they don't feel like they need to do anything for
themselves.

---

[3] For additional evidence supporting our claims, see Morin (1996).

When juxtaposed with the usual pandering statements from politicians and many elite observers regarding the noble, diligent, capable, and yearning-to-be-involved masses, these amazingly forthright self-assessments are jarring and revealing. People themselves believe that people aren't very bright, they don't care, they are lazy, they are selfish, they want to be left alone, and they don't want to be informed. People are self-effacing. They do not need to gloss over their shortcomings, as politicians must gloss over people's shortcomings. They know they should be involved in politics and they know they are doing damage by not being involved. They understand that their lack of involvement has made possible the very dominance of special interests that they despise. To be sure, some people feel they were driven out by flaws, real and perceived, in the system, but many concede that the professional political class did not commit a hostile takeover. Rather, the people admit that the politicians were invited in. Moreover, people recognize that the influence of the professional political class is at least partially beneficial. Thanks to representatives, people do not need to be constantly bothering with a lot of issues about which they do not care. Since individuals are often too uninformed, unmotivated, or narrow to exert appropriate political influence, politicians *should* make the decisions for us, at least that is the sentiment of a surprising number of focus group respondents.

People do *not* universally agree that they have been forced out of politics. A large number, in fact, would prefer to have nothing to do with politics and therefore readily admit that they opted out. They support a division of labor in which others are designated to deal with political matters so that ordinary people can go on with their lives. Unlike academics, most people are not consumed with a desire to figure out ways in which ordinary Americans could become more involved in politics. Consider the following focus group exchange.

Michelene: When I leave here, when I walk out this door, I'm not going to volunteer for anything. I'm not going to get involved in anything. I mean I know this. I'm not going to pretend I'm some political activist. I'm lazy. I'm not going to do it. I'm too busy obsessing on other things going on in my life.
Robin: That's how most people are.
Michelene: I am. So somebody's got to do it and I don't care how much money they [politicians] make, you know. . . . I don't resent the money because I don't want the job. I'm not interested in it.

While the general thrust of Michelene's sentiments is similar to those of many, many others, she goes farther than most. Most people *do* resent the money that is made by politicians and most are not willing to turn over all decision-making authority to them. Indeed, even in the face of people's quite negative perceptions of the American people and the desire for others to take care of political problems for them, most people (again, unlike Michelene) still seem to want to shift power from institutions and elected officials toward ordinary Americans. Explaining this unusual combination of sentiments is, in many respects, the key to understanding the kind of government people want, and this challenging task is the one we tackle in the next chapter.

6

Americans' Desire for Stealth Democracy

Whereas in Chapters 4 and 5 we stuck closely to the data, reporting survey and focus group results on citizen sentiments toward various aspects of the political system, in this chapter on the larger picture of people's process preferences we take some interpretational liberties. This is by necessity. After all, determining why so many Americans appear to want to empower a group of which they think so little (ordinary people) is not information that can be readily obtained via a pat survey item. As such, our interpretation of admittedly circumstantial data should be taken for what it is. At the same time, it is only fair to point out that the widespread belief that the American people want to empower ordinary people because they believe they would do a better job making political decisions than elites is based on an interpretation as well – or, as we argue below, on a serious misinterpretation. Regardless, unraveling the American people's perceptions and preferences on this point is the key to understanding the kind of governmental process they really want.

Many people do not believe their fellow citizens to be particularly noble, trustworthy, informed, or competent. At the same time, two-thirds of the American public believes the input of these flawed citizens should be increased at the expense of input from elected officials and political institutions. But even as the people call for giving more influence to people like them, they make it clear that they would prefer not to be much involved in political decision making. When it comes to politics, many people want, as one focus group participant put it, "to be left alone." But if this desire to be left alone is as common as we imply, how can nearly 84 percent of American adults support greater use of direct democracy in the form of ballot initiatives and referenda?

Our explanation of this puzzling confluence of views is relatively straightforward. People's most intense desire for the political process is that it not take advantage of them by allowing certain entities such as special interests and elected officials to reap personal gains at the expense of ordinary people like themselves. Increasingly, scholars are realizing that the desire to avoid being played for a sucker is an intensely held human motivation (for a good review, see Guth and Tietz 1990). And rank-and-file Americans believe the existing structures of American politics allow ordinary people to be played for suckers. Their strongest and most earnest political goal is to get power away from self-serving politicians. But identifying who should *not* have power is easy; identifying who *should* have power is another story. Conventional wisdom holds that people want to shift power to the people; our view is that this alleged populist instinct, this apparent desire to empower ordinary people, is largely if not entirely chimerical.

Not far behind "giving more power to selfish elites" on the list of disliked political procedures is "getting more personally involved." People indicate greater enthusiasm for more political involvement when popular democracy is presented as the only alternative to dominance by self-serving elites. As it becomes apparent in the unfolding of this chapter, we believe that if people were convinced that a third option were possible – namely, government by non-self-interested elites – they would take it in a minute. In pointing this out, we are not implying that people are typically prepared to articulate a developed sense of their procedural preferences. But articulated or not, it is vital to know roughly where the people do and do not want to go procedurally. We are certain that as much as they would like to weaken existing, allegedly self-interested elites, people do not want to empower ordinary Americans. Populist reforms will not lead to a more popular and legitimate government because they are not what the people want.

STEALTH DEMOCRACY

As is apparent from the evidence presented in Chapter 5, many people do not find politics intrinsically interesting. They do not want to reengage with the political process. They do not want to follow political issues because they do not care about most issues. As a result, people most definitely do *not* want to take over political decision making from elected officials. As Cronin (1989: 228) admits,

"Americans overwhelmingly endorse leaving the job of making laws to their elected representatives." We would take this observation one step further: Americans do not even want to be placed in a position where they feel obligated to provide input to those who *are* making political decisions. People appear to want to be more active and involved in politics only because it is one of the few ways they can see (or the only option presented to them) of stopping decisions from being made by those who directly benefit from those decisions.[1] People often view their political involvement as medicine they must take in order to keep the disease of greedy politicians and special interests from getting further out of hand.[2]

If Americans could have their druthers, representatives would understand the concerns of ordinary people simply because they are ordinary people themselves and because they spend time among other ordinary people. No public input would be necessary. How is such a system democratic? The people want to be certain that if they ever *did* deign to get involved, if an issue at some point in the future happened to impinge so directly on their lives that they were moved to ask the system for something, elected officials would respond to their request with the utmost seriousness. This, to many people, is as democratic as they want their political system to be; they do not want a system that is characterized by regular sensitivity to every whim of the people (and that thus expects and requires an attentive and involved public), but, rather, a system that is instinctively in touch with the problems of real Americans and that would respond with every ounce of courtesy and attentiveness imaginable if those real Americans ever did make an actual request upon the system. This form of latent representation, of stealth democracy, is not just what people would settle for; it is what they prefer, since it frees them from the need to follow politics. For this to happen, though, people need

---

[1] In a famous essay written in the early nineteenth century but only recently translated into English, Benjamin Constant (1988 [1819]) argues that it is good that citizens no longer need to spend much time on politics. That way they can spend more time on private activities like commerce and they can "hire" representatives to look after politics. As such, Constant perfectly anticipates the mood of many modern Americans. Constant, however, believes the people are foolish if they do not look after the people they hire to look after politics. We argue that Americans are eager to avoid even this responsibility and become frustrated when they feel obligated to "look after" their representatives.

[2] There is even evidence that those who believe politicians are acting selfishly are *more* likely to participate in politics because the need to check elite power is greater (see Hibbing and Theiss-Morse 2001).

to be assured that decision makers are interested in them as people, are potentially open to popular input, and are not benefiting materially from their service and decisions. This desire for empathetic, unbiased, other-regarding, but uninstructed public officials is about as distinct as possible from the claim that people want to provide decision makers with more input than is currently done.

IF I DON'T CARE ABOUT AN ISSUE, OTHER REAL PEOPLE PROBABLY DON'T, EITHER

A key factor causing many Americans to be attracted to the deferential, "don't bother me" political processes we have described is their disinterested attitude toward most issues on the political agenda (see Part I) and their belief that most other Americans are similarly disinterested. Psychologists and others have consistently found that people often perceive a false consensus.[3] That is, people tend to see their own attitudes as typical so they overestimate the degree to which others share their opinions. This pattern almost certainly applies to perceptions of issue interest as well. Those who are not interested in any political issues tend to believe that most other ordinary people are not interested in any political issues, either. Those who are interested in, say, education policy overestimate public concern about education and underestimate public interest in other policy areas.

Evidence for such a pattern is found in the national survey. We asked respondents to identify "the most important problem facing the country." Responses were coded into 34 possible categories (see Appendix B). The most identified problem (crime) was mentioned by just 82 of 1,263 respondents (6.5 percent). Seventeen problems were viewed as most important by at least 20 respondents. In short, in the first half of 1998 at least, there was nothing approaching a consensus on the most important problem facing the nation. But when we asked respondents whether they believed "the American people agreed on the most important problem facing the country," 39 percent said that "most" Americans did and another 41 percent said that "some" Americans did, leaving only one out of five saying that "very few" Americans did. The perceived level of consensus on

[3] See, for example, Ross, Greene, and House (1977); Noelle-Neumann (1984); Montgomery (1992); Moscovici (1992); Doise, Clemence, and Lorenzi-Cioldi (1993); Baker et al. (1995); Glynn, Ostman, and McDonald (1995); Stringer and Thomas (1996); Parker (1997); and Glynn et al. (1999).

society's most important problem is decidedly greater than the actual level of consensus. Beliefs about extensive consensus among regular Americans were apparent in the focus group sessions as well. A participant named Lisa spoke for many when she concluded, "in the end, a majority will want the same thing, the same end." And another claimed that "80 percent of the people think one way."

Relatedly, people believe, perhaps correctly, that there is a general societal consensus on major goals. Since people agree on the big goals – affordable medical care, a growing economy, a balanced budget, a secure retirement program, an adequate defense, less crime, better education, and equality of opportunity – they believe a properly functioning government would just select the best way of bringing about these end goals without wasting time and needlessly exposing the people to politics (see Morone 1990). Indeed, the people's lack of desire to become informed on (at best) all but a few issues makes it difficult for them to comprehend any legitimate justification for intense disagreement on other issues. Consequently, when it is apparent that the political arena is filled with intense policy disagreement, people conclude that the reason must be illegitimate – namely, the influence of special interests. After all, the reasoning goes, people like me could not be the cause of bitter policy disagreements on all those issues because we do not care that much, because we do not see their relevance, and because even when a particular policy goal is important to us we cannot understand why bickering over the details of proposed solutions is necessary.

People's tendency to see the policy world in such a detached, generic, and simplistic form explains why Ross Perot's claim during his presidential campaigns in 1992 and 1996 that he would "just fix it" resonated so deeply with the people. Since, according to the people's perceptions, Americans tend to agree on where the nation should go, and since getting there is merely a technical problem, is it any wonder that people have little time for policy debate and compromise? People's lack of policy interests leads them to view policies in an overly broad fashion (if consensus means only that few people want high crime, bad schools, and a lousy economy, then consensus does not mean much at all), which in turn makes it impossible for them to fathom how any elected official who claims to be in touch with the people could care so much about minute policy details, especially when these details involve a policy area that does not seem central to them. False consensus makes it difficult for the people to realize that even though it is not central to them, a given policy area may be central to someone else, and disinterest makes it difficult for people to realize that working out a detailed plan for *how* to achieve quality schools, crime-free streets, and low unemployment is the real (unavoidably contentious) question. Of course, there is a consensus on these objectives, but people's belief that policies designed to achieve consensual goals can be considered, compared, and adopted democratically without extensive disagreements is simply incorrect.

Too much has been made of Americans' middle-of-the-road position on individual policy matters. People who are unmotivated by policy debates tend not to know much about policy details and, when asked in surveys about these details, give neutral, middle-ground responses. It is true that Americans tend to be moderates on many issues (see Dionne 1991; Fiorina 1996), but it is also true that the appearance of moderation is exacerbated by the people's perfectly understandable lack of political awareness. People who adopt centrist positions on difficult policy issues tend to be less politically informed than people who adopt noncentrist positions (see, e.g., Zaller 1992: 102). A middle response is in many respects the safest response when information is lacking. If people would suddenly find the motivation to care about policy specifics, they would soon become both more informed and less moderate. Only from the dimness of people's policy-disinterested cave does the vision of consensus on real policy issues appear.

PEOPLE'S DISLIKE OF DEBATE, COMPROMISE, AND CONFLICT

People's overestimation of consensus affects the public's attitudes toward central elements of standard democratic processes in real-world (that is, nonhomogeneous and therefore somewhat conflictual) situations. Why should the public favorably view processes designed to resolve conflict if they deny the existence of legitimate conflict? If 80 percent of the people are in agreement, there is no need for debate and compromise. People would see democratic procedures as unnecessary and maybe even counterproductive because conflict is unnecessary and counterproductive. It turns out that this is exactly people's take on political debate and compromise.

Before providing empirical support for this statement, we briefly recognize an interesting group of people: those who simply are uncomfortable in the presence of political disagreement of any kind. For these individuals, the problem is not just that conflict appears to be the creation of special interests; it is that they just do not enjoy confrontation and disagreement, regardless of its legitimacy or relevance. We are in no position to state the portion of the American population so constituted but it is important to recognize that such people exist. One item in the survey asked respondents to agree or disagree with the following statement: "When people argue about political issues, you feel uneasy and uncomfortable." Perhaps using the phrase "argue" rather than "disagree" boosted people's tendency to concur with the statement. Nonetheless, it is noteworthy that 26 percent of all respondents agreed (some strongly) that political arguments in general made them feel uneasy. We all know people who become visibly uncomfortable when the conversation shifts to politics. For them, the problem is not the nature of political disputes so much as the fact that they occur at all – even among friends and relatives.

Conflict-averse individuals are interesting to our analytical scheme because they are quite likely to support the concept of stealth democracy (anything to make it less likely that they will have to witness political arguments and conflicts), but, unlike many other stealth democrats, their motivation for being supportive does not require them to believe that debate and compromise are bad. Theoretically, at least, these individuals may recognize that debate and compromise are absolutely essential, but they still want to do everything they can to avoid seeing these activities, perhaps by boxing government decision making and putting it in a corner. In any event, as many as one out of four American adults appears turned off by political argumentation regardless of how dignified or noble it might be.

But the main source of the desire to make government a less visible part of people's everyday lives springs from people who do not mind political arguments in theory but who are convinced political arguments are unnecessary. Our prediction is that, primarily because of their perceptions that the people agree on the big-picture goals and that policy specifics are irrelevant to all but special interests, people will see little need for or value in the democratic processes of debate and compromise. Two of the items in the survey most directly speak to this matter: "Elected officials would help the country more if they would stop talking and just take action on important problems" and "What people call compromise is really just selling out on one's principles." Responses are reported in Table 6.1.

As can be seen, the public overwhelmingly preferred action (86 percent) over debate. Perhaps it is not surprising that people prefer

Table 6.1. *The public's beliefs about debate and compromise (%)*

	Elected officials should stop talking and take action	Compromise is selling out one's principles
Strongly agree	23	8
Agree	63	52
Disagree	13	38
Strongly disagree	1	2
Strongly agree and agree	86	60

Source: Democratic Processes Survey, Gallup Organization, 1998.

doing something to talking about doing something, and these results do not necessarily mean that the public is antidebate, but even with this wording it is somewhat surprising that there is not more support for talking through problems and hearing diverse sentiments before plowing ahead. Moreover, another item asked people whether they believed "officials should debate more because they are too likely to rush into action without discussing all sides." Even with the mention of the negative alternative (rushing into action), 43 percent still viewed debate unfavorably. Attitudes toward compromise were barely more positive. Well over half of the respondents agreed that compromise was the equivalent of selling out on principles rather than a needed concession to legitimate opposing interests for the sake of obtaining some kind of solution. Again, this single question cannot allow us to conclude that the public hates compromise. To be sure, in certain contexts people support compromise, and perhaps a term such as negotiation would lead to more positive responses. But the results presented here do nothing to disabuse us of our suspicion that the people prefer politics to include minimal debate and compromise, regardless of the groups doing the debating or compromising.

The comments made by focus group participants serve only to underscore the belief that political disagreements detract from the process. In responding to a general question on the strengths and weaknesses of government in the United States, a participant named Ben said:

I'll tell you just right off the bat the thing that I don't like, or maybe I just don't understand it, is . . . where it seems like you have someone over here and someone over here and they're always fighting, although they're both supposed to be working for this common good. You know they're always, "well he said this and you said that," you know, bickering, and it doesn't seem like there's so much concern about where we're going rather than where each other's been.

Others expressed the same sentiment: "We need to have more decision making structure so that there's not so much bickering in government" and "Congress bickers all the time between the two parties, and they're always struggling for the power, rather than taking care of the issues."

The people's impatience with deliberation and compromise is an important element of the American political system. For most theorists, deliberation and compromise are at the heart of the democratic process. How else would people with initially divergent opinions come to agreement, short of having an agreement imposed upon them from a nondemocratic source? Our results suggest analysts need to recognize that even though Americans say they want democratic decision making, they do not believe standard elements of it, such as debate and compromise, are either helpful or necessary.[4]

FONDNESS FOR NONDEMOCRATIC
DECISION-MAKING STRUCTURES

If our interpretation of people's procedural preferences is correct, if they are not suspicious of the concept of elite decision making generally but, rather, only suspicious of those elites who are able and willing to serve selfish interests, then people's desire to stay out of the political process should lead them to be surprisingly open to empowering any elite they believe will not be particularly selfish. From the results presented so far, it is obvious that the public believes current elected officials and other politicians are irreparably self-serving. Is it possible for them to envision elite decision makers who are not? To be sure, this is a difficult image to conjure, but three items in the survey make an attempt. These items are important

---

[4] In this sense, journalist Clive Cook (2000: 2444) has it wrong when he speculates that if citizens were ever asked what they wanted from the political system, they would reply, "give us an honest debate and choices between alternatives, and we will take more of an interest." Our results show that citizens do not want to see more debate and would take less of an interest if more debate – honest or otherwise – were provided.

enough to our argument that we spend some time addressing them. They read:

1. Our government would run better if decisions were left up to successful business people.
2. Our government would run better if decisions were left up to nonelected, independent experts rather than politicians or the people.
3. Our government would work best if it were run like a business.

While none of these statements advocates replacing democracy with a dictatorial style of government, it is fair to say that support for business-type approaches to governing or for turning authority over to something as amorphous and unaccountable as "nonelected, independent experts" instead of "politicians or the people" suggests moving in a different direction than the populist reform agenda widely attributed to the public today. Giving more political influence to successful business people and to unelected experts would entail a significant diminution in the influence of the run-of-the-mill American. If the populist argument is right, surely, the American people, with their desire for the people to play a bigger role in political decisions, would reject such notions out of hand. If we are right, however, these less-than-democratic options would appeal to a substantial number of people.

As is evident in Table 6.2, surprising percentages of people respond favorably to the mention of decision-making structures that are not democratic and not even republican. It may be possible to discount the enthusiasm of people for suggestions of running

Table 6.2. *Public attitudes toward less democratic arrangements (%)*

	Leave decisions to successful business people	Leave decisions to nonelected experts	Run government like a business
Strongly agree	4	3	10
Agree	28	28	50
Disagree	59	60	37
Strongly disagree	10	9	3
Strongly agree and agree	32	31	60

Source: Democratic Processes Survey, Gallup Organization, 1998.

government like a business (as seen in column 3, 60 percent think this is a good idea). The concept of a smoothly running, directed, coordinated entity, moving with the efficiency demanded by market competition, may be so attractive to people that they respond in the affirmative without taking into consideration that the decision-making processes of most businesses are not accurately described as democratic. But answers to the other two questions are more difficult to dismiss. Nearly one-third of the respondents agreed that the political system would be better if "decisions were left to successful business people," and a similar percentage agreed the political system would be better if "decisions were left to nonelected experts" rather than to politicians or the people. (The mention of people in the item makes the response all the more surprising.) Some people, of course, liked both the expert and the business people options, but cross-tabulation indicates nearly 48 percent of all respondents agreed with at least one of these two less-than-democratic options.

Just short of half the adult population in the United States sees some real benefit to transferring decision-making authority to entities that are, for all intents and purposes, unaccountable to ordinary people. The question thus becomes, How can 68 percent of the population want to shift the political process so that ordinary people have more power (see Fig. 2.2), while 48 percent respond favorably to the idea of rendering the input of ordinary people all but irrelevant? Obviously, one solution is that the bulk of people who support the idea of empowering the people are not the same ones who support all but removing the people from the decision-making process. If this is so, it would be reasonable to expect a strong negative correlation between the desire to give more influence to the people and the desire to give more influence to entities that are not even accountable to the people. Alas, no such relationship materializes. The correlation between the desire to shift power to the people and the desire to give authority to unelected experts is -0.01 (n.s.), to give authority to successful business people is 0.02 (n.s.), and to run government like a business is actually a *positive* 0.12 ($p < 0.01$), meaning there is a tendency for those very individuals who want to give more authority to ordinary people also to want the political system to run like a business.

Perhaps the situation is better seen graphically. To do so, we return to the process space continuum introduced in Part I, running from direct democracy to institutional democracy. If we place people on this spectrum according to their fondness for nondemocratic

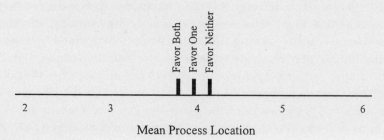

Figure 6.1. Process space locations of people who favor neither, one, or both nondemocratic process alternatives.

decision processes, an interesting pattern appears. As is apparent in Figure 6.1, those respondents who expressed a preference for both unelected experts and successful business people paradoxically also have stronger preferences (on average) for direct democracy than do those who expressed a preference for only one of the nondemocratic options. And those who responded negatively to both nondemocratic modes of decision making are further from the direct democracy pole than those who favor nondemocratic decision-making structures. Though the differences are not substantively great, they are statistically significant ($p < 0.01$) and they suggest that, far from being diametrically opposed, the apparent desire to empower people often cohabits with the desire to empower entities virtually unconnected to the people.

How can this situation be explained? Of course, people are perfectly capable of holding contradictory beliefs. They may want to reduce taxes and increase governmental services without increasing the national debt. They may want less government regulation but protection against dirty air, unsafe products, and misleading business practices. People's desire to increase the influence of ordinary people yet also increase the influence of business people and unelected experts may simply be another manifestation of the people, somewhat unrealistically, wanting it both ways. Perhaps this is true, but there may be something deeper at work.

We believe the key to explaining how large segments of the public can want to give more influence to ordinary people and also to business people and unelected experts is recognition that many Americans accept the (related) notions that (1) ordinary people are more or less in agreement on the fundamental goals for the nation and (2) governing is, therefore, basically a management problem of determining how best to achieve those goals. The first notion was most famously expressed by Rousseau (1946 [1762]) and, as we have seen, remains a popular myth among both academics and the populace. A general will exists and is visible if elites, special interests, and other counterproductive elements are kept at bay so that the noble and consensual instincts of the rank and file are allowed to emerge.

Since the people agree on societal goals, no conflict need exist, and governing is reduced to the mechanical process of implementing a good plan for attaining these goals. Determining appropriate policy action thus requires no (and, in fact, is likely to be harmed by) elaborate institutions and powerful elected officials. Burke's trustees, with their industry and judgment, are not needed (1949 [1774]). Their industry alone is quite enough. Better yet, why not turn to unbiased, perhaps even scientifically informed experts to figure out the best way to achieve the public's goals? In so doing, the people are empowered and democracy is not weakened. James Morone (1990) may have best captured this aspect of the American belief system. He points out that the combination of "direct democracy with scientific administration is a contradiction only when observed from liberal ground. If, instead of clashing interests, the people really did share an underlying communal good, then both methodologies served the same end" (126).

Contrary to conventional wisdom, people like the concept of objective bureaucrats making their technical decisions. If people are responding to a perception that bureaucrats are taking advantage of people by not working diligently, opinion may be negative, but the general notion of a dedicated bureaucratic elite calling the shots on the means to achieve the consensual ends, even if there is not direct accountability to the people, is attractive. On the basis of his Federal Reserve Board service, Alan Blinder (1997: 115) recognized that "the real source of the current estrangement between Americans and their politicians is the feeling that . . . elected officials are playing games rather than solving problems." He believes that the people want more public policy decisions "removed from the political thicket and placed in the hands of unelected technocrats" (119; see also 126). Independent commissions and the like are always appealing to the people, and presidential candidates frequently compete to be the first to propose such ideas. People want to avoid government by people who act selfishly, not government by experts and elites (see Spence 1999).

The public's accepting attitude toward government by experts is perplexing to many observers. Michael Kryzanek (1999: 64) remarks that "already in most industrial democracies the bureaucratic elite . . . has pushed aside the elected segment of the government and now makes the key decisions about public policy and national direction. Under this model efficiency and specialization replace the uncertainties associated with democratic politics. What is more distressing is that there don't appear to be many complaints about government run by bureaucrats." Of course there are few complaints. This is what the people want, as long as the bureaucrats are not personally benefiting from the decisions they make. Why should people find government by bureaucrats distressing?

Reliance on independent experts, on successful business people, or on consensual ordinary people all move decision making away from clashing interests. Some people have a simple, definite aversion to conflict, and for them clashing interests are the source of discomfort.[5] But even many of those who handle conflict in stride believe that most political conflicts are unnecessary trumped-up affairs traceable to the influence and narrow interests of powerful groups. After all, the people do not have strong feelings on policy minutiae, so any conflict must have been fabricated by self-serving elected officials and their ilk. In fact, people believe the very existence of conflict is a sign that elected officials are out of touch with ordinary Americans. Remember the comments of Ben, who lamented that "it seems like you have someone over here and someone over here and they're always fighting, although they're both supposed to be working for this common good." For Ben and many others, the common good should be self-evident, and how to achieve the common good is a management problem to which there is a readily attainable, perfectly acceptable, or perhaps even best, answer. The notion that debating among elected officials may actually be necessitated by their responsibility to represent the interests of diverse constituencies across the country is rejected by most people.

The important point in the people's thinking is that anybody *not* connected with biased special interests and self-serving elected officials would basically arrive at the same place. That is why the public is remarkably cavalier about giving more power to unelected experts

[5] See our earlier results and also Hartz (1955); Noelle-Neumann (1984); and Eliasoph (1998: ch. 2).

or to unelected business people. It is the same reason that ostensibly populist Americans give a puzzlingly warm embrace to extremely rich candidates. A 1992 Harris poll found that 55 percent of respondents agreed with the statement "Because Perot is a billionaire he won't be influenced by the special interests who make big campaign contributions." The people are comforted by the thought of a decision maker who is clearly not motivated by money and perquisites. They would rather center the political process around such individuals even if it limits accountability on the issues. Because many people have limited interest in most issues, accountability is not a pressing concern for them.

MEASURING AND EXPLAINING PREFERENCES FOR STEALTH DEMOCRACY

In a stealth democracy, governmental procedures are not visible to people unless they go looking; the people do not routinely play an active role in making decisions, in providing input to decision makers, or in monitoring decision makers. The goal in stealth democracy is for decisions to be made efficiently, objectively, and without commotion and disagreement. As such, procedures that do not register on people's radar screens are preferred to the noisy and divisive procedures typically associated with government.

Measures of support for each of the many disparate components of stealth democracy are unavailable, but the survey items described earlier in this chapter would seem to provide a reasonable start. Specifically, supporters of stealth democracy believe debate is not necessary or helpful, they do not view compromise favorably, and they are willing to turn decision making over to entities that are largely, perhaps completely, unaccountable but that promise efficiency and an absence of contention. Thus, for our purposes, stealth democratic tendencies are indicated if a respondent (1) agreed that "elected officials would help the country more if they would stop talking and just take action on important problems," (2) agreed that "what people call compromise in politics is really just selling out on one's principles," and (3) agreed either that "our government would run better if decisions were left up to nonelected, independent experts rather than politicians or the people" *or* that "our government would run better if decisions were left up to successful business people." While an admittedly imperfect measure, people who are dismissive of debate and compromise and accepting of government

Table 6.3. *Prevalence of stealth democratic characteristics*

Those with . . .	Number	Percent of all respondents
No stealth democratic traits	83	6.5
One stealth democratic trait	302	23.8
Two stealth democratic traits	538	42.4
All three stealth democratic traits	345	27.2
Total	1,268	99.9

Source: Democratic Processes Survey, Gallup Organization, 1998.

by detached entities are clearly in possession of some of the core attitudes we are associating with supporters of stealth democracy.

The distribution of people on these measures is presented in Table 6.3. It is rather remarkable to us that only 7 percent of the national survey respondents are completely devoid of stealth democratic attitudes; that is, only about one in fifteen Americans values political debate and compromise and recoils from government by experts or successful business people. On the other hand, 27 percent hold all three stealth democratic attitudes and 42 percent have two of the three. At the least, the conclusion has to be that Americans' support for standard features of democracy such as deliberation, compromise, and accountability are substantially more tepid than is usually imagined.

What accounts for the fact that some people are markedly more favorable than others toward stealth democracy? We do not pretend to have a complete answer to this question, but if the arguments presented earlier are correct, then people who simply are uncomfortable with political disagreement, who believe most Americans agree on the political agenda (or at least on the most important item on that agenda), and who have virtually no interest in political issues should be more inclined to support political procedures in which they (and other ordinary people) did not have to take an active part. The reason conflict-averse individuals should prefer stealth democracy is obvious: Any method of reducing political disagreements is bound to make such people happy. And it would also be rational for those who believe Americans agree on the items most in need of governmental attention or who are too disinterested to appreciate the importance of policy details to be accepting of stealth democracy.

It is important to notice that only one of these three conditions (conflict-aversion, perceptions of agenda consensus, or political disinterest) needs to be present to push someone toward stealth democracy. If an individual is uncomfortable in the presence of political disagreement, it does not really matter whether he or she sees consensus or is politically interested, because conflict aversion on its own is enough. Thus, our key independent variable indicates whether or not political disagreement is disliked, unnecessary, or uninteresting and is dichotomous. It is coded 1 if a person "feels uneasy and uncomfortable when people argue about political issues," believes "most" people agree on the most important problem facing the country, or expresses "no" or only "slight" interest in politics;[6] people who have none of these three attitudes or perceptions are coded 0. For shorthand, we refer to this variable as "negative view of political disagreement."

In addition to this independent variable, we rely upon a standard battery of demographic and political controls to help us understand variations in support of stealth democracy. More specifically, we include variables for gender, age, income, race, education, party identification, and political ideology. The relationships between several of these control variables and preferences for stealth democracy are interesting in their own right. The results obtained when our measure of support for stealth democracy is regressed on the main independent variable of interest as well as the eight control variables are presented in Table 6.4.

Beginning with the control variables, none of the demographic variables accounts for variations in support for stealth democracy. The coefficient for years of education may be the most surprising to many readers. It is reasonable to expect education to encourage an understanding of the necessity of debate and compromise and the importance of democratic accountability and thus for Table 6.4 to indicate a strong, negative relationship between education and support for stealth democracy. Instead, although the sign of the coefficient is negative, it is not even significant at the more permissive

[6] We repeated our procedures using an additive combination of these three variables, and the results are very similar, but the conceptualization used in Table 6.4 seems more consistent with theoretical expectations. Moreover, we substituted a more elaborate measure of specific policy interests (drawing on whether respondents claimed to "feel strongly" about preferred approaches to the policy areas of welfare and environment), but the complicated operationalization produced results similar to the basic interest measure, so we stick with the formulation described in the text.

Table 6.4. *Explaining support for*
stealth democracy

Variable	b	s.e.	p
Gender	−0.02	0.02	0.26
Age	0.003	0.04	0.94
Income	0.04	0.04	0.29
Race	0.04	0.03	0.11
Education	−0.05	0.03	0.17
Democrat	−0.08	0.02	<0.01
Republican	−0.01	0.02	0.77
Ideology	0.15	0.04	<0.01
Negative view of disagreement	0.07	0.02	<0.01
Constant	0.53	0.04	<0.01
F	6.85		<0.01
Adj. R^2	0.05		
N	999		

Source: Democratic Processes Survey, Gallup Organiza-
tiion, 1998.

0.10 level, meaning we cannot confidently state that, compared with
those lacking a high school degree, those with many years of school-
ing are less likely to support stealth democracy. One possible explanation for this disturbing situation is that education may be collinear
with the "negative views of political disagreement" variable. In other
words, education may be associated with a willingness to tolerate
political arguments, to be interested in politics, and to recognize that
"most" Americans do not agree on the most important problem
facing the nation. This explanation does not withstand analysis. The
correlation (Pearson's R) between education and "negative views
of political disagreement" has the predicted negative sign but is not
large: −0.19. Education seems to be related to people becoming
more interested in politics, more realistic about the extent of agenda
diversity, and more comfortable with political disagreement, but it
does not seem to be related to less support for stealth democracy.
When the regression is run without "negative view of disagreement,"
the coefficient for education's effect on stealth democracy is still
statistically insignificant.[7]

[7] Given the importance of this relationship, we looked at the effects of education
on the individual components of support for stealth democracy. In the multivariate

As described previously (Hibbing and Theiss-Morse 1996), we believe at least part of the explanation for the fact that additional education does not clearly lead people to be less supportive of stealth democracy is the unfortunate emphasis in most schools on consensus. Difficult, contentious issues are often avoided in schools for reasons that are as understandable as they are lamentable. State legislatures, school boards, administrators, some teachers, and many parent organizations have apparently come to the conclusion that any program realistically confronting public opinion diversity promotes conflict and therefore is anticommunity and perhaps antifamily – as if the only way we can have successful social units is to pretend that everyone thinks the same way.[8] Numerous foundations contribute to the problem by pouring money into civic education programs that teach only the details of governmental structure and badger students to participate (without giving them good reasons to do so). Unfortunately, these programs ignore conflict appreciation, so why should students come away with an understanding view of debate, compromise, and accountability?

In Chapter 1, we described results from an experiment conducted by Amy Gangl that showed that, when they were exposed to clear, even nasty, conflict, people actually were led to care about issue positions. When conflict was muted, people's issue positions were irrelevant.[9] Extrapolating from these results to current educational strategies, if the message students receive is that no meaningful conflict exists among the American people, is it any wonder students' issue positions are largely irrelevant to their political attitudes and behaviors (see Chapter 1)? By adopting a head-in-the-sand approach to conflict, the educational community is unwittingly facilitating the lack of issue relevance in American politics and is encouraging students to conclude that real democracy is unnecessary and stealth democracy will do just fine.

specification, additional years of education do lead to more favorable views of compromise and to less support for government by "experts," but education does not lead to more favorable views of debate or to heightened suspicion of government by successful business people.

[8] When she was a student in secondary school, political scientist Diana Mutz was involved in an innovative program designed to teach about conflict and how to deal with it. She reports that the program was sacked because of fears that it was proconflict and anticommunity (Mutz, personal communication).

[9] There is a parallel here to Ansolabehere and Iyengar's (1995) finding that campaign ads that play on conflict by comparing the records of each candidate are more informative to voters than ads that focus on only one candidate.

Returning to Table 6.4, it is time to discuss the nondemographic variables. Since it would be a mistake to assume the effects of party identification are linear, we included separate terms for Democratic party identifiers (34 percent of the sample) and Republican party identifiers (26 percent). Those identifying with a third party (a surprising 12 percent) or as Independents (29 percent) constitute the excluded term, so the coefficients for the major parties reflect the extent to which major-party identifiers are different from Independents and third-party identifiers (which, for the sake of simplicity, we refer to as nonpartisans). Interestingly, though nonpartisans appear slightly more supportive of stealth democracy than partisans, Republicans do not differ significantly from them. The odd-person-out is the Democratic identifier. Other things being equal, Democrats are significantly less dismissive of debate and compromise and are more suspicious of unaccountable forms of decision making. The surprisingly high level of sympathy in the American public for stealth democracy cannot be laid at the doorstep of the nonpartisan, since nonpartisans are not much different from Republicans (this conclusion holds true for each of the three component parts of the stealth democracy measure). And the aversion of Democrats toward stealth democracy is difficult to explain, since the effect is independent of "negative views of disagreement." In other words, the effect cannot be explained by the possibility that Democrats are more comfortable with political arguments than Republicans, see less consensus than Republicans, and have more interest in politics than Republicans.

In point of fact, Democrats are actually less comfortable in political arguments, have a less realistic view of the lack of consensus in the United States, and have less interest in political issues than Republicans. Democrats tend to have the traits we would associate with stealth democrats, yet Democrats tend to be the most averse to stealth democracy. Even in the bivariate specification, Democrats are less supportive of stealth democracy, but when the "negative view of disagreement" variable is included as a separate term, the difference between Democrats and the rest of the sample is, as can be seen from Table 6.4, substantial. What is it about Democrats that makes them more averse to stealth democracy? One obvious possibility is Democrats' historic antipathy toward successful business people. Since one of the possible ways we allowed people to indicate support for stealth democracy was to state that government could be improved by turning decisions over to "successful business people," perhaps

Democrats' distaste for the business community manifests itself as distaste for stealth democracy. While reasonable, this explanation fails. We ran the identical regression equation to that presented in Table 6.4 except that the "successful business people" item was not included in the dependent variable (support for stealth democracy). As was the case in Table 6.4, the coefficient for Democrats was strongly negative and statistically significant, while the coefficient for Republicans was not significantly different from nonpartisans. Apparently, there are deeper reasons that Democrats do not like concepts we are associating with stealth democracy.[10]

The main variable of interest in Table 6.4 is the one called "negative view of disagreement." It distinguishes those respondents who are not comfortable around political arguments, believe there is strong agenda consensus in the United States, or are politically disinterested. The presence of any one of these traits strongly encourages stealth democratic attitudes. As expected, people who are made uncomfortable by political disagreement or who feel it is unnecessary are more likely to believe that we can do away with debate, compromise, and accountable procedures. Willingness to govern via a stealth democracy, not surprisingly, will diminish if we can get people to tolerate political arguments, if we can show them that consensus does not exist regarding the issues that people believe need to be addressed, and if we can convince them that political issues are important.

Our claim is not that most people hold a tightly integrated set of process preferences, thereby allowing us to label them stealth democrats. People's thinking about governing processes is generally not developed enough for this to be the case. Rather, our survey respondents (and focus group participants) made it clear that they are unenthusiastic about representative, not to mention direct, democracy. In this sense, the central point is less that Americans have a compelling desire for a particular method of governing called stealth

[10] As would be expected, some multicollinearity exists between party and ideology (the Pearson's R is 0.31). But, of course, multicollinearity does not affect the sign or size of the coefficient, it only inflates standard errors, which raises the possibility that some coefficients will appear insignificant when they are not. Since party and ideology are both significant even with the multicollinearity, the danger to misinterpretation is not severe. Just in case, we ran the regression with the party variables but not ideology and with ideology but not the party variables. No features of the equation were appreciably affected by the removal of the variables, so we focus on the results with both included.

democracy than that most are only casually committed to traditional democracy. They think and say they are deeply committed, but when pushed, it becomes apparent that they do not have much understanding of the realities of real-world democratic politics. Most merely equate democracy with freedom and have not thought any more about the matter. They certainly have not taken on board the distasteful elements inevitably associated with democratic processes in diverse societies. These are the lessons people must be taught, not so that they will love democratic government – real democracy is not lovable – but so that they will tolerate and appreciate it.

Thus far we have skirted an issue that is of obvious importance to political scientists: representation. We have asserted that stealth democrats are not wary of unaccountable decision makers, and even prefer them to more accountable forms of decision making. Does this mean many Americans do not care about representation? In the next section we return to the argument we made in Part I that Americans do not care much about most policies. Since they are not policy-oriented and since they believe there is a consensus on the relevant matters facing the political system, we need to think about representation in more than a policy-congruence sense.

REPRESENTATION

By emphasizing process over policy, it may appear we are denigrating the importance of representation, which in most formulations involves a match between the people's policy preferences and the policy actions of those in power. This view of representation, we argue, is misguided. We believe the people want representation to provide them with something quite different from policy consequences, something that fits quite easily into their understanding of how the political process ought to work.

We begin by reemphasizing the extent to which people do not have a range of specific policy preferences that they expect officials to enact (see, e.g., Miller and Stokes 1963; Popkin 1991). Recent research underscores this point. Jon Dalager (1996: 509) discovered that among respondents claiming to have voted in the 1988 Senate elections (a presidential election year), "almost three-quarters of the electorate [could not] correctly recall even one of a number of issues raised in the campaign." Since less than half of the eligible electorate typically votes in modern-day on-year congressional elections, we are left with the conclusion that a tiny percentage of American adults is policy-driven. Presidential elections may not be much better. A Pew poll found that, at least in the early part of the 2000 presidential campaign, "potential voters [were] basing their early preferences . . . more on broad impressions and personalities than issues." They found that people were not even making "a connection between a candidate and his top issue" ("Poll: Voters Choose Persona over Issues" 1999: 7A). The absence of positions on a range of issues is one factor that permits stealth democracy to be an attractive set of processes to many people. Thus, what most people usually want out of their representative is not particular roll-call votes or policy outcomes. Although people may feel strongly about an issue or two and they may get outraged by an unusually salient vote or action, it is a rare day that issues get an official in electoral trouble.

Elections aside, people are not that displeased with the government's policies. Remember that 56 percent of our survey respondents were "generally satisfied with the public policies the government has produced lately." What is more, pleasure with public policies is hardly a guarantor that people will be pleased with government. Of those respondents who indicated they agreed with recent governmental policies, 28 percent disapproved of the federal government, and of those who disagreed with recent policies, 29 percent approved. These 57 percent are people whose perceptions of government policies do not determine their attitudes toward government. No doubt there are many others whose approval or disapproval of policies and of government match but do so only because of chance or projection.

Much previous research has noted that people want more than issue representation out of government. This message has been ably sent by some of the classic works on Congress,[11] but our results – particularly, the focus group results – allow us to elaborate the general point in important ways. We believe what people want in terms of representation is not congruent roll-call votes but a general sense that those in government understand and care what life is like for ordinary people. Many people now do not believe government understands them, and the people most likely to feel this way are not those one would think to do so.

Richard Fenno's (1977) detailed description of the view of the representational process held by members of Congress demonstrates the extent to which the members realize that policy details and policy

[11] See Mayhew (1974); Fiorina (1977); and Fenno (1978).

congruence are not the prime desires of most citizens. When asked why he felt compelled to attend a local event back in the district, one member said, "People want to see the congressman – me. . . . I could have sent the most scholarly person I could find to make a more erudite, comprehensive and scholarly exposition than I made. If I had done so, the people there wouldn't have enjoyed one bit of anything he said. And they would never have forgiven me for not being there" (902). People do not necessarily want certain policy outputs; they want decision makers to care. But this quote came from a member Fenno took to be emblematic of a "person-to-person" style. Are constituent desires different in an "issue-oriented" constituency? Apparently not. When Fenno's prototypical issue-based member was asked what was important to his constituents, he said, "People don't make up their minds on the basis of reading all our position papers. We have twenty-six of them because some people are interested. But more people get a gut feeling about the kind of human being they want to represent them" (904). Exactly – and people's gut preference is to be represented by someone like them or, at the least, someone who understands them. They do not want someone who seems more interested in arcane legislative procedures and unusual, special, or what the people take to be minority-opinion concerns.

Whereas protecting minority rights and guarding against a tyranny of the majority have been important concerns of political analysts (see, e.g., Guinier 1994), the people are convinced representation is threatened from the opposite direction. Some 70 percent of our respondents in the national survey *disagreed* with the statement that "the current political system does a good job of representing the interests of all Americans. . . ." But, more notably, displeasure with the current system of representative government tends not to spring from perceptions that minority views are going unheard but, rather, from perceptions that minority views are dominating the political scene. Thus, many believe the underrepresented group is not those with unpopular (i.e., minority) opinions but, rather, those holding the majority opinion. As Margaret Levi (1998: 91) observes, "there is a danger . . . that institutions meant to protect minorities are perceived by majorities as discriminating against the majority." She is absolutely correct.

Statistical analysis of the kind of people likely to complain that the interests of all Americans are *not* being represented reveals that they tend not to be the "outs" of society but, rather, with an exception or two, the "ins." This situation is most easily seen for race. We divided

Table 6.5. *Perceptions of quality of representation by race*

	Whites (%)	People of color (%)	N
Current system does *not* represent all Americans	70	59	861
Current system represents all Americans	30	41	406
N	1,058	209	1,267

Source: Democratic Processes Survey, Gallup Organization, 1998.

the sample into whites and nonwhites so we could determine which group was most likely to agree that "the current system does a good job representing the interests of all Americans, rich or poor, white or black, male or female." As indicated in Table 6.5, people of color are actually more likely than whites to approve of the current status of representation (the correlation is 0.075, which is significant at the 0.01 level). With regard to race at least, minorities in the United States are more pleased with representation than is the majority. Moreover, the less educated and the young are more likely than the more educated and older people to approve of the current representational system, and men are not more likely than women to give high marks to the current system of representation (though it is true that those with higher incomes view representational patterns positively). So, if anything, the group generally seen as ascendant in American society – well-educated, middle-aged, white males – is the one most likely to believe the current system is *not* representing the interests of all Americans, though these relationships are all fairly weak.

The somewhat surprising result that "minority" groups are more likely to believe all interests are being represented becomes less so when we turn to the focus group comments. Consider the following two exchanges that came from an earlier wave of focus groups we conducted in 1992 on attitudes toward Congress.

Bob: When the President says I think we need to do this for the country blah blah and all that, they [members of Congress] ought to see if they can do it rather than work hard not to do it and kill it, right?
Delores: But that started a long time ago when they allowed the protestors and the demonstrations to come in front of the White House or wherever. They pitch their little thing and confuse the whole issue. And then everybody gets all excited and this has to be acted on.

Bob: The government has to listen to the 10 people who feel this way but that's only 10 out of millions. . . . We are the silent majority.

Molly: I think the vast majority of Congress's members have no idea really what the people's wishes are.

Steve: They are in touch with the extremes. Those are the people that they listen to and they're the ones that pull their strings, right? But the majority doesn't scream and shout.

The people are convinced that small numbers of individuals, either because of their ability to attract attention or, more likely, because of their money and contacts, can succeed in capturing government, thereby leaving "the silent majority" out of the loop – ignored and frustrated.

The reason dissatisfaction with current representational strategies is not concentrated among those belonging to racial minorities or those with dissenting policy views is that most people are not primarily concerned with achieving their policy objectives on a range of issues. Instead, people seem much more concerned with knowing that those in power understand what it is like in the ordinary world and can identify with that world's trials and tribulations. We were quite surprised at the extent to which people do not expect elected officials to solve all of the problems affecting them personally or the nation at large. People know that many problems are beyond the control of elected officials and that others are devilishly difficult. But while they may not demand solutions to these problems, they do demand respect, sensitivity, and understanding. One of the most emotional comments on this point came from Jean in one of our more recent focus group sessions.

The reality is until you've walked a mile in my very worn sneakers then you [cannot understand me]. . . . We're more in touch with reality than anybody in Washington or [her state capital]. I know in my heart of hearts I'm doing all I can; raising two kids by myself. . . . I know I represent a large majority of the people.

And two other participants even concocted a strategy for getting politicians to learn about the people they should be representing.

Tammie: They should send a politician . . . with a mom that works, you know, two kids, no husband.

Andrea: A waitress job.

Tammie: Go live with her for a week and deal on a daily basis with what she deals with and see, you know . . . just things like that. I think they should be more in touch with the people.

Jean, Tammie, and Andrea are not expecting that even the most enlightened government would be able to solve the very real difficulties peppering the lives of so many people. But they would feel much better about government if they were convinced that the people in it understood their plight.[12] People are less concerned with governmental solutions than they are with knowing that decision makers understand what it is like to walk in very worn sneakers at a waitress job. But too many people are convinced that decision makers know only what it is like to walk in wing-tips at lavish cocktail parties. This is what people want changed about government, not specific policies.[13]

But, to return to an earlier claim of ours, how can people imagine that unelected experts and business people would represent them in such a fashion? Surely, they are as unlikely as politicians to have walked in a single mom's sneakers. True, but in our formulation, empathy is a secondary concern. Before someone can empathize with our situation, that person must stop focusing on his or her own. In this sense, item number one on the people's procedural agenda is to try to get someone in power who either does not have the ability or the desire to act self-interestedly. For many people, even after the Enron collapse, the phrase "successful business person" evokes images of an individual who is already successful and, more important, who has not sought political power. Whatever else, such people at least did not begin with the intention of taking advantage of us and that puts them ahead of politicians, since politicians made a concerted effort to gain power. It is this desire for power that sets politicians apart and that makes people suspicious. As we pointed out before, most ordinary people believe that, if they were magically placed in a position of political power, they would be just as self-

[12] Lind and Tyler rightly observe that politeness and empathy are key parts of procedural justice (1988: 214; see also Lerner 1981).

[13] In one sense, Bill Bianco (1994) is on the right track in stressing that constituents want to trust their elected officials. But he believes the goal of constituents is to "ensure that their representative does what they want" in policy terms, so they "look for ways to increase the chances" they will so act (13). The evidence from our survey and focus groups leads us, on the other hand, to the conclusion that manipulating representation in such a fashion is far more than the people want to do. Trust for them is simply believing the representative will not act in a self-serving fashion and thus will (by default if nothing else) act in the interest of ordinary people. Of course, by stressing trust as a policy matter, Bianco is in good company. See Arnold (1990), for example, though Fenno's (1978) focus on a presentation of self (as the same kind of person as the constituents) comes much closer to the needed emphasis on procedural matters.

serving as the politicians are. But politicians' motivations make them suspect, particularly when the current system, in the opinion of the people, provides motivated individuals with a plethora of opportunities to be self-serving.

Although people are willing to cut some slack to a representative they believe to be personally attached to them, the prevalence of money, special interests, and office perquisites in the modern American polity means people are extremely reluctant to believe that the kind of representation they want can be provided by anyone who craves the power of elected office. Even if the eventual policy decisions are the same, people would rather thrust power at someone who does not want it than someone who does. After all, if the decision maker is not there by choice, people are less likely to conclude that the driving force of the decision maker is to take advantage of his or her position. People would like constraints to be put in place that would make it impossible for elected officials to become rich by serving. Failing this, they would prefer to secure officials who do not begin with a desire to seize the reins of power. In an ideal world, these officials would not be self-serving and they would also be empathetic. Successful business people and independent experts, though not necessarily empathetic, are perceived to be competent, capable individuals not in pursuit of power. That is enough for many people, or at least it is better than the kind of representation they believe they are receiving now.

STEALTH DEMOCRACY REDUX

Ordinary people have a different view of politics than political elites. The people believe that Americans generally agree on overall societal goals. While they realize that different opinions exist on the best way to achieve those goals, they are convinced there is a reasonable way of proceeding that can be divined by hard-working, unbiased, intelligent people. In so believing, the American people are viewing the governing process as the marriage of Rousseau's general societal will and the progressives' confidence in scientific implementation processes. More important, perhaps, is what the people do *not* believe the governing process should be. Some are not eager for candidates to offer any proposals at all (remember the focus group participant who noted that if politicians have their own "agenda," they may not be as attentive to the needs of the people). Many others do not believe politics should entail a competition of ideas, with candidate

A offering one set of ideas and candidate B offering another. Many people are not convinced a legitimate opposition is central to good government, because if governmental procedures were working properly, then the opposition would be opposing the consensus will of the people, and how could such a stance be legitimate? People do not see a need for political debates and brokered decisions. They simply do not believe debates and compromises are necessary, since we all want the same general things, since the best way to achieve those things will be readily apparent to those who study the problems in an unbiased way, and since the little details of policy are not that important anyway. To put it simply, the people yearn for the "end of politics" (Schedler 1997).

Political elites, on the other hand, tend to believe the ideal democracy is characterized by an excited commotion, with diverse ideas and new proposals being offered and tested in the stimulating crucible of public debate. Sides are picked, battles are fought, debates are held, and the resulting compromised outcome by definition reflects an appropriate synthesis of legitimate conflicting forces (see Dahl 1956). Crick (1992: 18) sees government as "the open canvassing of rival interests." If politicians sound too much alike (Brody and Page 1972) or if they focus their campaigns on their (and their opponents') families or personal traits such as integrity (Ansolabehere and Iyengar 1995), analysts see this as a failure of the process, a deviation from proper, issue-based politics. Remember, in Converse's well-known formulation (1964), citizens' political capabilities are judged by their ideological understanding, their issue constraint, and their issue consistency. Citizens lacking a coherent ideology (i.e., lacking a set of issue beliefs that hang together in some fashion) are judged to be deficient.

But the people do not see failure in the same place analysts see failure. People equate the presence of dissenting policy proposals with the presence of special interests and the attendant demotion of the true consensual, general interest. As a result, the people believe competition and differences should not be revered as the sine qua non of good government but instead should be reviled as its bane. People do not want to have to meet under Rousseau's oak tree to resolve political issues; they want someone else to meet. But they want the people who meet to be intimately in touch with the realities of the lives of ordinary people – realities they believe to be generally universal. If this is the case, disagreements among those who meet will be virtually nonexistent, and deciding what to do will be quick and painless. Governing experts will implement decisions in the most efficient manner, and the public will not have to hear about delays, debates, compromises, gridlock, egos, and agendas.

To the extent the people *are* willing to be involved in politics, the motivation stems not from their desire to achieve a certain policy outcome but, rather, their desire to keep politicians from being able to get away with behaving in a self-serving fashion. This is an important difference. People are not sure what policies they want, but they know what processes they do *not* want – and those are processes in which people who are making political decisions are able to feather their own nests. People's political involvement, such as it is, is often driven by the perception that politicians and their special-interest ventriloquists are taking advantage of ordinary people (see Hibbing and Theiss-Morse 2001).

The Supreme Court is relatively popular not just because the justices hide their internal conflict from public view but mostly because their decisions are not perceived to affect their own material well-being. When the Court permits criminals to get off on technicalities or radicals to burn the American flag, the public, by wide margins, believes the decisions to be seriously wrong-headed. But approval of the Court persists because the situation of the justices themselves has not been improved by those decisions or any others they make.

A perfect illustration of the benefits derived by the Court from public perception of the motivation of the justices surfaced in the aftermath of the 2000 presidential election. When the Court decided in a contentious 5-4 vote (with an unusually personal attack on fellow justices contained in John Paul Steven's dissent) to give the presidency to George W. Bush, most observers predicted the Court's standing, even legitimacy, would suffer. Jeffrey Rosen, for example, felt the Court had put itself "in harm's way" by revealing that it is "no less ideologically divided than every other institution" (2000: 17). Elites were therefore surprised when, though the people saw the Court as divided as a result of *Bush v. Gore*, the realization did nothing to lower public approval. As Richard Morin and Claudia Deane (2001) noted on the basis of *Washington Post* data, little damage was done to public confidence in the Supreme Court. All other surveys in early 2001 showed the same thing. Our theory provides a clear explanation for Court approval thriving despite *Bush v. Gore*. The public may not have liked what the Court did and many may have realized for the first time that the Court is ideological, even political. But most people were not led to conclude that the justices' actions were designed to make themselves rich. Political conflict in and of itself is not despised by the people. Political conflict traceable to self-serving interests is.[14]

By way of contrast to the Court, when Congress votes on campaign finance, patients' bills of rights, congressional salaries, tax loopholes, tobacco subsidies, and pollution control, the public may or may not be upset with the particular outcome, but approval of Congress suffers regardless because the public is absolutely convinced that the decisions are attributable to the desire of the members to better themselves by securing reelection, by getting a trip to Maui, by getting rich, or by garnering a major contribution for their campaign coffers. The people are not always sure what decisions they want, but they are sure they want those decisions to be made for something other than self-serving reasons. Ironically, the more the public trusts elected officials to make unbiased decisions, the less the public participates in politics. The ideal form of government, in the opinion of many people, is one in which they can defer virtually all political decisions to government officials but at the same time trust those officials to be in touch with the American people and to act in the interest of those people and not themselves.

[14] This is a point missed by our earlier research (see Hibbing and Theiss-Morse 1995).

PART III

Should People Be Given the Processes They Want?

W HAT WE HAVE TRIED TO DO SO FAR is understand the political process the people of the United States most prefer, for better or worse, realistic or not. And we now know that Americans do not care much about most policies. They do not like conflict. They do not like special interests. They are not populists. They do not want to be more involved in politics. They do not want to keep a wary eye on self-interested politicians. What they want are caring, other-regarding, common-good-oriented decision makers. They want empathetic, non-self-interested decision makers (ENSIDs).

What do these empirical results mean for our understanding of democracy and how it ought to work in the United States in the early twenty-first century? Part III addresses this question. We should stress that we do not believe government by ENSIDs is feasible (though it is more feasible than those wedded to politics-as-usual imagine). And we should also stress that even if it were feasible, we do not think government by ENSIDs would be a good idea (but perhaps not as bad an idea as those same traditionalists imagine). The problem is that the currently popular alternative strategies for improving people's attitudes toward government are no better, and may actually be worse, than stealth democracy. We critically analyze some of these alternatives, including getting people more involved in volunteer associations and in deliberative democratic settings. By drawing on a wide range of research primarily from political science and psychology, we argue that pushing people to be more involved in politics and political decision making will not lead to better decisions, better people, or a more legitimate political system. Theorists are misguided if they think otherwise.

What is the solution? We realize our answers will be unsatisfactory to many, but there are no quick, easy fixes. One possible option is to pass laws that make it more difficult for elected officials to act in a self-serving manner. For example, we endorse passing campaign finance reform legislation. At the same time, we harbor little hope that such legislation would markedly improve public attitudes toward government, for without a *complete* eradication of all means for elected officials to appear self-serving (not just acquiring campaign funds), Americans will continue to believe that elected officials almost always act in a self-interested manner. It is in our nature to be suspicious of the motives of the powerful. The most promising, but not easily implemented, proposal is to educate citizens better on the need to tolerate conflict in a highly diverse, complex, modern, democratic political system. Only then will people better appreciate the usefulness of institutional arrangements that try to put together solutions by listening to many voices, including those of special interests, debating all sides of the issue, and compromising to reach a solution agreeable to many.

The purpose of Part III, then, is to look seriously at the contemporary democratic theory literature given the empirical results we detail in Parts I and II. The key question of this final part of the book is, Which reforms do or do not hold promise for making the United States government better? As becomes apparent below, we are convinced that many of the reforms being pushed by political theorists and others have been formulated without due attention to the kind of political system the people want. Consequently, these reforms are unlikely to improve the system and may very well damage it. In Chapter 9, we take up the kinds of reforms suggested by people's procedural preferences. Before that, however, we present (in Chapter 7) and critique (in Chapter 8) many of the currently popular reform proposals, paying special attention to the two proposals most discussed in academic literature: getting the people more involved by having them deliberate or by encouraging them to join groups, clubs, and organizations.

7

Popular Deliberation and Group Involvement in Theory

Just what is it about the political system that needs improving? Political theorists have long been convinced that a successful democratic governmental system will accomplish three tasks: (1) It will make good decisions; (2) it will be perceived as legitimate; and (3) it will help the people in society become better people. In considering systemic reforms, as we do in this chapter, we are not implying that the American political system is a failure; rather, we are recognizing only that the extent to which any democracy is accomplishing these three tasks can always be improved and that every effort should be made to do so. But the first goal of any reformer should be to do no harm, and, on the basis of the findings presented in Part II, we fear that the reform proposals currently attracting the most attention would actually do significant harm.

REFORMING (OR IMPROVING) AMERICAN POLITICS

Ideas for improving the political system are probably about as numerous as people, but to help organize the various types of changes that could be preferred, we offer Figure 7.1. In this figure, the governing process is divided into two steps: predecision consideration and the decision itself. The key players in each step can either be the people themselves or elites. Though overly simplistic, this conceptualization at least makes it possible to categorize reforms according to the particular procedure advocates want to modify.

Four Governing Processes and Possible Reforms

Elites Consider, People Decide. Beginning with the upper-right quadrant of the figure, some governing processes entail preliminary discussions

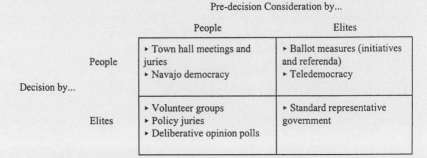

Figure 7.1. Categories of democratic procedures, with examples.

and consideration by elites but leave the final decision to ordinary people. The clearest example of this would be the referendum process (currently operating in 26 states) in which state legislatures discuss and formulate language addressing a particular problem, but then leave the final decision to the people of the state who have the opportunity to vote yes or no on the proposal. Initiatives are proposals that originate outside the legislature and (like referenda) are voted on by ordinary people, so they may belong in the upper-left quadrant, but the actual operation of initiatives indicates that many proposals emanate from elite segments of society or at some point are commandeered by elites in (frequently expensive) contests to influence the final decision of the voters (see Magleby 1984; Broder 2000).

Numerous writers believe American politics would be improved by expanded use of this form of direct democracy. Cronin (1989: ix–x), for example, argues that "a country willing to share more political power with its citizens will find a citizenry willing to participate in the workings of government." Gerber (1999) believes that ballot measures, or even just the threat of ballot measures, serve as a useful prod to needed government action (Lascher, Hagen, and Rochlin 1996 have a decidedly less favorable view). While seeing some negatives to the initiative and referendum process, Bowler, Donovan, and Tolbert (1998: 264–70) contend that it is not, as some have averred (see Gamble 1997), a threat to minority rights. Citrin's (1996) account is quite balanced, but he does see the use of ballot measures as responding to the people's "positive yearning for voice – for the chance to be heard and to participate" (290).

Even more enthusiasm exists among political writers these days for utilizing modern telecommunications technology to give people the opportunity to make direct decisions on policy matters. Though these technologies could be employed in many different fashions (as we see below when discussing the lower-left quadrant), the relevant procedure at this point works as follows. Similar to the standard referendum or elite-driven initiative process, elites formulate and present proposals to the people, who then, in the comfort of their homes, use the Internet or a television with a coaxial cable to register their preference on the proposal. Variations of teledemocracy are being widely discussed and considered (see Grossman 1995; Morris 1999; and Becker and Slaton 2000, to name a few). To be sure, some of the proposals for teledemocracy involve communication among ordinary people, but generally this communication is of the "on line" variety and thus is quickly discounted by supporters of real, face-to-face deliberation. Under most teledemocracy procedures, face-to-face deliberation is limited to elites.

Regardless of the specifics, advocates of teledemocracy tend to be wildly enthusiastic about the prospects afforded by advances in communications technology, as is indicated by Ornstein's (2000: 15) summary: "The advent of the internet has thrilled and excited a core of populist and direct democracy advocates who have become the leading proponents of 'cyberdemocracy.' The Net, they say, is the key to freeing citizens from the bonds of so-called representative democracy." Many of these advocates believe citizens' heightened role in the system would lead ordinary people to feel empowered and to pay more attention to politics. Even setting aside any perceived advantages of cyberdemocracy, many observers simply view it as increasingly inevitable in light of technology and people's presumed desire to play a more active part in politics (see Naisbitt 1984; Rosenthal 1998; Morris 1999; Solomon 2000).

Elites Consider, Elites Decide. When, however, the elites not only formulate the proposals but also decide on the proposals, governmental procedures are best described as standard representative government, the lower-right portion of Figure 7.1. Placing responsibility for both proposal consideration and proposal selection in the hands of elites is the usual procedure in the United States and in virtually all democracies.[1] The justification for such an approach was

---

[1] Besides the twenty-six states in the United States, only Switzerland makes extensive, regular use of ballot measures, though this could be changing (see Butler and Ranney 1994).

perhaps most famously stated by James Madison, who saw the need to "refine and enlarge the public views by passing them through a chosen body of citizens" (Federalist no. 10). Similarly, Edmund Burke (1949 [1774]: 115) spoke glowingly of the "mature judgments" and "enlightened conscience" of elites.

Since consideration and decision by elites already make up the main governing process in the United States, it might make sense to assume that supporters of such a process would not be eager to see any reforms. Not so. In fact, advocates of representative government are remarkably open to reforms, since many of them believe that current problems with the system stem not from the general practice of deferring to elites but from the particular manner in which elites consider and decide upon proposals. Thus, defenders of representative government could eagerly pursue campaign finance reforms, gift-giving restrictions, and other limits on special interest influence so that elite considerations and decisions would be (or would appear to be) based more on the merits than on money. Relatedly, those sympathizing with representative government might urge steps to make elite consideration more decorous, civil, and useful. Brady and Theriault (2001) believe dissatisfaction with Congress to a great extent springs from members' tendency to engage in unnecessarily shrill, extreme, and partisan debate (see also Uslaner 1993). Indeed, experimental work by Funk (2001) shows that people respond more favorably to civil debate than to hostile debate. People who believe representative government is the best procedure quite often are among the most active in seeking reforms in the way elites consider and decide upon policy proposals.

People Consider, Elites Decide. For all the interest in campaign finance reform and expanding direct democracy by the use of ballot measures or the Internet, even more energy and academic interest have been devoted to procedures in which the people are involved in a richer fashion at the earlier stage of the governing process – the consideration and formulation of policy proposals (the left side of Fig. 7.1). We begin with procedures providing for the people's participation in consideration while elites make the final decision, the lower-left quadrant.

The primary motivation behind these procedures is that the system would be improved if people were more involved. Advocates do not believe it sufficient when people are limited to making a final decision either on the candidates who will become decision makers or on policy decisions themselves. Benjamin Barber (1984) refers to such procedures as "weak democracy." What he and many others prefer is strong democracy, which he describes as "public reasoning ... in the participatory mode," as "ongoing civic participation," and as ordinary people involved in "deliberation" (151). Kettering Foundation official (and former Cabinet member) David Mathews (1994) echoes this desire for the people to be intimately involved with the consideration of policy proposals, for them to deliberate. To underscore this point, he uses the American jury system. "Deliberation ... is what makes twelve of our peers a group to whom we literally give life-and-death powers. We don't just trust twelve people with those powers under any condition. We only trust them under the condition that they deliberate long and carefully. The same is true of democratic politics" (111).

In this quadrant, people's role does not extend beyond deliberation. Elected officials are still responsible for making final decisions, but those who favor this general style of political process desire reforms that would allow elected officials to be informed by rich and sustained deliberations on the part of ordinary people. How would this occur? Specific proposals are incredibly numerous, incredibly diverse, and incredibly imaginative. Here, we only scratch the surface.

Perhaps the most discussed method of increasing people's presence in the "consideration-formulation-deliberation" stage is somehow to increase their involvement in the many volunteer organizations existing around the country. Drawing on the work of James Coleman (1990), Robert Putnam has popularized the concept of social capital, a reservoir of expectations, obligations, and trust that builds up as a result of satisfying interactions with other people in informal settings and especially in group activities. More important, perhaps, Putnam makes claims for the ability of social capital to boost political capital. He believes social capital plays a big role in "making democracy work" (1993) and that the United States is experiencing political difficulties because of a decline in social capital (1995). Putnam painstakingly documents the post-1960 decline in Americans' associational involvement with their fellow citizens and pleads that we "find ways to ensure that by 2010 the level of civic engagement among Americans then coming of age in all parts of our society will match that of their grandparents" (2000: 404). Journalist David Broder (1996: 4) is in general agreement with Putnam, saying that "unless more Americans start working with each other on shared civic enterprises, and learning to trust each other, the formal government of this nation will probably lurch from one credibility crisis to the next."

The hope is not that citizens take over authoritative political decision making but that they become more active in groups which would, in turn, foster skills (see Verba, Schlozman, and Brady 1995), interests, and, as a result, communication with those who *do* make political decisions. In this way, citizens would be more active in the formulation and consideration of policy proposals. Others, however, believe that the existing group structure, as varied as it is, is not sufficient to provide decision makers with a sense of people's preferences. They advocate special structures to fulfill this need.

James Headlam (1933) calls for the empaneling of "citizen issue juries." Political theorist Robert Dahl (1970) urges the use of "mini-populi." Sociologist Amitai Etzioni (1972) wants to merge sampling and electronic communications to find out what ordinary people are thinking. Similarly, Ivor Crewe and Martin Harrop (1986) want to create an "Electronic 500" (see also MacDonald 1986). And James Fishkin (1991, 1995) has actually experimented with deliberative opinion polls in the United Kingdom and the United States.[2] The uniting goal of all these ideas is to obtain something approximating a random sample of people who are then provided information and a special opportunity to discuss the topic at hand. As a result, the group will be able to engage in informed deliberation that will be much more valid and much more useful than standard public opinion surveys, since the latter usually entail relatively uninformed opinions and never provide for deliberation among citizens. The contention is that if real decision makers could see informed but otherwise typical people deliberating with each other on the key issues of the day, those decision makers would be better able to act in the real interests of the people (see, esp., Fishkin 1995: 161–76; McCombs and Reynolds 1999).

People Consider, People Decide. The most radical reform proposals would not stop with people deliberating prior to turning decisions

---

[2] Some advocates see the real potential for modern communications technology, not in allowing the people to render a final decision (as we discussed pursuant to the upper-right quadrant), but in allowing people to deliberate with each other rather than making the final decision. As Ornstein (2000: 15) described the goals of such individuals, they want to reduce Congress to a chamber that merely "waits for public instructions before making any decisions."

over to elites. They would instead entail ordinary people considering and formulating proposals and then making a final decision on the proposals as well. Existing institutions of representative government would not be necessary, as the people would engage in rich, pure direct democracy.

The best illustration of such an approach to governing is the classic New England town meetings. The way these work is that residents of the town attend periodic meetings, discuss issues affecting the town, and then vote to determine the specific approach that will be used to resolve those issues. Discussion and decisions are made entirely by ordinary people and not by any designated set of elites. The American jury system provides another example of the people both considering and deciding, since it involves ordinary Americans discussing the evidence of a case and then deciding the outcome. As with town meetings, consideration and discussion are not preliminary to elites making the decision but rather to ordinary people making the decision.

An important variant of these strategies is when no distinction is made between the consideration phase and the decision phase. A good example of this approach is Etzioni's (1996: 221) description of "Navajo democracy, in which dialogues continue until all members of a tribe embrace a given position." This is a style of consensus decision making in which no voting or other formal decision-making structure is necessary. Instead, discussion proceeds until the decision is apparent. This is similar to the approach advocated by Amy Gutmann and Dennis Thompson (1996). They believe that all problems, even incredibly difficult moral disputes, can be worn down and conquered by the deliberative process. People just have to stay with it long enough (and follow some rules that we discuss below in this chapter). As they put it, when citizens disagree, "they should continue to reason together" (1). But the key point is that, whether consideration and resolution are viewed as two separate steps or one in the same, procedures in the upper-left quadrant do not require elite involvement. The people do it all.

Taking Stock

Having assayed the various procedural options of democracy as well as examples of reform strategies employing these options, it is apparent (if it were not before) that the range of democratic forms is incredible. Accordingly, we are not be able to evaluate each and every form in light of the findings we reported in Parts I and II of this book. But we evaluate what seems to us to be the primary concern of political writers early in the twenty-first century, and that is to get ordinary people more deeply involved in the political arena, with deep involvement understood to mean something more than voting Democrat or Republican or voting for or against Proposition X.

As such, we do not have a great deal more to say about the procedures listed on the right side of Figure 7.1. This is not because these proposals are less important – indeed, locating ways to make representative democracy more palatable to ordinary people or determining the degree to which people should be involved directly in the decision-making stage of the political process is profoundly important. But popular involvement in the consideration of political matters is the central concern for us for two reasons: first, because of the extent to which it dominates discussions of how to improve the American polity; and second, because it requires the people to invest more of themselves in politics, and our empirical results speak directly to the people's willingness to make a greater investment in politics.

In the remainder of this chapter, we present the justifications theorists (and some empiricists) have offered for getting the people more involved in voluntary associations and in political deliberation. Then, in the next chapter, we hold the theorists' contentions up to the light of empirical work, much of it recent and much of it utilizing various experimental designs. We find that reality casts a dark cloud over theoretical claims that popular involvement either in volunteer organizations or in serious deliberation benefits the political system. As a result, in the last substantive chapter of the book, Chapter 9, we take a more careful look at the kinds of procedures that *would* improve the American political system in light of people's perceptions and lack of political motivation.

THE ALLEGED BENEFITS OF GREATER INVOLVEMENT IN VOLUNTARY ASSOCIATIONS

The siren call of social capital as a way to understand the decline of civil society in the United States has enticed many political scientists and pundits. There is something decidedly appealing and hopeful in the idea that so many of society's problems can be remedied by getting people to be more socially engaged. Social capital, according to James Coleman (1988), is a resource available to a society, much as physical capital and human capital are resources. Social capital develops in the relations among people. We discuss the arguments behind social capital, in particular, Robert Putnam's version of this idea.

According to Putnam (1993, 1995, 2000), social capital is the product of dense social networks, which he associates with active and involved membership in voluntary associations. Numerous studies have shown that members of voluntary associations are better democratic citizens: They are better informed, more politically active, more efficacious, and more supportive of democratic norms, and they have greater self-respect and are more politically skilled (see, e.g., Almond and Verba 1963; Verba and Nie 1972; Milbrath and Goel 1977; Verba et al. 1995). Putnam (1993) argues that voluntary association membership generates even greater rewards for society itself, including greater economic performance and more effective government performance.

Why is voluntary association membership so beneficial to individuals, political systems, and the society as a whole? According to Putnam (2000: 134), "the touchstone of social capital is the principle of generalized reciprocity – I'll do this for you now, without expecting anything immediately in return and perhaps without even knowing you, confident that down the road you or someone else will return the favor." People directly engaged with other people in voluntary associations develop this sense of generalized reciprocity because they learn to trust others and they learn to generalize this trust to people they do not know (what Putnam refers to as "thin trust"). Generalized reciprocity is essential to civil societies because it lowers transaction costs and lessens frictions. When people trust one another, they can more easily navigate their daily lives and more efficiently transact business. Governments can expend fewer resources to obtain the same outcomes if they are not constantly using resources to enforce laws and punish lawbreakers. If people are trusting of others and have a sense of generalized reciprocity, they will create a better society by being more willing to take care of others' welfare and by giving time and money to good causes (117).

Putnam's concern is that there has been a decline in voluntary association membership (see Putnam 1995, 2000). Fewer Americans are involved in groups that allow their members to interact directly, such as bowling leagues, Elks clubs, and Parent-Teacher Associations. Instead, if Americans do join groups, they join those that are faceless, such as the American Association of Retired Persons, the

Environmental Defense Fund, and the American Civil Liberties Union. People are nominal members of these groups, paying their dues but not being actively involved. They do not engage directly with other members and therefore cannot develop generalized reciprocity or trust. More broadly, Americans are increasingly engaged in individualistic, private pursuits. Democratic society suffers, according to Putnam, when people do not interact with their fellow citizens.

The solution to the problem, according to social capitalists, is to get more people involved with each other, and one way to do that is to get them to become active members of voluntary associations. Getting people more involved in individualistic pursuits, such as national interest groups or even voting, will not give democratic society the boost it needs. Other theorists concerned about the individualistic tendencies in American democracy are those who promote political deliberation. For them, involving people in deliberative settings will take care of many of modern democracy's ills.

THE ALLEGED BENEFITS OF ENHANCING POLITICAL DELIBERATION AMONG ORDINARY PEOPLE

Voting, whether it be for a candidate or on a policy proposal, is generally a private, individual act. Modern political commentators tend to react quite negatively to this atomistic, individualistic version of democracy. Indeed, for a growing number of political observers, the essence of true democracy is not individual-actor decision making but decisions that are made only after intense, sustained, social interactions.[3] Deliberation has become the concept de jour of political theorists and in some cases has taken on nearly religious overtones. Exhortations to deliberate seem to be everywhere. All problems are the result of a "failure to communicate," and if something is wrong with a democratic polity, insufficient deliberation must have been the cause. After all, when a problem develops, is it not best to talk about it in hopes that it can be resolved? Who could deny the benefits of deliberation? Thus, whether it comes by people being more involved in voluntary groups or by creating new fora for discussing policy problems, the goal of many theorists is to increase the amount of interaction and, especially, deliberation among ordinary people.

---

[3]Though see some of the essays in Macedo (1999) for negative assessments of deliberative decision making.

Better Decisions

Perhaps the most obvious alleged benefit of democratic deliberation is that it leads to better decisions than would have occurred if there had been no deliberation. This sentiment is manifested in Condorcet's Jury Theorem (1994 [1785]). According to this theorem, each person on the jury has private information; that is, information the others never had or did not retain. If each person reveals this private information to others on the jury, the decision subsequent to deliberation will be a step above that which would have occurred had no deliberation taken place. A similar, if less formal, justification is offered by Abramson (1994: 205) when he characterizes deliberating juries as "collections of wisdom [in which] . . . people change their minds not out of expediency but because their views actually have shifted through hearing the views of others."

The logic leading to the conclusion that deliberated decisions will be better decisions extends well beyond the jury box. After all, "two heads are better than one" is a general-purpose aphorism. It is only common sense. What could be more reasonable than believing that decisions are improved by bouncing ideas off of others and sopping up information they provide? John Rawls (1971: 359), for example, makes the straightforward point that "discussion is a way of combining information and enlarging the range of arguments" and will therefore "improve matters." Benjamin Page (1996: 2) agrees: "Since policymaking is complicated and full of uncertainties, an individual citizen's personal experience and reflection, alone, can get her or him only so far. Sound political judgment requires exchanging knowledge and ideas with others." James Fishkin (1995: 28) is thinking along these same lines when he asserts that decisions made in scattered isolation are decisions based on "partial knowledge, partial arguments, and unanswered misrepresentations." And Robert Dahl (1989: 104–5) equates deliberative decisions with "enlightened understanding" and the opportunity for citizens to "discover and validate."

Sometimes, the justification for deliberation is not that resultant decisions will simply be better informed but that they will be more sensitive to the needs and concerns of others with whom one has deliberated.[4] Benjamin Barber (1984: 152), for example, writes that "[c]ommunity grows out of participation . . . civic activity educates

---

[4] This sentiment is found in many of the works of communitarians.

individuals how to think publicly as citizens." He takes making citizens capable of public thinking as "a single, crucial end" (197). In fact, Barber believes that participating in democratic deliberation leads people to think not of "me" but of "we" (153). In this, of course, Barber is closely following Rousseau, who saw the democratic process as a way for a person to reaffirm partnership with the general will (Rousseau 1946 [1762]).

Better (That Is, More Legitimate) System

Not only do theorists assert that democratic deliberation leads to better decisions, they also argue that it encourages people to view decisions as more legitimate and valid. If people have the opportunity to be involved in the decision or if they at least believe the decision was based on an inclusive and responsible debate of the relevant issues, they may feel better about processes and decisions (Ely 1980: 181). Recent writings connecting legitimacy to democratic deliberation are plentiful.[5] To provide two examples, Seyla Benhabib (1994: 26) points out that people may "accept the . . . will of a . . . process that has been fairly and correctly carried out," even if there are "grave doubts about the rationality of the outcome," and Iris Marion Young (2000: 5–6) believes "the normative legitimacy of a democratic decision depends on the degree to which those affected by it have been included in the decision-making process."

Scholars of the legislative process, not surprisingly, have been particularly interested in the connection between deliberation (among representatives rather than ordinary people, in this case) and legitimacy. Why, they have asked, are legislatures so omnipresent when few of them have real power? The usual answer is that visible, open, democratic deliberation, such as that typically occurring in legislative bodies, makes people feel better about the governmental process, so legislatures help secure legitimacy.[6] As summarized by Packenham (1970: 530), the belief is that, traditionally, the existence of a legislature has "reduced tension, provided reassurance, and generally enhanced satisfaction with or acquiescence with . . . government." People need to know, or at least need to think, their voices

[5] See, for example, Manin (1987), Cohen (1989), Dryzek (1990), Tyler (1990), and Keohane (2001: 10).

[6] This theme can be found in the writings of Beer (1966), Packenham (1970), Loewenberg (1971), Loewenberg and Patterson (1979), and, especially, Wahlke (1971).

are being heard, and representative assemblies are probably the most realistic way to achieve this eventuality. In modern mass democracies, where face-to-face interaction among ordinary people seems to be prohibited by geography and by population size, legislatures act as a vital source of system legitimacy – of diffuse support, to use Easton's (1965) well-known phrase.

Unlike the claims that people's involvement in deliberation leads to better decisions, the belief that such involvement makes people feel better about the system actually has some empirical basis. As Lind and Tyler (1988: 170) put it, "one clear finding from research ... is that people like to have an opportunity to present their views before policy decisions are made." Tyler, Rasinski, and Spodick (1985) conducted three experiments and all supported this conclusion. In the first, they found that within a random sample of people who had recently been defendants in an Illinois traffic and misdemeanor court, those who felt they had been given the opportunity to present evidence in their case were more satisfied with their experience, regardless of whether they won or lost their case, than those who felt they did not have voice. In the second experiment, students in an introductory psychology class were asked questions about a class they had taken the previous term. Those who felt they had input into that class, in terms of demonstrating their knowledge and influencing the grade they received, evaluated the class more favorably regardless of their grade. And finally, in the third experiment, random groups of students were asked to read different scenarios about a city council. In one the council solicited citizen input before making a budget decision, and in the other, citizens did not have much opportunity to speak to the council. Once again, where the process allowed public input, respondents tended to react more favorably and the decision itself was of less consequence.

Tyler's (1990) later work on why people obey the law even more directly tests the hypothesis that if people have voice in a process, they will view the decision itself as legitimate even if the decision is undesirable. Tyler contacted people in the Chicago area who had recent experience in the legal system and asked them about their level of satisfaction and the degree to which they felt they had some input into their case. He found that people who believed they had a voice were much more accepting of an adverse decision. Tyler concludes that procedural justice, and, in particular, allowing citizen input, is a logical way to get people to feel better about their experiences with government and the like. Echoing Marx, he even worries that the effect is so powerful that decision makers will become skilled in coopting people by only pretending to allow them a voice (Lind and Tyler 1988).

Better People

A final justification frequently tendered by theorists is that the very act of being involved in issue-based discussions makes better people, regardless of what it might mean for the quality of public policy or for the system. Such involvement, claimed John Dewey (1927: 148), is necessary for "the full development of human beings as individuals." This belief in the personal edification and improvement function of deliberative democracy has been around for centuries.[7]

Rousseau, for example, is often identified as an early adherent of the notion that involvement in the give and take of political discussions would improve people, but this encapsulated version is not directly on target. Rousseau lived much of his life as a recluse, and his *Discourse on Inequality* can be read as contending that society has failed and that anyone involved in society will be doomed to unhappiness. But by the time he wrote *The Social Contract*, Rousseau had concluded that it is possible to live in society without forgoing the individual freedoms he deemed so important. In fact, Rousseau (1946 [1762]: 262) believed that social order could be an improvement over the natural state of man in that it "substitutes justice for instinct in behavior, and gives to his actions a moral basis." Association with such a society can change a person from a "limited and stupid animal into an intelligent being" (263). How will this magic be performed? In the process of interacting with others on societal and political issues, a person's "ideas take on a wider scope, his sentiments become ennobled, and his whole soul elevated" (263). It is easy to understand why Rousseau is held up as an early leader in recognizing the ability of democratic deliberation to improve the people doing the deliberating.

But this conclusion falls short of providing an accurate feel for Rousseau's ideas. The trouble is, Rousseau believed the positive effects of this kind of societal interaction would accrue only in a very specific (and unusual) kind of society. First of all, the society has to be based on a common interest and governed on the basis of that common interest (256). Lacking this common interest, all that

---

[7]See Tocqueville (1951 [1848]: vol. 1: 252), Mill (1977: 68), and many others.

remains is an aggregation of individuals and not a true society. Not surprisingly, a true society in Rousseau's eyes can happen only when the society is small, technologically and economically simple, and socially homogeneous. Thus, Rousseau had hopes that a true society could come to pass among the people of mid-eighteenth-century Corsica (for whom he drafted a constitution); he would, no doubt, be more pessimistic about the prospects for a true society among the people of the early twenty-first-century United States.

Rousseau had no time for representative assemblies, arguing, instead, that legislatures should be composed of the whole people assembled, such as can be found in the assemblies of the Swiss Cantons and New England towns. The ideal political arrangement for Rousseau is "groups of peasants deciding the affairs of State beneath an oak tree" (384). But Rousseau did *not* support open communication among these well-shaded peasants; rather, he believed there should be no communication that might be construed to encourage divisions of interest, development of factions, or anything not based on the general will (390). The goal was not, as it is for some deliberative democrats, getting in touch with the unique problems and concerns of our diverse fellow citizens, but, rather, reconfirming the tenets of the general will shared by all of society. Anyone behaving otherwise should not be involved. This is not a vision of society that would be endorsed by the American Civil Liberties Union. The plight of real, minority views and people is assumed away since there cannot be any diversity in a true society. This sleight of hand leaves Rousseau with a far different view of the edifying potential of deliberation: not to expose people to other views or to make them more empathetic to those who are different from them, but to make sure people remain in touch with a unitary general will.

Even more than Rousseau, perhaps the name most readily associated with the ability of democratic processes to improve and educate people is John Stuart Mill. Mill was convinced this relationship existed, and to support his hypothesis he cited the intelligence of Athenians during their democratic period and the cleverness of nineteenth-century Englishmen. The latter phenomenon, he was certain, existed because English citizens occasionally took part in democratic situations such as juries and parish offices (1977 [1861]: 290). Mill contended that participation in public affairs would educate participants and have an invigorating effect on them. As James Carey (1987: 14) has more recently stated, "the public will begin to reawaken when they are addressed as a conversational partner and are encouraged to join the talk rather than sit passively as spectators."

Yet while Mill valued deliberation, he conceded that if democratic systems were to be practicable in anything but the smallest communities, personal, peasant-level involvement in political discussions could not be a prerequisite. Unlike Rousseau, Mill was quite comfortable with representative democracy, believing that the process of "periodically elected deputies" (1977 [1861]: 305) would still involve the people broadly enough to generate the alleged beneficial consequences. In fact, in direct contrast to Rousseau, Mill was quite elitist. He believed that only a very few people would have original thoughts and that "these few are the salt of the earth" whose presence keeps the human condition from being nothing more than "a stagnant pool" (1977 [1859]: 78). Though they both believed democratic involvement leads to self-improvement, Rousseau and Mill had quite different notions of what self-improvement entails and what kind of involvement is necessary to achieve this improvement.

In the modern era, this concept of self-improvement through political participation has been adopted with gusto by communitarians and deliberation theorists. Pateman (1970), Barber (1984), and Etzioni (1996), to name just a few, contend that if people play a vital role in decision making, they will become better informed, they will be more open to the ideas of others, they will become better debaters, they will be more cooperative, and they will be better people. One of the more enthusiastic champions of this point of view claims that, were citizens to be directly involved in deliberation, "America would see an immediate and invigorating rise in interest in politics. . . . Politics would be on the lips of every man, woman and child, day after day. As interest rose, a demand would be created for more and better sources of news" (Wolff 1970: 36–7).

Although most modern writers seem to agree with Rousseau in terms of the type of participation necessary for self-improvement (intimate rather than indirect involvement) and with Mill in terms of the nature of the improvement that results (broad-based, empathetic, and educative gains rather than merely a melding with the general will), disagreement is substantial. Moreover, the claims made by modern writers for popular deliberation extend well beyond personal improvement. Given their breadth and diversity, we conclude this chapter by summarizing the assertions of modern theorists regarding greater popular involvement in politics. We break them down into two overarching categories: communitarians and deliberation theorists.

COMMUNITARIANS AND DELIBERATION THEORISTS

The communitarian movement, which flowered in the 1970s and 1980s, is best seen as a reaction to liberal individualism (see Avineri and de-Shalit 1992). Whereas liberalism stresses universal morality and the autonomy of each individual, communitarianism tends to follow Hegel by casting its lot with collections of individuals who share particular values.

For many communitarians, deliberating and interacting with our neighbors not only leads to better decisions, a more legitimate politics, and better people, but improves communities and therefore society itself. David Mathews (1994: 2), for example, writes that "working together with others to solve common problems recreates a sense of community." This sense of community is desirable because communities give our lives meaning and are morally good (see Taylor 1992). The value of people's lives "is only a reflection of and is derivative from the value of the life of the community as a whole" (Dworkin 1989: 497). Communitarians trace society's problems to a lack of community so are eager to recreate the sense of community they believe existed in a halcyon era (see Putnam 2000).

For some communitarians, a sense of community is actually a prerequisite for meaningful deliberative involvement. Sandel (1996: 5) believes that "to deliberate well about the common good requires . . . a sense of belonging, a concern for the whole, a moral bond with the community whose fate is at stake." As a result, Sandel continues, "to share in self-rule . . . requires that citizens possess . . . certain qualities of character or civic virtues" (5–6). It is unclear what should be done when such values are absent. Presumably, since they are a precondition for self-rule, a nondemocratic mode of decision making would be required.[8]

Communitarians themselves are a diverse lot. Etzioni (1996), for example, thinks it desirable for people to change to a different, small community if they do not approve of the views of their current

[8]Communitarians often maintain consensus is really present if we look hard enough for it, and they go to great lengths to concoct methods of fabricating consensus. See, for example, Kay (1998).

community, whereas Sandel (1996) sees no reason why communities have to be small and contends that the entire United States could be a national community. More traditional communitarians blanch at the notions that attachment to the values and virtues of one community could be traded in willy-nilly for the values of another or that values could be watered down sufficiently to attract the active allegiance and participation of 270 million diverse people, so it would be a mistake to leave the impression that communitarians are, well, a community.

Communitarians are less concerned with the precise nature of people's interaction with other people than with interaction occurring. This is one of many things that sets communitarians apart from deliberation theorists. As the label implies, deliberation theorists have thought long and hard about the preferred nature of people's interactions and deliberations. Perhaps the leading figure in this movement has been Jurgen Habermas. Like the "Navajo democrats" we met earlier, Habermas (1984: 42) contends that consensus will result "if only the argumentation could be conducted openly enough and continued long enough." The difference is that Habermas sets down some very specific deliberation guidelines that must be met if a consensus solution is to result. For example, all participants must be equal and their actions must be rational (a rational action is one for which everyone agrees there was a good reason). If there is a dispute about rationality, it must be resolved by norms that are themselves "acceptable to all who are potentially affected by the norm" (Habermas 1987: 49). In other words, participants must agree upon the rules of evidence so that something approaching a scientific process of verbal exchange is achieved (see also Chambers 1996: 136). Irrelevant information and bad logic will be driven out; useful information and tight logic will allow the group to move to a unified conclusion (Habermas 1996). The great advantage of Habermas over Rousseau and many communitarians is that he can discard the extremely questionable notion that there is a single general will just waiting to find expression. For Habermas, people begin from what seem to be vastly different positions but through reasoned discourse they can arrive, democratically, at the same place.

In their important work, *Democracy and Disagreement,* Amy Gutmann and Dennis Thompson (1996) use terminology different from Habermas's but express similar ideas. Like Habermas, Gutmann and Thompson believe disagreements, even incredibly divisive moral disagreements, can be worked out through the deliberative process. For this to happen, however, evidence the deliberators introduce must be consistent with scientific rules and must not, therefore, be based on unverifiable or unchallengeable notions (52–94). Supporting a point by invoking faith in a supreme being would not be following this tenet of "reciprocity." The similarity between Habermas's "ideal" deliberation and Gutmann and Thompson's reciprocity-based deliberation is apparent.

John Dryzek (2000) offers a contrasting view. He contends verbal interaction among people does not need to follow restrictive rules to be beneficial. He values humor, anecdotes, even rambling remarks, and prefers the phrase "discursive democracy" to "deliberative democracy." As he puts it, "political equality, human integrity, reciprocity, publicity, and accountability are undeniably important values, but the best way for people to learn these values is through the practice of deliberation rather than through being told that they must abide by these principles" (47). Dryzek believes wide-open communication is better suited to solve complex social problems because "it provides for coherent integration of a variety of perspectives" (173).[9]

So, communitarians want to eliminate conflict by denying any exists (Sandel 1996; Kay 1998), by breaking into small, homogeneous groups where it does not exist (Putnam 2000), or by prohibiting discussion of contentious topics (Etzioni 1996: 104–5). Deliberation theorists admit that conflict exists and that society is not well served by pretending it does not. They believe that deliberation, if conducted properly, makes it possible for people to work through conflict to the benefit of individuals and the collective. But they are at odds over the "proper" conduct of deliberation. Rousseau (1946 [1762]) wants to permit only comments that are consistent with the belief that there is a general will; Habermas (1987) and Gutmann and Thompson (1996) want to permit only comments that meet rational, scientific, and fairness standards; and Dryzek (2000) wants to permit any and all comments, no matter how irrelevant.

CONCLUSION

In this chapter, we have summarized the various approaches to democratic government and reform proposals relevant to those

[9] Presumably, Putnam and others in the "join more groups" school would have some sympathy for Dryzek's points, since discussion in most informal group settings is more likely to be discursive than rational.

approaches. Numerous views exist regarding the proper role for ordinary citizens in a democracy. We paid particular attention to the arguments of those who believe either popular involvement in group activities or in deliberation is the solution to the dilemmas facing democracy. Many theorists have emphasized the ability of personal group involvement and deliberation to lead to better decisions, to lend legitimacy to the system, and to improve the people so involved.

The strong consensus on these points is somewhat surprising, given that theorists have vastly different perceptions of a "good" political system. Some believe all that is required of a good system is for the people in it to be in touch with a general will; some believe it consists of working toward consensus after beginning with very diverse specific wills. Some believe the end result is to create a sense of community by cooperating on problems together; some believe the deliberative process itself is the end. Some think deliberation has to be direct; some see nothing wrong with electing deputies to do our deliberating for us (Madison, of course, went so far as to say deliberation by elected deputies was preferable to direct deliberation). Some are communitarians; some are liberal individualists. Some are glad that each community has its unique deliberative style; some think deliberation must be governed by universal norms of conduct.

Regardless of these differences, the core notion is that greater popular involvement is what is needed to improve American democracy. Absent this involvement, democracy is superficial, thin, and certainly undesirable. Any other form of democracy is cold, impersonal, and unsatisfying. To interact with fellow group members, residents of a community, or inhabitants of a nation is the essence of being a democratic citizen – or so we are told by the advocates of deliberative democracy. Though this position seems to be commonsensical, in the next chapter we make the case that, in light of people's desire to avoid politics, democratic procedures entailing sustained personal involvement may not be preferable to other forms of democracy.

8

The Realities of Popular Deliberation
and Group Involvement

The fact that there are many forms of democracy means there are numerous ways for the people to be involved in politics. Political theorists believe people would enjoy politics if only the system would allow them to get involved in an appealing political forum. Theorists further believe the political system would be improved if people played an active role in the consideration of various policy proposals – if people would get together and work collectively on matters, discussing them, learning from each other, and striving for a common goal. Only then, theorists argue, will people learn to trust each other, to appreciate the needs of other people, to care about politics, and to trust the government. Two very different strategies have been advocated for facilitating the needed interaction with other individuals: getting people more involved in self-selected, volunteer groups and creating environments in which diverse people are brought together to deliberate on policy matters.

In contrast to theorists' speculations, the results presented in Part II indicate to us that people's dislike of politics runs deep and is unlikely to be eliminated if they would only get involved with other people in political procedures. Some people react negatively to any political dispute. Many more believe politics is largely unnecessary, since they are convinced there is a popular consensus on important national goals and do not care about the specific means used to achieve those goals. People get upset with government because politicians spend too much time on unimportant matters, not because politicians vote down issues about which people care. Misplaced attention indicates to the people that politicians are not in touch with what really matters to ordinary Americans (remember, people tend to believe that if a topic is not important to them, it is probably not important to other ordinary people). As long as the government is involved in many matters and individuals care about few, they will consistently perceive the government as misplacing its attention and as being out of touch.

This means that just getting people more involved in politics is not going to do any good, absent making them understand that Americans as a group care about a variety of issues and have different ideas for attacking those issues. We believe stronger political involvement will not make people more trusting, more tolerant, more other-regarding, or more supportive of government. In fact, it may even be the case that such involvement, in and of itself, will make people more upset by immersing them in the very political arena they dislike so much. In sum, our findings lead us to exactly the opposite set of expectations as those offered by normative theorists. They believe increased interaction with other people will boost political capital and otherwise enhance people and the political system. We believe increased interaction will not boost political capital at all and may very well do damage.

Fortunately, in recent years a growing number of scholars has begun to test the claims of political theorists regarding the consequences of political involvement. In this chapter, we summarize the findings that bear on the ability of increased interaction to improve the political system. In doing so, we separate the two main strategies proposed: getting people more involved in existing groups and forcing people to discuss politics in more diverse deliberative settings. This separation is necessary because the two strategies are so different and, accordingly, have unique strengths and weaknesses. We turn first to findings regarding the consequences of group involvement and then, in even more detail, to those bearing on the consequences of people deliberating with others. In each case, the clear conclusion of empirical research is that enhanced involvement in politics does not have the benefits theorists claim.[1]

GROUP INVOLVEMENT

Are Putnam and the other advocates of more group participation[2] correct in their belief that such activities will create political capital?

---

[1] To be sure, some recent theorists have raised serious questions about the benefits of enhanced popular involvement in democracy. See Ackerman (1980, 1989); Riker (1982); and Mueller (1999).

[2] See, for example, Barber (1984); Mathews (1994); Broder (1996); and many others.

Careful study of the nature of these groups undermines the logic behind such expectations. The best work in this area has been done by sociologist Nina Eliasoph (1998). By systematically observing many volunteer groups of the kind championed by the social capitalists, Eliasoph documents that members of these groups typically are socialized to oppose "debating, talking, pretentiously holding forth" (45). One group member "assumed that when activists got up on the public stage, it must be for the purpose of getting attention, not for instigating public discussion" (143). Eliasoph's summation is right on target: "In an effort to appeal to regular, unpretentious fellow citizens without discouraging them, [the groups] silence public-spirited deliberation" (63). "In practice, the way they tried to show that good effective citizenship was possible was to limit their circle of concern and try not to care about issues that were not close to home" (83). So, "instead of discussing potentially upsetting issues, most meetings featured in-depth discussions of practical fundraising projects" (31). Eliasoph observed one meeting at which a participant committed the faux pas of raising a difficult, controversial issue. After a long silence, the chair of the meeting said dismissively, "I'm sure someone'll be coming to talk to you to figure out a solution" (33).

It is apparent that real groups often work to shut out divisive voices in the unlikely event they arise, but very often such voices are never even heard in the first place. The fact that voluntary community groups are self-selected means that members tend to look and think the same, leading to what Mark Peel (1998: 339) calls "the communitarian fallacy of homogeneity." When interaction occurs in such a context, the local results are comforting, but the implications for the larger picture are truly alarming. Diana Mutz and Jeffrey Mondak's (2001) work discovered that "voluntary associations provide very little exposure to dissimilar political views. . . . precisely because they are *voluntary*, these associations are characterized by extreme homogeneity" (11; see also Beem 1999 and Mutz 2001).

This point is illustrated nicely by Robert Axelrod's (1997) imaginative computer simulation of "the dissemination of culture." As he describes it, when interactions are "based on self-selection, people will tend to interact with others who are already quite similar to them on relevant dimensions. . . . Such self selection could result in an even stronger tendency toward both local convergence and global polarization. . . . The implications for resolving the tensions inherent in a multicultural society are problematic" (174). Problematic would seem to be an understatement. Axelrod's pictures of societal devolution, based simply on the assumption that people prefer to associate with people with whom they share at least one trait, are disconcerting (157). An original Madisonian multiplicity is gradually reduced to just three "regions," and, more to the point, complete stability eventually arrives to these three regions because, after a large number of iterations, "members of adjacent regions have absolutely no features in common" (156).

This is not the kind of society any of us want, and Axelrod's simulation confirms Margaret Levi's (1996: 49) shrewd observation that "by themselves dense networks support localism. . . . they promote trust of those you know and distrust of those you do not." Indeed, the dangers of substantial voluntary group membership are apparent in Berman's (1997) finding that Weimar Germany had an incredibly rich voluntary associational life but that it was composed too heavily of bonding rather than bridging groups and thus could not stop, and perhaps facilitated, Hitler's rise. Strong in-group bonds sustain rigidity and bigotry (Blau 1974; Mutz 2000).[3]

A sense of community can be a wonderful thing, but if it develops only because members screen out dissenters, silence activists, narrow concerns, and stifle debate, it becomes a terrible thing. Voluntary community group activities may help us learn certain civic skills (see Verba et al. 1995) and they may accomplish commendable local objectives. Our point is only that they all too often do nothing to help people learn how to come to a democratic solution on divisive issues of the day. In fact, there is a real danger that voluntary group organizations will diminish people's ability to appreciate the challenges and frustrations of democratic governance. Rather than the needed understanding of politics in adversarial settings, these groups unwittingly promote misunderstanding. As Huckfeldt et al. (1995: 1049) find, "private citizens who confine their interactions within the boundaries of cohesive social groups remain secluded and largely unaffected by the larger climate of opinion."[4] The more participants see local groups make progress on noncontroversial, service-based goals, the more these groups tend toward government bashing: "Look what we did! Why can't those bozos in Washington do the same thing?"

This self-congratulatory air is apparent in the following attempt to justify why young people (like the author of the passage) do not vote.

---

[3] As Sullivan, Piereson, and Marcus (1982) recognize, tolerance presumes disagreement, so tolerance cannot be successfully enhanced by dealing with people who already share our views.

[4] See also Huckfeldt and Sprague (1995).

"While our generation may seem more apathetic and less informed, we volunteer more, and we're more spin-savvy and independent-minded. . . . Just because we don't vote doesn't mean we don't care" (Murphy 2000: 41). One of the young people Murphy interviewed asserts that "most of the things I do for my community, I don't need to rely on Congress to get done for me." Another said that "volunteering is much more important than voting and it involves a much more serious commitment," and Murphy cites poll data indicating young people believe volunteering is a more effective way of bringing about change than voting (43–4). The tone indicates a complete absence of understanding of the challenges of governing and an apparent belief that if we all just become active in groups close to our heart, the country would work just fine. It betrays a failure to appreciate, to use Ridout and Espino's (2000: 6) example, that "it is easier for a group to get speed bumps installed in a neighborhood" than to come up with a nationwide plan for dealing with air pollution.

When people *are* confronted with diversity, they often withdraw from politics or fail to become more trusting. Diana Mutz's (2000: 1) empirical work consistently shows that "people whose political networks involve greater political disagreement are less likely to participate in politics." As a result of this finding, her conclusion that "people avoid politics as a means of maintaining social harmony" (4) is perfectly reasonable (see also Ulbig and Funk 1999). Similarly, the results of Ridout and Espino (2000: 6) show that only for groups that concentrate on noncontentious local issues does level of activity correlate with trust. To the extent group involvement facilitates social capital, it appears to result from the fact that such activity encourages people in their desire to believe that "everybody else is like me."

An important distinction needs to be made between social and political capital. They are not the same, not even positively related, and on occasion are inversely related to each other. Consider the following statement, representative of current wisdom on the condition of American government: "unless more Americans start working with each other on shared civic enterprises, and learning to trust each other, the formal government of this nation will probably lurch from one credibility crisis to the next" (Broder 1996: 4). The empirical evidence, on the other hand, shows that working together on shared enterprises does little to improve the credibility of government or the level of trust in fellow citizens (but see Brehm and

Rahn 1997).[5] Norris (1996: 479), for example, points out that "it is not self-evident that turning off the television, and talking with our neighbors, or even going bowling, is necessarily the best way of addressing the long-term problem of confidence in American government." Stolle (1998: 521) actually finds that the longer people belong to groups, the *less* trusting they are. La Due Lake and Huck-feldt (1998: 569) also raise questions about the politically relevant consequences of social capital, and this leads them to conclude, as have we, that not all participation is desirable: "Political activity cannot be meaningful unless it is informed." So we should not be surprised that Brehm and Rahn (1997: 1018) find that "civic engagement negatively affects confidence" in government. How could volunteer groups be expected to develop political capital if the groups' primary concern is maintaining an "egalitarian method of building a sense of togetherness" (Eliasoph 1998: 43) by trying "hard not to care about issues that would require too much talking to solve" (23)? As Newton and Norris (2000: 65) state, "whatever voluntary associations may or may not do for social capital, they seem to hold little importance for political capital."

Putnam and others have presented evidence that joining groups may increase social capital, although even here the fact that the results are not from randomized experiments makes it impossible to reject the counterhypothesis that a certain kind of person has higher levels of social capital to begin with and also is more likely to participate in groups (see Uslaner 2001). Sorting out the causal order, if any, requires better panel data than are currently available. The closest researchers have come to this approach is work done by Martin and Clairbourn (2000). Using the panel data of Jennings and Niemi, they find that group membership in one wave does not predict trust in a succeeding wave. This result is a serious blow to the claim that group membership has an independent effect on trust and other political variables.

The evidence that joining volunteer organizations helps people to appreciate the diversity of society's political views or the difficulty of coming to a solution in the face of that diversity is virtually nil. This is why some of the more careful surveys of research in this area con-

[5] The inability of civic engagement to help political attitudes should have been apparent to Broder (1997: 8B) when he realized just a few months later that "we're not such a nation of civic slugs after all." How can the low credibility of government be due to Americans' failure to work together on shared enterprises if they are actually doing a fair bit of such work?

clude that "a person's degree of social trust or level of civic engagement [has] little or no direct effect on his or her confidence in government" (Putnam et al. 2000: 26), and, more broadly, "there is not a close or consistent association between social and political trust, between social trust and political behavior, or between activity in voluntary associations and political attitudes of trust and confidence" (Newton 1999: 185). Thus, it is hard to avoid the conclusion that "social capital is not necessarily translated into political capital" (Newton 1999: 185–6).

In advocating more group membership activity, Mathews (1994: ch. 7) refers to it as "politics that is not called politics," but it is clear from the above that the reason it is not called politics is because it isn't. As Bernard Crick (1992: 18) points out, politics is the "open canvas of rival interests." If there are no "rival" interests among the members of a volunteer group, as Eliasoph's work indicates, politics cannot occur. People can become involved in such groups without having to face up to the fact that different Americans have different priorities and that government has a tough assignment in dealing with this diversity.[6] As a result, group activity usually does little if anything to promote the kind of political capital that is truly needed in the United States.

GETTING PEOPLE TO DELIBERATE MORE

The obvious inadequacies of voluntary groups have led many theorists to devise mechanisms through which potentially dissimilar people can get together to discuss political issues. We discussed several of these imaginative procedures, including policy juries and deliberative opinion polls, in Chapter 7. In light of the inability of volunteer groups to improve political capital due, we believe, to the fact that such groups do not help members appreciate and deal with diversity, it is perfectly reasonable to attempt to manufacture situations in which deliberation occurs among people who are not particularly alike. Participation in a discussion of policy issues with a random sample of fellow Americans should be a wonderful way to see the different concerns people hold as well as to see the difficulty

---

[6] Bridging groups have real potential to help on this front, as Putnam recognizes, just as bonding groups have real potential to do harm. After making the important distinction between bridging and bonding groups, Putnam (2000: ch. 1) drops it. At no point does he perform separate analyses of bridging and bonding groups. He should.

of pleasing everyone in the group. The instincts of the people who propose such ideas are correct in the abstract. Unfortunately, in specific practice, getting people to participate in discussions of political issues with people who do not have similar concerns is not a wise move. The reasons are numerous and usually related to the difference between deliberation in the ideal and the real worlds.

To their credit, deliberation theorists are quite candid about the fact that they are describing something other than a realistic exchange. Habermas (1987) uses the phrase "ideal speech situation" and Gutmann and Thompson (1996: 3) explicitly state that "actual deliberation is inevitably defective." But at some point recognition alone becomes insufficient. What good does it do to describe a type of situation that everyone agrees never occurs in the real world?[7] The assumption of these scholars seems to be that whereas less-than-ideal speech situations will generate fewer benefits than ideal speech situations, any verbal interaction, however imperfect, is better than nothing. In short, the prevailing assumption is that deliberation is a "no-lose" situation.[8]

We challenge this assumption and believe that deliberation in the real world can be and often is dangerous, a point recognized previ-

---

[7]As Frederick Schauer (1999: 24) accurately states, "choosing decision procedures in a nonideal world should involve some empirical evaluation of the likely consequences and outcomes of the alternatives." Stokes (1998) offers a balanced account of the pros and cons of deliberation in the real world (see also Johnson 1998). Bohman's (1996: 132) laudable goal is to show that deliberation can work in nonideal settings, but in the end he provides no evidence, only hopeful assertions. He is reduced to empirically groundless calls for "more participation in social life generally."

[8]Gutmann and Thompson (1996: 44) recognize the dangers of deliberation: "It may be feared that extending the domain of deliberation has the risk of creating even greater conflict than it is intended to resolve.... More issues come to be seen by more citizens as matters of principle, creating occasions for high-minded statements, unyielding stands, and no-holds-barred opposition.... Moral argument can arouse moral fanatics." But they justify their continued faith in deliberative democracy in the face of these "real risks" by claiming that "no democratic political process can completely avoid the risks of intensifying moral conflict" (44) and by persisting in their enlightenment belief that "the assumption that we know the political truth can rarely if ever be justified before we deliberate.... By refusing to give deliberation a chance, moral extremists forsake the most defensible moral ground for an uncompromising position" (44–5). While we agree with Gutmann and Thompson on the dangers of people claiming that truth has been revealed to them, the more relevant point is that many people *do* believe truth is revealed, not discovered. We cannot assume away these people.

ously by others (see Riker 1982; Ackerman 1989) but all too often ignored. As is indicated by the empirical evidence we are about to summarize, real-life deliberation can fan emotions unproductively, can exacerbate rather than diminish power differentials among those deliberating, can make people feel frustrated with the system that made them deliberate, is ill-suited to many issues, and can lead to worse decisions than would have occurred if no deliberation had taken place. While inconsistent with the expectations of theorists, all of these findings are right in line with what we reported in Part II. People dislike political disagreements or think them unnecessary. They would rather continue with their comfortable fantasy that all Americans pretty much have the same political interests and concerns than come face-to-face with someone who seems reasonable but who has different interests and concerns. People get frustrated by details and many simply tune out of the exchange because they feel uncomfortable or inadequate discussing politics.

To organize the many empirical findings bearing on the consequences of political deliberation, we use the three main reasons democratic theorists have offered for getting the people more involved: improving decisions, improving the (legitimacy of the) political system, and improving people. We take them in that order.

Does Deliberation Lead to Better Decisions?

To begin to understand the full impact of deliberation on decisions, we return to the case of juries. Recall that proponents of deliberation view juries as pristine illustrations of its advantages. Twelve people arrive at a better decision by sharing private information in an open, discursive setting, weeding out inappropriate information and building on valid points, talking until a consensus is reached and justice is rendered in the form of a decision superior to that which would have resulted if the jurors had cast their votes in isolation.[9]

Interestingly, those who have been instrumental in shaping the current legal process in the United States clearly have reservations about free and open discussion among ordinary jurors. This is why the process attempts to limit the private information jurors may have acquired prior to the beginning of the trial. Potential jurors are eliminated from the pool if they display preexisting information about

---

[9] In Brazil, jurors promptly cast secret individual votes after hearing the evidence. No deliberation is permitted and the majority rules (Abramson 1994).

the case or parties in the case. Those who make it onto the jury are often told by judges during the trial to banish certain points and evidence from their memories and at the end of the case are given specific instructions about what they can and cannot consider. Jurors are sometimes sequestered so that they are less likely to encounter additional information that they might share with others on the jury during deliberations. In short, jurors are circumscribed in what they hear, what they know, and what they can discuss. These restrictions are clearly at odds with the view that participants should each have the "opportunity to raise issues, voice objections, and enter new alternatives into the discourse" (van Mill 1996: 734).

Why, then, would these constraints be applied? The restrictions placed on juries bespeak a fear that, if given the chance, jury decisions would be influenced by all sorts of wild, extraneous, and irrelevant facts and beliefs. Jurors are forced to stick only to what legal professionals determine are the "real" issues and "legitimate" evidence, because there is concern that regular open debate would lead to the consideration of inappropriate factors. Are these fears merely the product of an arrogant legal process that delights in demeaning the capabilities of ordinary people relative to legal professionals?

Unfortunately, the restrictions described above are needed. Consider the following case involving the real-life jury experience of one of the authors of this book. Since in this case jurors did not follow the instructions of the judge, it provides a window into what might happen if juries were at liberty to do what they wanted. The facts of the particular case involved a twenty-five-year-old mother whose car was hit by a train at an intersection. Though the mother, who was driving, survived the collision, her child, a passenger in the car, was killed. The mother claimed the railroad was at fault because the intersection was improperly maintained and was therefore unsafe. She sued the railroad for damages, primarily damages due to the loss of companionship she suffered as a result of the tragic death of her child. The railroad argued the intersection was safe and that, even if it were not, the mother merited no money for loss of companionship because there was evidence she was a casual drug user (not on the day of the accident) and had been involved in an extramarital affair. The jury was charged with deciding (1) whether or not the railroad was culpable in any fashion for the accident, and, only if the answer was yes, (2) the value of the lost companionship.

Of course, the woman's sex life and other private pursuits were totally irrelevant to the matter of the intersection's safety and should have come into play (according to common sense as well as the instructions given to the jury) only if the jury deemed the railroad partially culpable for the accident. But two members of the jury brought up the woman's habits during discussions of the intersection and accident. What is more, this information, which in a properly functioning speech setting should have been driven out by relevant information, took on an ever-increasing presence in the jury's deliberations, even among jurors who had not initially mentioned anything about sex and drugs. Visions of a child ignored by a hedonistic, philandering parent were so strong that real evidence about the distance of unobstructed vision at the intersection and the train's speed were driven out. The jury ultimately decided to award the woman only $250, just enough to cover the cost of her child's funeral. Even in the contrived world of American juries (where efforts are quite consciously taken to structure deliberation), it cannot be assumed that inappropriate points will be ignored and legitimate evidence will rise to the fore. Quite the contrary.[10]

In more natural settings, without the protections that have been built into jury deliberation, the irrelevant is even more likely to drive out appropriate information in group discussions. Popkin (1991: 218) is right when he argues that "new and personal information, being easier to use, tends to drive old and impersonal political information out of circulation." Public opinion research consistently finds that people pay most attention to the personal, the titillating, the unusual, and the exciting. The irrelevant often trumps the relevant. For example, despite serious allegations and convincing evidence during Watergate, public opinion did not turn against Richard Nixon until the tapes revealed he routinely used profanity in the White House. Bill Clinton's popularity took a serious hit when air traffic was delayed because he was receiving a haircut in Air Force One. Later, people became more likely to say he was doing a good job as president after the Lewinsky scandal brought him under attack first from Kenneth Starr and then from Congress. If public opinion focused on the relevant, Nixon's efforts to cover up the burglary would have been more important than his proclivity for locker room banter with aides, just as Clinton's policy actions, not his haircuts

[10] For more evidence of problems with Condorcet's jury theorem, see Austen-Smith and Banks (1996). And for evidence that the example just described is consistent with conclusions of systematic research on jury selection, see Kerr, MacCoun, and Kramer 1996.

and perceived victimization, would have been the key factor in the public's opinion of his performance as president.[11]

John Zaller's (1992) work on survey response casts further doubt on people's ability to give thorough, dispassionate consideration to issues. Zaller's findings follow those of Converse (1964) in suggesting that respondents typically are influenced by information that is most accessible in their minds – usually something that happened recently, not the most compelling and appropriate bit of evidence that may be buried deep in their brains. And there is little reason to believe such a pattern of relying on easily remembered but perhaps tangential information surfaces only when an interviewer happens to be on the telephone. In many circumstances, particularly deliberative ones, people are easily manipulated and are susceptible to points that are not relevant or logically consistent – especially if those events deal with the sensational.

Individual opinions do not become less problematic in the context of deliberative settings. Group environments may even lead to worse decisions (see Janis 1982). We fully agree with Lupia and McCubbins (1998: 226–7) when they write,

> were persuasion and enlightenment the same things, deliberative environments would indeed be the ideal solution to the mischiefs of complexity. Regrettably, they are not the same. Deliberation differs from enlightenment when the most persuasive people in a group are not knowledgeable or . . . have an incentive to mislead. . . . The mere construction of a deliberative setting does not guarantee that the cream of the collective's knowledge will rise to the top.

Thoughtful adjustment to previously held beliefs is not common, and when it does happen it is often not the result of reasoned argument and relevant information. As our jury example illustrates, opinions are often altered by irrational, rather than rational, factors. And the example provided is not an aberration. The "most influential book ever written" on jury deliberations concludes that "deliberation changed votes less through the force of reason and more through peer pressure and intimidation" (Abramson 1994: 197, summariz-

[11] In another example of a bias in the public's information usage, Frank Baumgartner and Bryan Jones (1993: 118–24) show that major catastrophes generate far more attention than ordinary events even though the sum total of the damage done by these ordinary events (like car accidents) far exceeds that done by catastrophic events (like airplane crashes).

ing the findings of Kalven and Zeisel 1970: 488). This being the case, the edifying potential of deliberation is unrealized.

Research from Solomon Asch and Muzafer Sherif provides the psychological underpinnings of one problem with the deliberative setting: people's tendency to conform. Asch (1951) and Sherif (1935, 1937) discover in separate experimental studies that people have a strong urge to conform to the group even when minimal pressure is put on group members. Whereas Sherif finds that subjects conform to a group decision when there is no clear right answer, Asch shows that many people conform to a group's obviously wrong decision. Verba (1961: 22) summarizes their findings: "When the opinions of other group members are revealed to the individual, even if no other pressures are applied, he will change his views to conform more closely to that of the group. This takes place even in those cases where the group opinion is not objectively more correct than that of the individual *or is objectively wrong*" (emphasis added). Subsequent research has attempted to clarify how and why conformity works as it does, but the fact remains that people are readily willing to conform in group settings.

Research on polarization effects suggests that group decisions can differ significantly from individual decisions, and not always for the better. According to Fiske and Taylor (1991: 498), "Many people think that groups represent the voice of reason and compromise; decisions made by committee are supposed to be safer than decisions made by individuals. A closer look at group decisions reveals that this is not at all the case." After group deliberation, individuals' attitudes become polarized toward more extreme alternatives. For example, individuals who have a tendency to take more risk will come to a much riskier group decision after discussion. This phenomenon is known as the "risky shift" (Stoner 1961, cited in Fiske and Taylor 1991). Similarly, individuals tending toward caution will make a much more cautious group decision (McCauley et al. 1973). A good example of polarization effects comes from Myers and Bishop (1970), who conducted an experiment on people's racial attitudes. They found that unprejudiced students became more unprejudiced after a group discussion (moving +0.47 on a seven-point scale), whereas prejudiced students became more prejudiced after a group discussion (moving a much greater −1.31 on a seven-point scale). Group discussions affect collective outcomes, but not always for the best.

The media are unlikely to offer much help in raising the level of discourse. The media are more than eager to contribute to people's thirst for the personal and irrelevant. Authors of stories in the media delight in regaling the public with explanations for why politicians do what they do. They attribute base motives to virtually any act (see Kerbel 1999). Issue-based discussions become rare as policy disputes are replaced by aspersion casting. Reporting on appropriate public policy takes a back seat to tales about which politicians will benefit from certain strategies – tales the people are predisposed to accept. Evidence of rational discourse is hard to find in sound bites. Overall, the current tenor of political debate in the United States does not inspire confidence in the ability of ordinary people to engage in deliberation – and the orientation of the media is not the only reason. In fact, we believe the major reason is the lack of motivation of the American people. As Kuklinski et al. (2001: 413) point out, people who lack motivation tend to make bad judgments.

Does Deliberation Lead to a Better (That Is, More Legitimate) System?

Deliberation theorists argue that

> deliberation contributes to the legitimacy of decisions made under conditions of scarcity. Some citizens will not get what they want, or even what they need ... [but] ... the hard choices that democratic governments make in these circumstances should be more acceptable even to those who receive less than they deserve. ... Even with regard to political decisions with which they disagree, citizens are likely to take a different attitude toward those that are adopted after careful consideration of the relevant conflicting moral claims. (Gutmann and Thompson 1996: 41–2)

We agree that citizens will have a "different attitude" toward decisions adopted after open deliberation of conflicting moral claims. We just happen to think that often their attitude will become more negative rather than more positive.

But what about Tom Tyler's experimental evidence (summarized in the last chapter) that showed participation or voice in the process made people feel better about outcomes, even if the people perceived the outcomes themselves as negative? As it turns out, the legitimizing capabilities of "voice" apply only under limited circumstances. In fact, under standard political circumstances the evidence shows voice typically diminishes, rather than enhances, legitimacy. The best work in this area has been done by R. L. Cohen (1985). Cohen correctly observes that most of the evidence for the positive effects of voice has been generated in studies of legal arrangements[12] or other situations in which the decision maker has no vested material interest in a particular outcome. Opportunities to participate in these situations unquestionably make people feel better about the process and the outcome.

But Cohen discovers that as soon as the setting is shifted to one in which the decision maker, or allocator, might receive differentiated payoffs depending upon the decision rendered, any salubrious effects of voice vanish and are replaced by "frustration" effects (see also Folger 1977). The evidence is clear that when the allocator and the recipient are in more of a zero-sum relationship, a real danger exists that people will perceive a process permitting voice to be insincere. This only makes sense. Imagine two situations, both involving a person (A) making a decision that benefits A at person B's expense. In one situation, A makes the decision without any input from B. In the other situation, A makes the decision after B has made an impassioned plea for an outcome more beneficial to himself. Is it not likely that B would be less accepting of the outcome in the second situation? After all, B's opportunity to provide input into the decision makes it certain that A was aware of B's plight. A looked B right in the eye and decided against B and for A. Is there any reason to expect that such a situation would produce anything other than frustration effects? In the eyes of participants, the opportunity for voice was obviously nothing but a sham.[13]

These results are incredibly damaging to Lind and Tyler's (1988) contentions about the beneficial consequences of voice. They try to

---

[12]Thibaut and Walker (1975); Tyler, Rasinski, and Spodick (1985); Tyler (1990).

[13]Another important reason Tyler's research on reactions to legal procedures cannot be generalized to attitudes toward government is the degree to which the participant sees the outcome as relevant. Obviously, a person cares about the outcome of his or her own court case, but as we saw in Part I, many people do not have strong feelings about most of the issues on the government's agenda. Attitudes toward government are harmed when people see officials fighting over issues that are of little relevance to the observers, even if the observers are encouraged to offer an opinion on these matters about which they care little. And as Diana Mutz (1992: 19) wisely observes, the perception of politics as distant has been exacerbated by the nature of modern existence: "[P]olitics has long been peripheral to most people's day to day concerns, but the nationalization of American mass media has inadvertently furthered the perception that politics is something 'out there,' divorced from day to day life experiences" (see also Mutz 1998).

pass them off by claiming that if Cohen had permitted "stronger voice" in the process, subjects would have been happy. "Even under conditions of severe conflict of interest . . . any relatively strong procedural justice difference will produce higher satisfaction and distributive fairness" (183–4). But they offer no evidence for this contention and it seems more likely to us that stronger voice would lead only to stronger frustrations with a high-handed and selfish decision maker.

Lind and Tyler (1988) also try to refute Cohen's contentions by saying the frustration effect "is a very rare phenomenon indeed" (183) and that frustration effects tend to occur "only when there are other reasons to be suspicious of the procedure" (201). They further claim that people have a "tendency to believe that procedures function as they are said to function" (184). This is the key difference between our position and that of Lind and Tyler. Far from being "rare," we believe that such situations are the norm, certainly in the political arena. People are incredibly suspicious of the motivations of political decision makers. People believe almost every action by members of Congress is produced by selfish desires: to get reelected, to raise campaign money, to get a free trip overseas or some other gift, or to increase the chances of receiving a cushy, well-paying job upon leaving Congress. The accuracy of people's perceptions is not at issue here, only that these negative perceptions of politicians' motives are extremely common. People are always looking for ulterior reasons for the actions of decision makers, and unless heroic constraints are in place (such as those surrounding judges), they assume such base motives are present.

Evidence that voice in nonlegal political settings leads to feelings of less legitimacy can be found in several places, including Tyler's own research on politics. He hypothesizes that the perceived ability to "make arguments to" or to "influence decisions of" a political body (such as Congress) should lead an individual to be more favorable toward that body, but he finds that this relationship never materializes. In fact, the relationship is always negative and sometimes reaches statistical significance (see Tyler 1994; Tyler and Mitchell 1994), suggesting that the greater a person's perceived involvement with a political entity, the less that person tends to like or respect that entity. In standard political situations, then, the research indicates that participation generally leads people to be more frustrated and to view the process and outcome as being less legitimate, not more.

Further evidence that inclusive procedures do not increase and may decrease satisfaction in standard political situations can be found in recent experimental work. As mentioned above, Amy Gangl (2000) created an experimental setting by having respondents read passages describing different styles of congressional process. Some subjects read of a legislative process that was procedurally fair (neutral decision makers, balanced discussion of the issue, and a wide variety of voices included). Others read of a legislative process that was procedurally unfair (self-serving decision makers, combative discussion of the issue, and only one side included). Gangl's results show that, as she predicted, the "neutral, balanced" process markedly increased subjects' perceptions that the process is legitimate, as did the "non-self-serving decision maker, combative" process.[14] But Gangl was perplexed to find that the "people have voice" process elicited no significant increase in perceived legitimacy. In fact, the sign was usually negative. But such a result is perfectly consistent with mounting evidence that voice, whether it be weak (vote) or strong (deliberative), does not make people feel better about political processes. People want neutral, non-self-serving decision makers, and if they can get them without having to participate themselves, they will be happy.

Michael Morrell (1999) presents similar results employing a completely different experimental approach. Rather than having subjects read about a process, Morrell had them actually participate in one of two possible processes. His hypothesis was that "citizens participating in strong democratic procedures will have higher levels of collective decision acceptance than citizens participating in traditional [i.e., weaker] liberal democratic procedures" (302). But he was surprised to discover that the participatory decision-making process did not lead to heightened satisfaction or to perceptions that the process was more legitimate. In fact, in some manifestations of the

---

[14] Care must be taken not to place too much emphasis on the quality of debate in determining people's satisfaction with the process and outcome. While, as shown by Gangl and also by Funk (2001), people respond more favorably to balanced, civil, constructive debate than to shrill and unbalanced debate, the more interesting point is that when a group being exposed to no debate is included in the experiment, the subjects in that "no-debate" control group accord the greatest legitimacy to the process (Morris and Witting 2001). In other words, people respond more favorably to a process with no debate at all than to one with either civil or not-so-civil debate. People are sending the message that improving the level of political debate is a good idea but getting rid of political debate is a better one.

experiment, the subjects involved in the participatory process saw the process as less legitimate and, accordingly, were less satisfied with it.

Morrell accurately concludes that his results "do not support Barber's contention that strong democratic procedures will create greater collective decision acceptance" (310), because "the group using traditional liberal democratic procedures showed greater levels of collective decision acceptance, assumption reevaluation, and group satisfaction than the group using strong democratic procedures" (313). Morrell's attempted explanation for his findings is directly in line with our beliefs. Participatory procedures "require participants to open themselves up in ways with which they may not be comfortable" (317) and "can create an atmosphere of disconnection and dislike. Rather than bringing citizens together, these types of structures of participation can only exacerbate already present divisions" (318). Tali Mendelberg's extremely thorough literature review of the psychological research on the consequences of citizen deliberation in politics comes to a very similar conclusion. Noting that deliberation typically brings inequality and greater conflict, she characterizes the empirical evidence for the benefits of citizen deliberation as "thin or nonexistent" (2002: 4).

This pattern of results is not confined to the experimental laboratory. For example, Greenberg's (1986) analysis of the consequences of various levels of worker involvement in workplace governance leads him to conclude that participation in coop affairs and decision making plays no role in workers' sense of satisfaction. And when local administrators in five cities went to great lengths to involve their citizens in policy making by devolving decisions to neighborhood levels and reducing participation costs, participation rates (and almost certainly levels of perceived legitimacy) were unchanged (Berry, Portney, and Thomson 1993).

On top of all this, people are frustrated by the plodding pace and inefficient nature of government, something largely attributable to deliberation. The central reason for inefficiencies is that democracy requires everyone to have their say. As Stark (1995: 96) puts it, "the more a system values giving everyone a voice . . . the less it can value speed and effectiveness. All those voices have to be heard." So in addition to the other delegitimizing elements of participation, it also is a direct contributor to the governmental inefficiencies people dislike so much.

Why do people approve of the Supreme Court more than any other political institution? Is it because people are routinely involved in Supreme Court decision making? No. The Court is more insular than any other political institution, and people like it for that very reason. People do not have to participate in or even see the deliberations of the Court (Hibbing and Theiss-Morse 1995). From the standpoint of preserving public support, Chief Justices Warren and Rehnquist were quite right to fight to keep the press as far away from the Court as possible.[15] If someone made a videotape of the justices vigorously debating in conference and showed it to everyone in the nation, people would not feel warmed by the frank sharing of views, whether the exchanges were characterized by reciprocity or not. If anything, deliberation reduces people's satisfaction; it does not increase it. This is true whether they are involved in the deliberation themselves or whether they observe others doing it. The relentlessly open quality of congressional procedures is one of the reasons Congress is among the least liked institutions, political or nonpolitical.

Does Deliberation Lead to Better People?

Are we as people improved when we deliberate with other people? There is one stream of empirical evidence that appears to be supportive of the argument that face-to-face interaction improves people – or at least makes them behave more sympathetically to others. In Stanley Milgrim's famous experiments on obedience, he found that people were less likely to administer what they thought to be a lethal dose of electricity to another person if they could actually see the person. Compliance was reduced even more if the experimental subject was required to physically push the "victim's" hand onto the electrode plate (Milgrim 1974; see also Tilker 1970). Similarly, Latane and Darley (1970) found that even a brief meeting with a person who later had a (simulated) epileptic fit greatly increased the likelihood that the new acquaintance would respond to cries of distress.

While face-to-face interaction is likely to heighten positive emotions such as empathy, it is also likely to heighten negative emotions. As Mansbridge (1983: 273) accurately points out, "in conditions of open conflict, the physical presence of one's opponent may...

---

[15] On December 5, 2000, the *New York Times* ran an editorial stating that by agreeing to televise its proceedings, the Supreme Court would "bolster the credibility and legitimacy of the institution" ("Televising the Highest Court" 2000: A30). This assertion is incorrect, to say the least.

heighten anger, aggression, and feelings of competition." As a result, "assemblies designed to produce feelings of community can . . . backfire." Gutmann and Thompson (1996: 42) concede that a greater reliance on deliberation will bring "previously excluded voices into politics" and that this in turn brings the "risk of intensified conflict." Amazingly, they see this as an advantage. "The positive face of this risk is that deliberation also brings into the open legitimate moral dissatisfactions that would be suppressed by other ways of dealing with disagreement" (42). If igniting the people's dormant disagreements is the positive face of deliberative democracy, we hesitate to consider the negative face.

The truth of the matter is that, as we saw in Part II, most people do not react well when confronted with opposing views. We want people to agree with us, and deliberation makes it more difficult to think everyone does. As mentioned in Chapter 6, psychologists have convincingly demonstrated that humans have a strong desire to engage in false consensus, to project their positions onto others.[16] After all, our positions seem sensible, so other sensible people must agree with us. When others disagree with us, we tend to denigrate their positions, to claim that their view is atypical and perhaps the result of some "special" interest rather than a true, real-American interest. Or else we harden our original stance. As Diana Mutz (1997: 107) discovered, "When exposed to the contradictory opinions of others, a person strongly committed to his or her viewpoint would be most likely to generate counter-arguments defending his or her initial position."[17] MacKuen (1990) finds that people will usually just clam up when they sense that their interlocutor is not a kindred spirit (see also Noelle-Neumann 1984). Whatever our response, research demonstrates that disagreement creates a negative psychological tension (Petty and Cacioppo 1981; Eagly and Chaiken 1993).

A major problem with deliberation, as people see it, is the inequalities that quickly surface in public discussions, especially given some people's distaste for conflict. The best examples of this come from studies of direct deliberative democracy in action: New England town meetings. Mansbridge's (1983) fascinating account of the events and sentiments surrounding town meetings in the real but fictitiously named New England town of Selby is the most revealing. After observing town meetings, Mansbridge interviewed many of the par-

---

[16] See Marks and Miller (1987); Mullen and Hu (1988); and Mullen et al. (1985).
[17] See also Patterson (1980); Kaplowitz et al. (1983); Geer (1989).

ticipants and concluded that the face-to-face deliberative version of democracy actually "accentuates rather than redress[es] the disadvantage of those with least power in a society" (277). The major reason for this exacerbation is simply variation in people's communication skills. As a retired businessman from Selby put it, "some people are eloquent and can make others feel inferior. They can shut them down. I wouldn't say a word at town meetings unless they got me madder'n hell" (62). Another said, "[W]e have natural born orators, don't we? I think we do. It's just the same as anything else. They carry more than their share of the weight" (83). A farmer had similar sentiments: "There's a few people who really are brave enough to get up and say what they think in town meetings . . . now, myself, I feel inferior, in ways, to other people . . . forty percent of the people on this road that don't show up for town meeting – a lot of them feel that way" (60; see also Eliasoph 1998: ch. 2). All in all, it is difficult to dispute Mansbridge's conclusion that "participation in face-to-face democracies can make participants feel humiliated, frightened, and even more powerless than before" (7).

The fact that deliberation in real-world settings tends to disempower the timid, quiet, and uneducated relative to the loquacious, extroverted, and well schooled is particularly difficult for deliberation theorists to swallow, since much of the theory's original appeal was based on its radical elan. True justice and democracy, the claim went, is possible only with noncoercive public debate. In the real as opposed to theoretical world, this position is patently unrealistic. Nancy Fraser (1989, 1992) and others convincingly point out that Habermas's model of radical, deliberative democracy would produce serious negative consequences for the influence of women and the lower, less-educated classes. For example, drawing on the work of Margolis (1992) and Tannen (1994), Susan Hansen (1997: 75) notes that "the content and style of political discourse is alienating to many women." Habermas himself has realized the error of his ways. His more recent work (1996) supports representative democracy after his early work (1973) was dismissive of anything other than direct popular participation. The chorus in the interest-group pluralism heaven may sing with a decidedly upper-class accent, but in direct deliberation heaven it sings with a decidedly white, male, educated, confident, blowhard accent.

As a result of disparities in elocution and willingness to speak publicly, a widespread perception in Selby is that a small group of people control decisions in the town meetings. The interviewees made countless references to "they." The following remark is typical: "If you don't say what they want to hear you're not even acknowledged. . . . If you don't agree with them, they don't want to hear you" (Mansbridge 1983: 69). Needless to say, when deliberative democracy repeatedly fosters this kind of reaction, it is not increasing the tendency of the people to view the political system as legitimate. If anything, it makes matters worse than would be the case with representative democracy or nondeliberative direct democracy (ballot propositions). Seeing the process up close led people in Selby to conclude that "no one *likes* each other" or there are too many "personalities involved" or "they get so darned *personal* at town meeting" (63).

The unwillingness to get involved in conflict leads to a spiral of silence (Noelle-Neumann 1984) in which only a small group of people speaks and the others seem to give their assent but really are scared to participate. Soon, many decide they will not even attend the deliberative sessions. Though systematic figures are difficult to marshal, there is little dispute that attendance at New England town meetings is down sharply across the region. Hampson (1996) notes that in Hampton, Connecticut, there would be 900 people at town meetings in the old days, 200 even a few years ago, and now only 50, with nearly half of them town employees or school board members. He continues: "The highlight of the political year used to be the town meeting where the budget was voice-voted up or down. But for the past five years voters have insisted the Hampton budget be approved via referendum" (2A). It is important to note that it is the ordinary town residents who ended deliberation on this key matter. No evil, aggrandizing power structure took away their opportunity to assemble. Rather, the people of Hampton did not want to meet on this issue, probably for the same reasons the residents of Selby had such negative perceptions of deliberative democracy: too much inequity, too much time wasted, and too much group think. The people were not forced out of deliberative politics, they put themselves out.[18]

Also important is the distinct possibility that the decline of the town meeting can be linked to growing diversity. Several of the residents of Selby, at least, spoke longingly of the days when long-term

---

[18] Fiorina similarly reports that in the New England town where he once lived, a movement sprang up to prohibit any proposal adopted at a town meeting from going into effect until it was approved in a townwide vote (personal communication). This movement was motivated by the (obviously correct) belief that those townspeople involved in the town meeting were highly unrepresentative.

residents made up the entire population of the town. For example: "[Selby] has always been such a peaceful town. But now these people come in . . . and then they just argue and won't trust anyone" (Mansbridge 1983: 68). Jack Gould's (1940) earlier study of New England town meetings came to much the same chilling conclusion. One participant told him that problems for town meetings arise when diversity is present. Difficulties are created, he said, because of "outlanders who speak different languages and whose . . . makeup is at odds with town meeting tradition" (60).

It is certainly possible that deliberative democracy could work if interests were primarily unitary but will fail when "these people come in" and government appears to be nothing but arguing. This is essentially the conclusion at which Mansbridge (1983: 276–7) arrives and we agree.[19] But we question the importance of a political process that can work only when "interests are similar" (277). As Andrew Schedler (1997: 4) notes, "politics presupposes plurality, homogeneity precludes politics." Virtually any governmental arrangement will work if all the people in the polity agree with each other. With that level of consensus, politics is unnecessary and perhaps impossible. But such a level of consensus on real issues in real-life politics is patently unrealistic.[20] Why create a decision-making structure that can work only in the fairy-tale, homogeneous, apolitical land of small New England towns of long ago or in voluntary organizations that come together because members already agree on a local, noncontroversial goal? Diversity is reality, but it brings people into conflict

---

[19] Consistent with these notions are the findings of Tali Mendelberg and John Oleske (2000). They closely observed two real-life meetings on school desegregation. One meeting had participants of various races, and the other was all-white. They found that "deliberation at the segregated meeting maintained consensus; but deliberation at the integrated meeting maintained the conflict between whites and others with people becoming angry and defensive," and the meeting ending in "alienation" (26–7). Relatedly, after describing "Navajo democracy," in which deliberation continues until the problem is solved, Etzioni (1996: 221) admits that it was tried in "several counterculture communes" and that the procedure failed miserably except when the "agenda was quite limited and the social bonds and normative preexisting understandings . . . were strong." Etzioni concedes that this approach will work only if people are willing to "leave some issues out of the debate" (104–5). Once again, it appears deliberation works only on easy issues or when there is preexisting agreement and homogeneity (see also Mansbridge's (1983: Part III) account of the "Helpline Crisis Center" when budget issues became difficult). Deliberation works only when it is not needed.

[20] Iris Marion Young (2000: 4) agrees.

with one another and people do not like conflict. Morris Rosenberg (1954–5) conducted interviews in Ithaca, New York, in the early 1950s. Several of his interviewees subscribed to the sentiment that "there is no harm in avoiding unnecessary conflicts" by staying away from politics (350). This sentiment, our evidence suggests, is a major reason people do not engage in politics.[21]

One final claim made by supporters of increased popular participation and deliberation is that interaction with other ordinary people will lead individuals to be more other-regarding. As Dryzek (2000: 21) puts it, through democratic participation people will become "more public-spirited, more tolerant, more knowledgeable, more attentive to the interests of others." Once again, however, empirical research casts doubt on the claim of theorists. Experiments by Adam Simon and Tracy Sulkin (2000) on people's generosity to others in small group settings confirm that "the presence of communication seems to encourage more exploitative outcomes" (16), a result directly at odds with the expectations of theorists. And real-life behavior seems consistent with these experimental tendencies. William Simonsen and Mark Robbins (2000) discuss the so-called "Eugene decisions," an effort to engage citizens in local decision making. They found that, contrary to expectations, the more citizens were involved in and knowledgeable about city decisions, the more they wanted to cut taxes and cut services, especially in planning, park maintenance, and building maintenance. They conclude that liberals should not support greater involvement by the public unless they are willing to see governmental programs cut. Presumably, if the study had been done in a city that was not so homogeneous (Eugene is 93 percent white), people would have been even more leery of government spending. In light of the findings reported by Simonsen and Robbins, one reviewer of their book wisely asks, "Do we really

[21] While people have probably always been put off by conflict they believe to be unnecessary, part of the public's dissatisfaction with politicians in recent decades may result from the fact that diversity in the United States is more apparent than it was several decades ago. Though it is impossible to say for sure, what happened in Selby to cause people to turn away from town meetings might have happened to the nation: Women, the poor, African-Americans, homosexuals, Hispanics, and others, have become significantly more noticeable in American society and politics. Diversity increases the system's attention to matters that seem not to concern the majority and may help to turn people away from democratic politics. The people's instinct is to dislike anything that makes it harder for them to pretend politics need not exist, and diversity tends to do just that.

need more participation if it is going to result in policies that fail to take into account the common good?" (Kraus 2000: 955).[22]

Deliberation will not work in the real world of politics where people are different and where tough, zero-sum decisions must be made. Democracy in authentic, diverse settings is not enhanced by town-meeting-style participation; it is probably diminished. Given the predilections of the people, real deliberation is quite likely to make them hopping mad or encourage them to suffer silently because of a reluctance to voice their own opinions in the discussion. Representative democracy at least affords representation to those who shy away from the give and take of politics. The bigger the role deliberation plays, the less influence such people have. When deliberation alone is expected to produce a result (as Gutmann and Thompson advocate and as is illustrated by Etzioni's "Navajo democracy"), people who choose not to participate in deliberation would be left with no input whatsoever.[23]

CONCLUSION

The evidence indicates that political capital is not increased when people join more groups or when they deliberate with people who do not necessarily share their views. For us, the essence of political capital is being able to deal with political disagreements in a constructive fashion or at least to appreciate the difficulties inherent in doing so. Why would joining self-selected, frequently homogeneous groups teach people about dealing with political diversity – especially when these groups typically pursue universalistic or at least noncontroversial goals? And why would thrusting people into settings where they come face-to-face with people who disagree with, and are different from, them and then requiring them to deliberate on political matters they would rather avoid make them happy, empathetic, other-regarding, and enlightened people? Why should they view such

[22] For an account of the negative consequences associated with unrealistic conceptualizations of what good citizenship entails, see Schudson (1998).

[23] For somewhat different reasons, rational choice scholars have also raised questions about the alleged beneficial consequences of deliberation, especially when preferences are dissimilar (see, e.g., Riker 1982; Austen-Smith and Riker 1987; Austen-Smith 1990). Relatedly, Fred Frohock (1997: 833–4) points out that public reason and deliberation "cannot resolve disputes" when "deep pluralism" exists. Mill (1977) went so far as to say true democracy was impossible in multiethnic societies.

a process as good and legitimate? The simple fact is that the "join more groups" strategy asks far too little of the American public and the "deliberate with people who are not like you" strategy asks far too much. The first does not expose people to sufficient diversity, and the second often dumps too much of it on them.[24]

Groups are useful for many purposes. Similarly, deliberation is going to have to be a part of any realistic democratic polity, so we do not want our remarks to be misconstrued. But the findings in Part II reveal that the core of people's dismissive views of politics, the reason many of them believe that stealth democracy is somehow preferable to real democracy, is their belief that political conflict is unnecessary and evil. And the empirical evidence just summarized regarding the consequences of group involvement and of exposure to deliberation indicates that neither of the main approaches currently being advocated by normative theorists holds much potential for getting people to deal with political conflict in a more realistic, comfortable, and accepting fashion.

If we are correct that neither volunteer groups nor forced deliberation is the solution to people's negative attitudes toward democratic realities, what is? As usual, pointing out the strategies that will not work is easier than identifying strategies that will, but the effort must be made. In the next chapter we review the potential benefits of decision-making strategies that focus less on the people than on elected officials and, specifically, on how those officials present themselves to the people. As such, our attention is on possible ways of making standard representative democracy (the lower-right quadrant of Fig. 7.1) more palatable to the people.

[24] As Morrell (1999: 319) notes, "strong democratic procedures may be too much to ask, at least for now."

9

Improving Government and People's Attitudes toward It

Regardless of how much the theorists muse and yearn, the empirical evidence consistently indicates that involvement either in volunteer groups or in rich, real deliberative settings does nothing to help people appreciate and deal successfully with the challenges of democratic governance. But showing that volunteer groups typically do not afford members practice in working through divisive issues in heterogeneous environments and that forced deliberation of divisive issues in heterogeneous environments often results in nothing more than frustrated participants and a delegitimized process is the easy part. The challenge is determining what should be done to help people gain this appreciation and ability. The goal of this chapter is to address this issue.

WE SHOULD JUST ACCEPT THAT GOVERNMENT WILL BE UNPOPULAR

Before discussing the reforms and changes that we believe will and will not help, we need to address the position that nothing need be done. This position holds that we should simply admit that government will often be unpopular and live with it.[1] Certainly, the U.S. government can survive being unpopular. It has done so for most of its 200-plus year history. But this should not be taken to mean that no costs are associated with the public's often intense negativism toward

[1] This is essentially the conclusion at which John Mueller (1999: 17) arrives when he states that "democracy can often work pretty well even if people generally do not appreciate [its] workings." Though we agree with nearly all of Mueller's other observations on the public's attitudes toward democracy, we disagree with this belief that a lack of appreciation of democracy is benign.

government. It is unfortunate that Easton (1965) led so many to view support, along with policy demands, as an input into the political system. It is better seen as a set of constraints within which political institutions and officials need to work. The black box of government rests on support, and when that support is thin, it rests uncomfortably and functions less well.

Sensitivity of elected officials to public disapprobation can lead those officials to avoid difficult policy matters. In the spring of 1998, the leadership in Congress worried that if it adopted an agenda that addressed difficult issues, the popularity of the institution and, with it, the majority party would plummet (see Hess 1998). So it followed a very conscious strategy of laying low. Former U.S. Senator Bill Bradley provides a vivid description: "Being part of government in a time of distrust like this is like walking across terrain where there are camouflaged pits with sharpened poles at the bottom, where at any moment you might fall through and be impaled. So you govern tacitly, by the latest focus group, the latest poll. You never pull back and try to figure out the bigger narrative, where the story is going and where it ought to go" (quoted in Broder 1999: 6B). If politicians are paralyzed by the (largely accurate) belief that any debate or contention will drag down the popularity of their institution and perhaps them (see Durr et al. 1997), then it would seem that public dissatisfaction with government is having deleterious consequences.

Evidence also abounds that quality candidates sometimes choose not to run for election or reelection to positions in unpopular institutions like Congress.[2] One former member of Congress explained his decision to leave Congress this way: "People just presume we are dishonorable. . . . Imagine living under a cloud of suspicion all the time. If you can do that, you can understand why some of us think serving in Congress isn't enjoyable." Another noted that "the vilification of the average politician in the eyes of the public is a very alarming trend. . . . Some people seem to think I should be ashamed to have served in the U.S. Congress" (Hibbing 1982: 55–6).

Several of the dangers of a sour public mood were made apparent in Chapter 3, where empirical work indicated that dissatisfaction with governmental processes decreased tendencies to comply with governmental outputs (i.e., the law). People may choose not to comply with laws if they are convinced the processes leading to the laws are deeply flawed (see Tyler 1990). And, of course, noncom-

[2] See Kazee (1994); Theriault (1998); and Cooper (1999).

pliance is extremely dangerous to the social fabric. Process dissatisfaction also increases tendencies to support reforms, many of which,
ironically, would make government even more disliked.

The polity will not crumble in the face of public distaste for politics (see Citrin 1974), but this does not mean the consequences of
such distaste are harmless. If dissatisfaction with government leads
to a lower quality of public servant, to serious societal problems
being ignored, and to people with so little respect for the governing
process that they do not feel compelled to comply with governmental edicts, it strikes us as wholly inappropriate to throw up our hands
and suggest we simply learn to live with the public's deep disgust for
its government.

ENHANCING EXISTING MECHANISMS
OF REPRESENTATIVE DEMOCRACY:
EXPOSURE TO POLITICS

If it is important to try to get the people to feel better about their
government and if intense personal involvement on their part is not
the answer, then what is? Many reformers who do not desire various
forms of strong democracy want instead to increase the extent to
which people are informed about and vote for officials in the present
representative system. In light of the findings we presented in Part
II on people's desire to avoid exposure to politics, both of these
strategies are misguided. We begin with people's exposure to politics. It would be impossible for a political system to be democratic
and at the same time make its decisions in secret. People need to be
able to learn about decisions, the reasons for and against, the ratio-
nale of decision makers, the evidence pro and con. But they will be
more pleased with government if they learn about these matters only
when they really want to do so. Some distance between representative and represented, what George Will (1992: 231) refers to as "constitutional space," is not a bad thing. Paul Light (1985) has described
in detail the process by which Social Security was reformed in 1983.
Nothing was happening on this contentious issue until a group of
seventeen moderate members of Congress began meeting (and
negotiating with the White House) in private. The "secret gang built
a compromise" (232). Of course, the compromise still needed to be
passed by the entire Congress (it was), but Light's point is that
without the secret maneuvering, no bill would ever have made it to

the floor. Anthony King (1997: 195–201) provides many similar examples of the value of the occasional executive session.

Our point is not that C-SPAN should be closed down or that all congressional committee sessions should henceforth be held in private, even though the evidence is clear that televising the legislative process causes people to be more negative toward it ("Ineffectual, Unloved, Exhausted" 1985: 40). People with a bird's-eye view of their interests being filtered generally do not like what they see. Whereas former House Speaker Tip O'Neill believed that "if the work of legislation can be done shrouded in secrecy and hidden from the public, then we are eroding the confidence of the public in [elected officials] and in our institutions" (quoted in Bach and Smith 1988: 15), our results suggest that it is exposure to the work of legislation that erodes public confidence. As long as people know the process could be viewed if they wanted to view it, there is no need to thrust it upon them. Americans detest linkage politics or vote trading of any fashion, preferring instead that each issue be considered in isolation and solely on its individual merits. Coming to resolution within these demanding constraints would be extraordinarily difficult for elected officials. The voraciously investigatory press, the Freedom of Information Act, and the plethora of "sunshine laws," so much in evidence on the modern American scene, could be scaled back without causing a crisis of democracy.

The people's preference for unobtrusive governmental procedures stands in stark contrast to the procedures advocated by deliberative democrats and utilitarians. Jeremy Bentham (1839) supported publicizing every move made by government because such a practice would, among other things, motivate public officials to do their duty. And Bentham believed that those who opposed publicity must assume citizens are incompetent (310–13). Neither of these assertions withstands scrutiny. We oppose publicity and do not assume citizens are incompetent, and, though Bentham is correct that publicity makes elected officials do something, the something they do may not necessarily constitute the kind of "duty" they should be fulfilling.

Consider the situation of modern members of Congress. Roll-call votes have always been a matter of public record, but when publications such as *Congressional Quarterly* began reporting attendance rates, things changed. A less-than-sterling attendance record is now guaranteed to generate a negative ad from the challenger in the next election. What is so bad about this? What is bad is that the difference between a 100 percent attendance record and a 95 percent attendance record is invariably a smattering of inconsequential quorum calls. Members would be doing something much more beneficial to the greater good by remaining in their offices or committee rooms, meeting with constituents, studying, or discussing issues with fellow committee members. But the pressures of publicity force them to dash off to vote on every nonissue, no matter how foregone the conclusion. Publicity is certainly a powerful tool for manipulating the behavior of elected officials. All too often, contrary to Bentham, it manipulates them to ignore their real duty of serving their constituents in the most valuable way possible.

Gutmann and Thompson (1996) devote an entire chapter to "The Value of Publicity." They recognize that secrecy may be necessary in some situations (like decisions of the Fed on interest rates). They also admit that there are "pressures toward superficiality in political campaigns" (124). In fact, in the course of this discussion they make an even more surprising concession that should have given pause to their general advocacy of deliberative democracy: "A political version of Gresham's law operates relentlessly in American democracy: cheap talk drives out quality talk" (124). This is precisely the kind of concern that leads us to conclude that centering a real rather than ideal political system around talk is a bad idea. Finally, they note that "the main contribution of publicity is not to make politics public-spirited but simply to make it public so that citizens can decide together what kind of politics they want" (127). Our question then becomes, what if the "kind of politics people want" is a system in which both publicity and "deciding together" are limited?

Following Rawls (who speaks of privatizing fundamental disagreements), van Mill (1996: 749) believes that "we can only arrive at a consensus if we deprive individuals of a lot of information." We would not go this far and our concern is less with whether or not people arrive at a policy consensus than with whether or not they revile the system. We are not proposing actively depriving people of information so much as pointing out that information and support are frequently inversely related. We should not look to new ways of exposing people to every nook and cranny of the decision-making process as a solution to people's negative views of government. People do not need and do not want to be satiated in politics. We can grant them their wish and improve opinion of the political system at the same time. Shortly after sessions of the British House of Commons began being televised, a survey found that for every respondent who claimed his or her view of parliament had improved due to broadcasting, four said it had declined ("Ineffectual, Unloved, Exhausted" 1985: 40).

ENHANCING EXISTING MECHANISMS OF REPRESENTATIVE DEMOCRACY: VOTING

For many reformers and academics, increasing the public's participation in elections is the supreme goal. Introductory textbooks now compete to see which one can do the most to encourage college students to vote and otherwise get involved. Vignettes are circulated of instances in which somebody, somewhere might have made a difference in the political process, and the hope is that the examples will inspire students to participate (Frantzich 1999). People's stubborn and continued lack of participation, in turn, is attributed to "government-imposed barriers to participation" (Johnson, Hays and Hays 1998: 4). Reformers seek ways to remove these supposed barriers.

Piven and Cloward (1988, 1996), for example, led the charge to make voter registration easier. Congress passed the so-called Motor Voter Act, making it possible for citizens to register when they were performing other "courthouse" functions. Registration levels skyrocketed, but, much to the chagrin of the reformers, voting levels barely budged and may have declined (for analyses, see Martinez and Hill 1999). Other registration reforms (such as election-day registration) have produced similarly dismal results. Many of these reforms were on the books for the first time in 1996, and as Stephen Knack (2001: 66) points out after a careful analysis, "the record low turnout in 1996 . . . understandably deepens the suspicions that many Americans simply are not interested in voting, however easy it becomes." He goes on to note that turnout in North Dakota, which does not even have voter registration, is only around 56 percent. Despite being the closest race ever (a close race usually increases turnout marginally), the presidential election of 2000 produced another disappointing turnout. Much talk was heard about how voters were taught by the 2000 election and its well-publicized postmortem that every vote matters, but we predict turnout will not be up significantly in 2002 or 2004.

If they say nothing else, our findings indicate that the basic reason people do not vote is not registration requirements or the demands of the voting procedure more generally. Much enthusiasm exists for Internet voting, mail voting, and other innovations (see, e.g.,

Johnson et al. 1998; Weberg 2000). Even if sufficient precautions can be taken against vote fraud and the serious security concerns associated with these procedures, once the novelty has worn off, turnout produced by "reformed" systems is unlikely to be much higher than that generated by traditional procedures. The real problem, of course, is the motivation of citizens and not the fact that voting unavoidably entails a few costs (for an extended treatment of the undesirable implications of the Internet for politics, see Sunstein 2001).

Realizing this, Arend Lijphart (1997: 1–14), former president of the American Political Science Association, goes one step further and calls for voting in the United States to be made compulsory. It is difficult to imagine a worse idea. The hope seems to be that, yes, the people hate politics, but perhaps they can be made to like it if we force them to be involved in it. As absurd as this notion is, the larger issue is why increasing voter participation, in and of itself, is taken to be the main goal of a viable American polity. John Mueller (1999: 182) is correct in asserting that "pursuit of participation for the sake of participation is rather quixotic," because "if people don't want to come, nothing will stop them," but he does not go far enough.

Our results suggest that securing participation at all costs while harboring a blind faith that participation will eventually lead to the kind of citizens we all want is not only quixotic but possibly dangerous. Recall one more time the focus group participant named Ernie, who finally decided to pay attention to the issues, to register, and to vote. But having done so he was angered because his voting did not lead to many of the changes he wanted. As a result, Ernie is embittered and completely cynical. Others voiced similar explanations for why they had stopped voting. Just as richer forms of involvement such as deliberation can lead to a frustration effect if the decision makers are deemed to be self-interested, weaker forms of involvement such as voting can have the same effect. If Ernie were convinced that his concerns lost out to the contrary concerns of other regular Americans, he would not have been as put-off, but he thinks his concerns lost out to self-serving politicians and their special-interest friends; consequently, he now has no time for politics. Why get people to participate if it just frustrates them and turns them away from politics?

Low levels of voting participation do not automatically indicate a flawed people or a flawed procedure for voting. They indicate a people for whom politics is not a high priority. If people were persuaded that their participation would help to eliminate self-serving politicians from government, they would participate in droves. For most Americans, with their tepid interest in issues, this is the only thing that will overcome their desire to stay as far away from politics as they can. But, sadly, since virtually all politicians offer agendas and "bicker," the public concludes that all politicians must therefore be self-serving. The automatic identification of all political conflict with self-interest must be ended before participation in politics can be expected to have beneficial consequences.

REDUCING THE ABILITY OF POLITICIANS TO BE SELF-SERVING

Most of all, the people want the individuals who make political decisions to be empathetic, non-self-interested decision makers (ENSIDs). And while empathy is nice, ridding the system of self-interested behavior is most important. People's perception is that in the current political climate, political decision makers are about as far from being non-self-interested as possible. We have argued that people are willing to sacrifice democratic accountability to obtain rule by those they believe would not be self-interested and that when people appear to want to empower ordinary people it is usually because they have been forced into a situation in which ordinary people are held up as the only alternative to rule by self-interested elites.

To illustrate, imagine three possible governing procedures:

1. Political decisions made by ENSIDs.
2. Political decisions made by the people themselves.
3. Political decisions made by self-interested decision makers.

Previous research has demonstrated convincingly that the people prefer option 2 to option 3. Option 3 is what the American public believes dominates the political system today, and we do not deny that the people would rather make decisions themselves than be played for suckers by the self-interested. But this willingness to get involved is something they would rather not do. If option 1 were a real possibility, people would gladly choose it, even at the loss of some democratic accountability. Absent strong issue positions, what good is accountability, anyway?

Thus, people give high marks to things that are light on accountability – the Supreme Court, the Federal Reserve Board, decision making by unelected experts or by successful business people, term limits for legislators. Presidential candidates compete to see who can be the first to suggest referring a problem (e.g., Social Security) to a bipartisan commission. If the people honestly believed that a decision maker could be trusted not to act (or was prohibited from acting) in a self-interested fashion, they would be comfortable with such an arrangement even in the absence of strict policy accountability.[3]

Is it possible to create a political system governed by ENSIDs, a system where decision makers are actually interested in the common good rather than their own selfish desires? We offer a qualified yes, although instituting such a system carries heavy costs. The people's preferred system is theoretically possible, but just because the people want something does not make it either desirable or practical. We are not even so sure that giving people what they want would, in the end, make them much less dissatisfied than they are now.

Are there any reforms that would make decision makers empathetic and non-self-interested? The main place to look is at the remuneration package given to elected officials. The public quite rightly sees two main sources of remuneration for public officials such as members of Congress. The first is the taxpayers of America, who provide salary and perquisites to members. The second is the special interests, who are believed to supplement members' official salary and perks with all kinds of gifts, campaign contributions, junkets, illicit presentations of cash, and promises of lucrative positions when members leave public office. People's most heartfelt wish for changing current political arrangements is that these two sources of remuneration for elected officials be reduced to the point that it would not be sufficient motivation to hold public office. We take each form of remuneration in turn.

Analysts sometimes claim that the public grossly overestimates the salary and perquisites of public officials and that public support would improve if only these misconceptions were corrected. Unfortunately, it is not that easy. In earlier research (Hibbing and Theiss-Morse 1995: 71–5), we found that the public underestimates the congressional salary by several thousand dollars and still feels members are substantially overpaid. Similarly, people believe far too many personal staffers are provided to members, even though they

---

[3] See Goodsell (1994) and Spence (1999) for more evidence that the people are quite supportive of bureaucratic expertise.

believe the number of staffers to be around six or seven, rather than the actual number, which is seventeen or eighteen. If the public were completely and accurately informed of the perquisite package received by, say, members of Congress, they would be more upset than they are currently.

Still, reductions in the salary and other perquisites of political decision makers is at least possible within the confines of the Constitution. Officials could be paid minimum wage and made to live more like ordinary people. The public would strongly favor such an approach and it could be done. Pundits should not waste their breath telling the people that the quality of public servants would decline and that without the perquisites public officials would not be able to do their jobs quite as efficiently. Since the details of policy proposals are not important to people, they are not particularly worried about getting the most competent people imaginable; good people with the right motives will do just fine, they think. And the people are convinced the process is already inefficient, so the notion that perquisites are needed to keep it from being inefficient is not a persuasive argument to them.[4]

[4]Though the longitudinal patterns in attitudes toward the government are too complex to explain simply, if our interpretation is correct, two factors that should not be overlooked in accounting for the precipitous decline in public attitudes in the late 1960s and early 1970s are the increasing professionalization of public service and the growing scope of government activities. This is not to say that the people are all political conservatives and want small government managed by amateurs but, rather, that, unwittingly, increased professionalization and scope make it easier for the people, rightly or wrongly, to conclude that elected officials have the opportunities and motivations to be self-serving. Relatedly, the fact that politicians have to work so hard to secure office these days makes the people even more suspicious. The opportunities for self-enrichment must be really good for all these people to knock themselves out trying to win that position. (As John Stuart Mill (1975/1861: 210) notes, citizens "care very little for the exercise of power over others . . . [but since] they are too well acquainted with the motives of private interest from which office is sought, they prefer that it should be performed by those to whom it comes without seeking.") It is not that politicians in the nineteenth century never served special interests, but it was rarer back then for people to become rich as a result of public service. Many of the best-known names of early American politics, such as Jefferson, Madison, and Webster, to name a few, were constantly in money trouble. Those who were well-to-do after governmental service (such as the Adamses) had usually been well-to-do before their government service. Today, government service, certainly in the eyes of the public, can lead to a radical transformation, if not when service begins, when it ends. Government service can provide an entree into wealth-generating consulting or lobbying work even as the ex-public servant is drawing a lucrative government pension.

The other source of perceived remuneration for political decision makers is more difficult to eradicate. People cling passionately to the view that special interests provide lucrative benefits to members of Congress in exchange for legislation beneficial to the special interests. Special interests funnel money into campaigns and, many believe, into the hands of elected officials, who then do their bidding. Special interests give members of Congress cushy vacations in the Bahamas and an opulent lifestyle in Washington, and by reaping such benefits, officials quickly lose touch with the American people. People would be wildly happy if laws forbade special interests from contacting members of Congress, from providing money or any other lavish benefits to elected officials, and from giving ex-public officials a job. Creating ENSIDs to a large extent means destroying special interests, but if Congress passed laws making special interest activities illegal, the people believe public officials would behave in a much less self-interested way.

But removing the perceived remuneration offered by special interests is virtually impossible without violating provisions of the Constitution, primarily the First Amendment. To be constitutionally acceptable, restrictions on interest group activity must necessarily be limited. Even if Congress at some point is successful in eliminating soft money contributions, interest groups would still be able to spend lavishly on "independent" ads for favored candidates. Even if Congress further tightened gift-giving restrictions (they are already quite tight), it would be impossible to eradicate all interactions with interest groups. Even if the limitations on former members' employment in the private sector were effective (since 1989 members of Congress have been minimally constrained by a largely ineffective one-year "cooling off" period; see Foerstel 2000: 515–19), interest groups would still have the opportunity to reward previous favors by employing erstwhile members as soon as one year after departure from Congress. The point is that, in light of the freedoms guaranteed in the Constitution, it is probably impossible to prohibit public officials from ever receiving any benefits from special interests. And with regard to campaigns, how can supporters be stopped from expressing their views about a candidate without violating the First Amendment? Special interests will continue to provide opportunities for elected officials to act in a self-serving manner even with certain restrictions in place.

Still, even these limited restrictions, such as serious campaign finance reform, might marginally improve public attitudes toward public officials, as might any method of making it difficult for special interests to provide rewards to government decision makers. Substantial reductions in the salaries and job perquisites of public officials might help, too. If our interpretation is correct, anything that serves to convince the public that political decision makers are not able to enrich themselves (so must therefore be trying to enrich the public good) should be considered.

But there is the rub. We do not believe the people can be convinced, even after serious reform, that politicians are behaving in a non-self-interested manner. ENSIDs may be what the people want, but since they tend to assume that anyone with the opportunity to be self-interested cannot be trusted, and since, as we have just seen, the Constitution would seem to make it impossible to remove all opportunities for officials to be self-interested, the possibility of attaining a situation in which the people are convinced that public officials are ENSIDs is remote.[5] The American people tend to agree with H. Ross Perot, who said, "Take any good, decent citizen, give him enough perks, privilege, and access, and he'll lose touch with reality" (quoted in Wilentz 1993: 35). One focus group respondent claimed, "It wouldn't matter if we [the people in the focus group] were in Congress. . . . We would act more or less just as they're acting." What makes elected officials different is opportunity, not personality.

Put simply, the people want to be assured that public officials' motivations for serving are not selfish, but they are extremely skeptical about any assurances they receive. As we mentioned in Chapter 2, one way process space differs from policy space is that people perceive process to be highly immovable. People do not believe elected officials will change a system from which they so clearly benefit. As long as opportunities exist for elected officials to act in a self-interested fashion, a great number of people will operate under the assumption that the prime motivation of officials is self-interest and that any process reforms will be window-dressing. This is a fact of life that politicians must face. People are incredibly suspicious of those

---

[5] Many Jeffersonians believe the people dislike government because ordinary citizens have insufficient protections against governmental power and insufficient rights for meaningful involvement in government. They have heaped scorn upon the Constitution and its principle author as a result of these perceptions (see, e.g., Richard Matthews 1995). It is somewhat ironic that the real reason people are unhappy with government is that the Constitution provides so many protections that elected officials cannot be immunized in the fashion desired by the people.

with the opportunity for self-enrichment, and they know political decision makers have a golden opportunity. People's fear of politicians enriching themselves may strike some observers as slightly irrational, but once the intensity of this fear is appreciated, the procedural changes advocated by the people become utterly rational.[6]

But we wish to go even further. Let's assume that opportunities for politicians to enrich themselves could be eliminated. Would people be happy? Yes, but not completely so. The government would still address a wide variety of issues, most of which people would find irrelevant and unnecessary, and it would therefore be involved in conflicts the people do not want to see. As we argued in Chapter 6, most people care about a few, if any, issues and project their disinterest onto other Americans. Why would the United States government spend so much time and money on, say, violence in the Balkans when it has little to do with what Americans care about? The answer, these people assume, is that special interests are inordinately influencing what the government does, creating conflict where there should be none. So even if remuneration packages could be eliminated for elected officials, the people would still believe public officials to be swayed by special interests. Campaign finance reform, smaller salaries, and a variety of limits on the benefits members of Congress receive would likely make people feel better about government, but their dissatisfaction would still be palpable simply because a democratic government in a highly diverse, complex nation is going to deal with issues many people see as irrelevant.

TEACHING PEOPLE TO TOLERATE POLITICAL CONFLICT

We support wholeheartedly certain reforms, especially campaign finance reform. People are disgusted by the role money plays in politics. Limiting its effect, within the confines of the Constitution, will help make people feel better about government, but we are afraid only marginally so. As we have argued, people harbor several misperceptions about the workings of democratic government, and they will interpret any attempts to reform the system within the context

[6] Rational or not, people's fear of being played for a sucker appears to be a core human motivation. See Barkow, Cosmides, and Tooby (1992); Alford and Hibbing (2001).

of these misperceptions. Further, we believe people's willingness to be satisfied with uninstructed ENSIDs as opposed to wanting to play a more active role in democratic procedures – in other words, their willingness to settle for stealth democracy – is based on or at least encouraged by these misunderstandings of democratic politics.

Perhaps the most important of these misunderstandings has to do with the perceived distribution of political views and concerns in the United States. Most people care about few, if any, issues on the government agenda, and so they tend to conclude that other ordinary people feel the same way. When they see disagreement taking place within the political arena, they assume the source of that disagreement cannot be ordinary people. To be sure, people are sometimes upset when they do not get their way on issues they care about, as is evident in the following focus group exchange.

Debbie: When we demand something, we still don't get it.
David: That is why we get disgusted and stop voting.

Debbie and David seem to think that they have a right to "get disgusted" if they do not receive every demand they make. Certainly, people like them need to be disabused of the notion that they should get everything they demand. They also need to be disabused of the notion that because they did not get what they demanded, no one did (or only special interests did). When many people make divergent demands, some people win and some people lose.

But our research suggests that, as spoiled and sophomoric as Debbie and David's attitude might be, a more prevalent and therefore even more dangerous attitude is made possible when people have no particular – or only very limited – issue demands in the first place. Suppose a person's only serious desire for the political system is that it improve the financial status of American farmers. When public officials devote substantial time to peace efforts in the Mideast, affirmative action in college admissions, tourism in Hawaii, protecting the spotted owl, the proper mix of union organizers' rights, and Albanian insurgents in Macedonia, the person who cares only about agriculture immediately concludes that the reason officials are doing so is due to special interest influence, not the influence of ordinary people. Analysts often suggest that people use the term "special interests" to refer to anybody adopting a position with which they disagree. This may be true, but we are suggesting an important addition: People use the term "special interests" to refer to anybody discussing an issue about which they do not care. As one participant in our earlier set of focus groups stated, "There are so many special interest groups that think their agenda is the most important and it's just uproar after uproar if they don't get attention from the president on down, such as the MIA group and the Right to Life group and so forth. And I just get so fed up with all this periphery being thrown at us that in my opinion it is not the president's job to address all of those things." People who care about veterans missing in action or abortion would vehemently disagree with this statement, but they would probably agree wholeheartedly if the groups mentioned were, for example, the National Corn Growers Association and the American Civil Liberties Union.

Instead of pretending all Americans are the same, the message needs to be communicated to people, probably through the educational community, that it is possible for an ordinary American to care about the Mideast, about tourism in Hawaii, about the spotted owl, or about racial patterns in college admissions even if others do not. Similarly, the message needs to be communicated that one farmer may believe the best way to increase income for the agricultural community is the Freedom to Farm Act, while another may believe the government needs to get back to having a systematic subsidy program. People must learn to accept that there is disagreement among Americans on how to resolve issues that are important to them and to accept that there is disagreement on which issues deserve to be on the political agenda in the first place.

Claims are frequently made that Americans are a consensual bunch because (1) they agree on goals and (2) they crowd the middle on the ideological spectrum. Both of these claims are misleading. Of course Americans share a desire for peace, a prosperous economy, low crime, good schools, and well-cared-for elderly. Is there a society in the world that does not exhibit general consensus on these goals? Consensus at this level of generality is banal, especially because people have divergent feelings about how to accomplish these objectives. But is it not the case that the absence of ideological extremists in the United States relative to most other countries makes for a more consensual politics? It is certainly true that the United States does not have a viable communist or socialist party and that there is no party on the right to parallel Jean Le Pen's National Front in France or Jorg Haider's Freedom party in Austria. But this point is largely meaningless to Americans, because few of them consistently think about the political world in left-right terms. All people in the United States could claim to be perfect ideological moderates, but if each of them cares at most about only an issue or two, and if the issue cared about is not identical across people, then such apparent consensus is nothing more than apparent. Remember, when asked to identify the most important problem in society, the answer receiving the most support was mentioned by only 6.5 percent of the respondents. The false consensus that really hurts people's views of the government is not the one that leads people to believe that everyone shares their policy belief but the one that says everyone shares their lack of concern about most of the issues the government is addressing.

A related misunderstanding that must be addressed is people's notion that any specific plan for achieving a desired goal is about as good as any other plan. This belief is clearly connected to people's reluctance to place much importance on many issues. People's preference is just to get an objective person to make a call and then to move on, preferably to something that matters. We found our focus group participants' disdain for issue discussions to be remarkable, but when we started reading the work of others (especially Eliasoph and Mansbridge) on ordinary people and politics, we realized we should not have been surprised. The key finding in these earlier works is that people want to avoid politics and they tend to think that people who do get involved in policy issues are showing off or worse.

All this is consistent with the observation made by Alan Wolfe (1998: 285) on the basis of his interactions with regular people: "What I heard as I talked to Americans . . . was a distaste for conflict, a sense that ideas should never be taken so seriously. . . . I wanted to join Harvard political philosopher Michael Sandel in telling them that democracy needs controversy." People need to be convinced that, while the common good may not be up for debate, the best method of achieving the common good is. Experts are not all in agreement; one solution is not as good as another; details matter. If people are ever going to tolerate politicians who are debating and compromising with each other on a range of issues, people must be convinced that the issues matter to other real people and that not all strategies for tackling each issue are equally effective.

One reason for hope is that, except for the group identified in Chapter 6 as being conflict-averse, most people are actually drawn to conflict. People love contests, people love athletic competition, people love television shows pitting one side against the other, people crave picking a side and being a part of a group with a shared concern. Why, then, since politics is laced with conflict, sides, shared concerns, and groups, do people despise politics? Because they believe politicians are playing them for suckers. If people paid good money for a sporting event but the athletes merely sat around and argued about whose agent was the most deserving, people would soon be as turned off about athletic competition as they are about politics. The theorists' problem is in thinking that forcing people to be involved in political processes that the people perceive to be irrelevant and biased would somehow have a beneficial effect – that people would eventually be drawn in or that their participation would lead them to conclude the process was fair and relevant. The empirical evidence indicates this is not the case. Theorists are putting the cart before the horse. Exposing people to a system they believe is flawed will only add to their frustration. If people are first convinced that the political system deals with issues that are relevant to some ordinary people and does so in a way that is not designed to benefit only politicians and special interests, then people's natural affinity for conflict, taking sides, and all the rest will kick in.[7]

Elsewhere (Hibbing and Theiss-Morse 1996), we have explained why we believe the current approach to education, with its emphasis on civics facts, volunteer service, and community unity, is wholly unable to show students the realities of political conflict. Grossman (1995: 239), for example, calls for civics education in all grades, teaching "from the earliest age the fundamental requirements and responsibilities of citizenship and the importance of fulfilling civic responsibilities." None of this would help public attitudes toward government in the slightest. Constitutional facts and impassioned pleadings to vote and to be good citizens are *not* the answer. A political system that people believe deals with relevant issues in a way that is not wired for the benefit of the decision makers *is* the answer. Thus, exposing students to the range of issue interests of people across the United States and simulations illustrating the challenges of coming to agreement in the face of divided opinion is what we need. The notion that such a curriculum could be perceived as anti-community is truly discouraging. Students will not become good citizens by memorizing lists of what a good citizen does but rather by recognizing that ordinary people have refreshingly different interests, that these interests must be addressed even when they appear tangential, that each issue has an array of possible solutions,

---

[7] This point is made forcefully in Rosenthal (1998: ch. 10); see also Wolfensberger (1999).

and that finding the most appropriate solution requires time, effort, and conflict.

To the extent the climate in schools these days encourages avoiding controversial political issues rather than teaching students to be comfortable in dealing with those issues, a great disservice is done to the students and to the democratic process. Students are left with only a saccharin civic side of politics and are thus made more likely to react negatively when in the real world they are exposed to the gritty, barbaric side of politics. Our educational system needs to work harder at teaching students to appreciate the difficulty of making decisions democratically.[8] As Elshtain (1995: 62) accurately points out, "Western democracies are not doing a good job of nurturing those democratic dispositions that encourage people to accept that they can't always get what they want." She continues, "if we spurn those institutional forms and matrices that enable us to negotiate our differences and to mediate them in civil and political ways, the result will be not more variety and pluralism but less" (xiii). Getting people more involved in volunteer groups or in participatory settings will not help people to appreciate that with political knowledge and caring come diversity, will not help people to see the need for debate and compromise, and will not make people more tolerant of disagreement on political issues. People's lack of concern about most policy issues is what leads them to the conclusion that there is popular consensus.

In sum, we all need to understand that if the American public knew and cared more about issues, there would be tremendous diversity. We have often been told that the people see special interests as anybody with an interest that differs from their own. Our claim is that the people often see special interests as anybody with an interest. Since government is filled with people who have interests, the people naturally come to the conclusion that it is filled with special interests. Teaching people to appreciate democratic processes designed to deal with diverse interests is an important step toward improving their view of government.

---

[8]This is quite a different thrust from the current infatuation with service learning. Getting students involved in tasks, while commendable, is not the same as getting them to appreciate the difficulties of making decisions. Even as staunch a defender of participation and involvement as Barber (1998: 194–5) realizes that "little can be expected from [service learning] unless it inspires a renewed interest in civic education and citizenship. Simply to enlist volunteers . . . will do little to reconstruct citizenship or shore up democracy."

CONCLUSION

Everyone seems to have an idea about the proper strategy for improving American democracy and, more specifically, for getting the American people to be more pleased with their government. Most of these recommendations, however, are predicated on the assumption that the people care so deeply about political issues that they would like to get more involved, if only the flawed and ossified system would let them.[9] Thus, modern political discourse is saturated with ideas for increasing people's opportunities to engage in political discourse, for using the "new media" to make it possible for people to spend their free time engaging in electronic town meetings and interactive debates on public policy, for providing the people with in-depth and detailed information booklets on all the political issues of the day, for opening up government even more so that the people can hold their representatives accountable by paying more attention to what they do, for putting more issues on ballots so that people can make more law themselves, for teaching students additional "civics" facts and assorted details about good citizenship, and for new advertising campaigns designed to get students to "just say yes to voting."

Our counterpoint is a simple one. The people do not care at all about most public policies and do not want to be more involved in the political process, so all of the proposals listed in the previous paragraph would only force people to be more involved in something they do not like. The people prefer a process that allows them to keep politics at arm's length. People seek this kind of system; they have not been forced into it by others. Their sourness toward government does not stem from the fact that they want to be more involved in it than they are but from the fact that they feel as though they need to be involved even though they would rather not be. But, human behavior being what it is, people also want to ensure that they are not played for suckers by those who *are* involved in politics, so their ideal system is one in which they themselves are not involved, but where they can be confident that decision makers will be motivated by a desire to serve the people.

In this chapter, we have discussed the obvious difficulties of building such a system, not the least of which is that people are

[9] Rational choice scholars and participatory democrats, so dissimilar in many other respects, are united by the assumption that people have a firm set of policy preferences.

predisposed to assume that those with power will use it selfishly if they have the opportunity, and the First Amendment virtually guarantees that decision makers will have the opportunity to act selfishly. What is more, we have asserted that people's willingness to say to government officials, in effect, "We don't care what you do on most policy issues as long as you don't do it in your own interest," is based on inaccurate assumptions about other people's interests as well as the nature of policy problems and solutions.

What, then, is the best approach for improving American politics and people's perceptions of it? The proposal we have outlined is imperfect but seems the most realistic. It involves elites meeting the people halfway. Public officials and elite observers must take seriously (or at least recognize) the people's intense desire to make it impossible for decision makers to act in a self-interested fashion. For their part, the people must take seriously the fact that political conflict is not necessarily an indication of a failure to serve the public interest. The former goal would entail reforms designed to lessen the opportunity of officials to be self-serving. The latter goal would involve a major reorientation of the message being sent by our schools (especially the social studies curriculum), by the media, and in general. In short, we must work to convince the people that political conflict often springs from them and is a good and natural part of any democratic political system. At the same time, elites must do better at viewing disputes about policy details from the people's eyes and at recognizing the location of politics in the people's priority system.[10] We do not underestimate the difficulty of accomplishing either goal but believe the effort must be made.

We hold no pretensions that a government of ENSIDs can magically appear or that people will suddenly become appreciative of democratic processes. The empirical results of our research indicate there is no reform proposal that will easily cure the ills of the system or the people. But our findings on people's lack of political motivation do urge caution on those who believe all we need to do is get people more involved in volunteer groups, in deliberative settings, and in politics generally. Such reforms will not have the intended positive effect, and will likely cause even greater harm to the system.

---

[10]The people rarely see instances in which government alters their lives directly. Those government programs that are used by large numbers of people – Social Security, Medicare, national parks and highways – seem routinized, so from the people's perspective little need exists for never-ending political debate and rehashing.

Epilogue

The data in Part I suggest that people care surprisingly little about most policies. The data in Part II indicate even more strongly that people would like very much to avoid politics. These empirical findings naturally lead (in Part III) to a questioning of the claims made by many theorists that the American political system can be fixed by getting the people more involved in the very policies and politics the people wish to avoid. When we looked for empirical evidence that greater involvement in either direct or indirect democracy has the beneficial consequences theorists predict, we found none and in fact found persistent hints that greater involvement in real politics can often have detrimental consequences. Reform proposals that are not based on a realistic understanding of people's attitudes toward democratic processes will certainly do no good and could do harm.[1]

---

[1] Those promoting novel participatory fora frequently claim that they were "successful," but it is not clear what success constitutes. Sometimes it appears success means only that people came together as specified (see McLeod, Eveland, and Horowitz 1998). Empirical tests are often based on less than scintillating hypotheses. As summarized by Johnson, Hays, and Hays (1998: 222), for example, Becker and Slaton discover that when citizens are encouraged to deliberate with family and friends about the polling questions prior to responding, they offer fewer "off-the-cuff" answers. It would be difficult for this to have been otherwise. To say the least, those utilizing new methods of getting the people involved in politics have not been particularly scientific in evaluating the actual consequences of those new methods (Fishkin's deliberative opinion poll may come closest to constituting an exception to this statement; see MacDonald 1986).

Even the Kettering Foundation's much publicized focus groups that were instrumental in popularizing the contention that ordinary people want to be more involved in politics and are starving for issue content have been called into question. Reporters from the *Economist* magazine attended one of the Kettering sessions in

Only two matters remain: some needed clarifications and qualifications, and a recommendation concerning future research.
Turning first to clarifications and qualifications, the evidence for our
claims is not ironclad, and we have probably stated our arguments
more boldly than we should have. Moreover, we fear that the nature
of our assertions combined with the understandably intense desire
of many people to make richly participatory democracy work will
render our claims ripe for misinterpretation. Thus, we ask for indul-
gence as we emphasize five clarifying points.

WE ARE NOT PEOPLE-DEMEANING ELITES

In questioning the ability of popular deliberation specifically and
participation generally to improve the political process, we open
ourselves to the charge of being elitists. Such a charge would be inaccurate. From Aristotle to Burke to Madison to Schumpeter, theorists
who have reservations about expanding the political role of ordinary
citizens are portrayed as elitists. Since these thinkers believe ordinary
people lack the requisite political skills, the elitist description is
not at all inaccurate. Burke (1949 [1774]: 7), for example, happily
admits, "I am not one of those who think that the people are never
in the wrong. They have been so, frequently and outrageously." And
he was fond of quoting *Ecclesiastes*: "[H]ow can we get wisdom that
holdeth the plow, and that glorieth in the goad; that driveth oxen;
and is occupied in their labours and whose talk is of bullocks?"
(Burke 1955 [1791]: 8). For his part, Madison (Federalist no. 10)
believed leaving the people in charge would result in "mutable coun-
sels." He spoke glowingly of the "enlightened views and virtuous
sentiments" of representatives. Lippman (1955: 39) was convinced
the people were incapable of transcending "their particular, local-
ized, and self-regarding opinions." And Schumpeter (1961: 285)
sought a way to limit the people's role in politics to "accepting or

Dayton, Ohio, and discovered that several of the participants (who were supposed to
be ordinary Americans) were actually Kettering employees, and several others were
included because they had a professional interest in the policy topic for that evening.
The situation led the *Economist* ("Building the Perfect Citizen" 1998: 21–2) to conclude that "the ordinary citizen still seems to have had very little to say for himself."
Solid, scientific evidence may eventually indicate that more participation in politics
leads people to make better decisions, to be more altruistic, and to be more supportive of the political system, but we have not seen any evidence to this effect yet.

refusing the men who are to rule them." Actions between elections such as "bombarding" representatives with letters should, he argued, be banned (295).

As is well known, early findings from the behavioral movement served only to strengthen suspicions about the ability of ordinary people to govern themselves. Stouffer (1955) discovered that community leaders were much more tolerant and accepting of civil liberties than was the mass public (also see McClosky 1964). Campbell et al. (1960) were struck by the extent to which people's political views lacked content and were the products of habit rather than rationality. And Lipset (1960: 121) detected what he referred to as "profoundly anti-democratic tendencies in lower class groups." The message appeared to be that democracy was salvaged only by elites and by the apathy of ordinary people.[2] As McClosky (1964: 376) so directly put it,

Democratic viability is . . . saved by the fact that those who are most confused about democratic ideas are also likely to be politically apathetic and without significant influence. Their role in the nation's decision process is so small that their "misguided" opinions or non-opinions have little practical consequence for stability. If they contribute little to the vitality of the system, neither are they likely to do much harm.

We do not necessarily share with these elitist sentiments a disparaging view of the American people. We do not think people are generally incapable of making political decisions or that they should be kept out of politics. If people want to participate in politics, we strongly encourage them to do so. What we believe, in fact, is that we ought to listen to the people, and when we do listen we hear that they do not want to be involved in politics. We think it hardly elitist to care about what the people say and not to push them into politics when they do not want to be involved.

By pushing people into politics, participatory, communitarian, strong democracy, and discourse theorists are in many ways elitists

---

[2] The rational choice school of thought also expresses skepticism that democratic voting and democratic deliberation lead to policy outcomes that are meaningful and accurate reflections of the public's views (see Riker 1982; Austen-Smith and Riker 1987; Austen-Smith 1990). Manipulations of voting structures and the prevalence of "cheap talk" are likely to produce biased outcomes, some rational choice theorists argue, as people may end up acting in ways that are not in their best interest as determined by their policy preferences.

themselves. While they believe people to be highly capable of fulfilling their citizen duties, they refuse to listen to what the people themselves have to say. Regardless of the precise activity they promote –
neighbors discovering the general will under an oak, right-thinking
citizens helping each other find the best answer, warm-and-fuzzy
interactions in coffee shops and local community groups, or eager
voters excitedly streaming to the polls to choose among candidates
and ballot propositions – they have all come to the conclusion that
they have the right to inflict their preferred process on a decidedly
unenthusiastic public. Granted, these thinkers believe that essentially
nonparticipatory politics such as that currently practiced by most
people in the United States is not what the people want but, rather,
is something they have been forced to accept because the elites have
haughtily pushed them aside, but they have arrived at this mistaken
view because they have not listened to the people's wishes. People
do not want to spend hours hashing out controversial issues with
their neighbors. If they did, they would. People do not want to join
more bowling leagues and service organizations. If they did, they
would. People do not want to study the issues and candidates in
preparation for going to the polls in greater numbers. If they did,
they would.

Elite observers often are so eager for a certain style of democracy
that they ignore what the people want. Page (1996: 5), for example,
recognizes that the large population of the nation and the complexity of modern issues "almost certainly necessitates a division of
labor in political expertise, policymaking, and communication. That
is . . . why we have a representative rather than direct democracy."
Exactly. But he goes on to say that "a vigorous democracy cannot
settle for a passive citizenry that merely chooses leaders and then
forgets entirely about politics" (5). Sure, but a passive democracy can
settle for a passive citizenry. Why should we assume the people prefer
a vigorous democracy? A vigorous democracy is the last thing people
want, and forgetting entirely about politics is precisely what they do
want. Why should people like Jean, who is already struggling in her
"very worn tennis shoes" to keep up with life's challenges, be saddled
with the unwanted obligations of a "vigorous" democracy? Reading
up on issues and extensively debating them or even being exposed
to others who are debating them is an additional burden she neither
craves nor needs.

Efforts to secure greater popular participation are unlikely to
succeed because the people have no desire to get involved in poli-

tics. Advocates of greater political participation should resist the urge to foist their political visions on the workaday American public and should instead take to heart what the people are saying. Participation in democratic politics is not costless and it is certainly not fun. Attempts to lure people into the political sphere by arguing the contrary will not work. Aside from pundits and academics, most people, quite understandably, do not enjoy the open conflict of interests that characterizes democratic politics. Only when people are convinced that democracy is conflictual, filled with compromises, and inefficient will they be positioned to make a sincere decision about the extent to which they want to be involved. Those who care about democracy should hope that many of these realistic citizens participate despite the frustrations of democracy but should also respect the decisions of those who do not. Ironically, those advocating greater public participation in politics contend that when it comes to policy, the people must be put in a position to get what they want. But for some reason when it comes to process, these advocates do not want to give the people any input. The people would rather not be more involved in politics, but the advocates *think* people should be more involved, and that is all that matters to them. Not only is this attitude high-handed, it is unfair to the American people.

The elitist bias among participatory democrats has been noted by others. Lynn Sanders (1997: 348) realizes that "ordinary citizens would not recommend solving political problems by means of deliberation, since some citizens are better than others at articulating their arguments in rational, reasonable terms" (see also Young 1996). But participatory democrats dismiss these concerns by saying that the problems of unequal representation in face-to-face groups "need to be weighed against the value of constructive deliberation of those people *who have the ability*" (Bell 1999: 84, emphasis added). If this is not an elitist attitude, we do not know what is, but theorists forge ahead with their "rich participation" style prescriptions. John Mueller (1999: 184–5) perfectly captures the prevailing intellectual drift in writing that "democratic theorists and idealists may be intensely interested in government . . . but it verges on the arrogant, even the self-righteous, to suggest that other people are somehow inadequate or derelict unless they share the same curious passion." And Russell Hardin (1999: 112) seems to concur: "It is hard to avoid the suspicion that deliberative democracy is the democracy of elite intellectuals. . . . It is virtually impossible to avoid the suspicion that deliberation will work, if at all, only in parlor room discourse or in the small salons of academic conferences. Far too much of real politics is about winning and losing. . . . Deliberative democracy clearly has the problem that Oscar Wilde saw in socialism. It would require too many evenings." We could not agree more.

It is true that supporters of these more participatory forms of democracy focus heavily on citizen participation in social movements rather than in everyday politics. Jack Walker (1966: 293), for example, is taken with "broadly based social movements, arising from the public at large." He sees them as "powerful agents of innovation and change."[3] Certainly, people's involvement in social movements can lead to important outcomes, such as those of the civil rights movement. Social movement activism might also be a positive personal experience for the participants. But this type of activity differs dramatically from involvement in day-to-day politics, which has been our focus. Social movement activists are passionate about the issue and it is this passion that draws them into the activity. They are not pushed against their will to get involved; they eagerly jump into the fray. Activists also agree on what they want the government to do, so they do not have to work out difficult compromises among people with completely opposing views. Granted, they do experience conflict with those on the other side of the issue, but this conflict is likely to reinforce the bonds among the movement members. So these movements may be well suited for ending an unpopular war, demanding civil rights, or expressing dissatisfaction with abortion policies, but we should not jump to the erroneous conclusion that getting people to be involved in day-to-day governing will be a similarly positive experience for the vast majority of Americans.

A related assumption may be that anyone who is not enthusiastic about expanding people's role in politics must be an ideological right-winger. We have several responses. First, there is little empirical support for this assumption. In Chapter 2 we showed that the relationship between liberal political beliefs and populist process beliefs is actually quite weak. More important, despite many liberals' expectations, involvement in the political process does not make people on average more other-regarding or likely to support additional government services (see Chapter 8). For those readers who care, we are both happily to the left of center and see no conflict

---

[3] Many other supporters of a more people-oriented democracy are similarly enamored of the success of social movements in the 1960s.

between our ideological persuasion and our willingness to point out that people do not enjoy politics and that they support participatory reforms only if it is the sole way they can get power away from those who are self-serving.

WE ARE NOT
POLITICIAN-DISRESPECTING POPULISTS

On the flip side, we wish to dispel the notion, taken away by at least one reader of an earlier draft, that we believe politicians are over-paid lackeys of special interests. This is the people's view, not ours. Since our book deals almost exclusively with the people's views of politics (and the implications of those views), readers may begin to take people's complaints for our complaints.

Again, for those readers who care, our own position on process space would put us quite close to "institutional democracy" and quite far from "direct democracy" (see Chapter 2). We think people tend to expect far too much of politicians (see Kimball and Patterson 1997) and we think the job of making important policy decisions in the face of a public that does not have strong policy preferences and that does not understand the need for political conflict is deserving of attractive salaries and additional public respect. No one can deny that politicians are on occasion self-serving, but people's faulty beliefs about the level of consensus and the lack of need for politi-cal conflict place politicians in an extraordinarily difficult, if not impossible, situation.

But the important point is not our thoughts but the fact that, whether any of us likes it or not, people are amazingly sensitive to being played for suckers (Alford and Hibbing 2001). Politicians are often in a position to do this, and as a result the people love to hate them. Telling people they should stop acting this way accom-plishes nothing because this pattern of behavior is wired into us very deeply (see Barkow, Cosmides, and Tooby 1992). Telling people to stop certainly would not advance the cause of politicians in the United States. In actuality, we harbor some small hope that by point-ing out that people's distrust of politicians is largely traceable to the position politicians hold rather than to specific actions they take, people could, if anything, become somewhat more understanding of them.

THE PEOPLE'S PROCESS CONCERNS DO NOT REQUIRE THEM TO BE INFORMED ABOUT PROCESSES

One common complaint raised against those, like ourselves, who emphasize the importance of political process is that the people do not know anything about process. This being the case, the logic goes, how could process be that important to people and how could it affect their political judgments? James Gibson (1991: 634–5), for example, in his critique of process advocate Tom Tyler's work, notes that "the disadvantage of the [process] argument is that it requires that citizens know something about the institution and how it operates . . . a formidable requirement for most citizens" (see also Gibson 1989).[4] Similarly, in response to earlier claims of ours that process was important, McGraw et al. (1999: 6) state that "people are notoriously uninformed about political institutions and processes" and that few "Americans have direct experience with institutional decision making procedures."

The notion that process perceptions can matter only if people possess an accurate view of procedural specifics is clearly mistaken. Most people are incorrect in their beliefs about how a filibuster can be ended or how the Supreme Court decides which cases to hear. But it is not necessary for people to be correct or even cognizant of the minutiae of process for their process views to be a powerful force in the formation of their judgments. To believe otherwise would be the same as claiming that people cannot act on the basis of policy preferences if their knowledge of current policy is superficial or mistaken, and this is obviously not the case. Consider that surveys show the American public, on average, believes that over 10 percent of all federal spending goes to foreign aid when in fact the real figure is about 1 percent (see Morin 1996). Even though people's perceptions are factually inaccurate, they still complain about foreign aid and urge that levels be reduced. In the same way, the fact that people's process preferences may be based on inaccurate perceptions of the process is completely irrelevant to claims that process

[4] Interestingly, Gibson's own research shows that, relative to other institutions, people are much more likely to ignore "bad" decisions by the courts than those by other institutions (Gibson, Caldeira, and Baird 1998). The key to understanding popular reaction is not the decision itself so much as the fact that some processes (like those employed by the Courts) make people more accepting of the decisions rendered.

matters to people. The important point is that, however inaccurate, the people do have process perceptions and, most important, process preferences.

What is more, the notion that process or procedural justice scholars believe that people are concerned with detailed matters of internal institutional operations is simply erroneous. Instead, these researchers generally want to know such things as whether the public perceives the process to have been open to public input (and sometimes to the input of a particular person), whether decision makers seem to take into consideration all sides of the dispute, whether decision makers are thorough and careful, whether decision makers consider all possible alternatives, and whether decision makers appear trustworthy and neutral (see, e.g., Tyler 2001). So conceived, process has nothing to do with the rules of parliamentary procedure or the structure of the White House Office, only with people's general perceptions of the decision makers.

Our own version of people's process preferences makes even fewer demands on the people. While we are firmly with other procedural justice researchers on the belief that process is important to people, we break with them regarding the belief that personal involvement in the political process is a source of satisfaction to the people. Other scholars believe that it is; we believe that it is not and that the only evidence it is a source of satisfaction has come from apolitical judicial-type settings where people believe decision makers do not have any stake in the outcome. In fact, in *political* situations, we believe people's process concerns come down to only one thing, and that is whether or not people believe decision makers are acting in their own self-interest. All the items about decision makers being thorough, collecting all the relevant data, considering all possible alternatives, and listening closely to the people can be thrown out (as we would have predicted, the effects of these concepts are usually weak or nonexistent, anyway; see, e.g., Tyler 2001).[5]

Process concerns are important to people but these concerns actually reduce to perceptions of the motives of decision makers, nothing more, nothing less. Far from requiring citizens to be students of the internal operations of political institutions, judgments influenced by process can be made by anyone who has an opinion of whether

---

[5] Items such as neutrality and trustworthiness, and perhaps even "consider all sides," have effects because they obviously are related to perceptions of whether or not decision makers are acting only to improve their own situation.

politicians are self-serving or not. We would encourage those who claim the common people are not knowledgeable enough to make process determinations to go to any bar in the country and ask the patrons whether they think politicians are out to benefit themselves or not. If the patrons say they do not know or have not thought about this aspect of process, this would be strong evidence that we are incorrect – but we are not worried.

PEOPLE ARE NOT AUTHORITARIANS

In Figure 7.1, we presented a two-by-two table to help organize the various types of democracy depending on the role people played in considering various proposals and then in selecting which proposals to adopt. The options ranged from the people being intensely involved in both consideration and decision making to the people turning both of these tasks over to elites, thereby requiring the people only to monitor elite actions and to change personnel when needed – practices amounting to standard representative democracy. The argument in this book is that, if they could choose their ideal political arrangement, a surprising number of Americans would select a set of processes that required even less of their involvement and attention than standard representative theory. We illustrate this by modifying Figure 7.1, as Figure E.1 indicates.

The key change is that, while in Figure 7.1 "elites" constituted a single category, in Figure E.1 they have been divided into two types. The first is the political decision makers currently perceived by the American public to be in power: somewhat accountable but also prone to self-interest. The second is close to the mirror image of the first: elites not accountable (or even visible) in the way political decision makers usually are but who are objective and unconcerned for their own selfish interests. What we are calling stealth democracy entails both policy consideration and policy decisions by this latter type of elites, and we believe this is the type of governing procedure most people want. People pay lip service to getting more involved themselves only because they rightly believe that acquiring objective (i.e., non-self-interested) decision makers is an almost impossible task. They simply want to check the ability of traditional elites to benefit themselves. But because people's hearts are usually not in it, procedures requiring more of them politically are inevitable disappointments in practice. Even in our focus groups, a flicker of enthu-

		Pre-decision Consideration by...		
		People	Accountable but partially self-interested elites	Objective but largely invisible and unaccountable elites
Decision by...	People	▸ Town hall meetings and juries ▸ Navajo democracy	▸ Ballot measures (initiatives and referenda) ▸ Teledemocracy	—
	Accountable but partially self-interested elites	▸ Volunteer groups ▸ Policy juries ▸ Deliberative opinion polls	▸ Standard representative government	—
	Objective but largely invisible and unaccountable elites	—	—	STEALTH DEMOCRACY

Figure E.1. Extended categories of democratic procedures.

siasm would sometimes be evident when populist reforms were first suggested, but it would quickly be doused when participants began discussing practical problems and began coming to terms with the commitment to politics that would be required of them.

If we left matters here, we may convey the impression that the people are authoritarians, preferring political decisions to be made by a detached dictator, albeit a dictator who had somehow been forced to be benevolent. Stealth democracy would not seem to be democracy at all. But we believe it is still democracy, and here is why. While people are not eager to provide input into political decisions, they want to know that they could have input into political decisions if they ever wanted to do so. In fact, they are passionate about this. But the difference between the desire to influence political decisions and the desire to be able to provide input if it were ever necessary to do so is substantial. On most issues, the American people do not want to play an active role in the shaping of public policy, but they do want to be assured that if an occasion should arise when they are moved to participate, their participation would be welcome and meaningful.[6] Too often, observers have missed this distinction and

[6]Almond and Verba (1963) make a similar point. They argue that people are generally disinterested in politics, but they want to know that the channels are open for them to participate if they become motivated to do so. The opportunity to participate needs to exist whether people ever take advantage of it or not. We take Almond

have equated the desire "to be heard when they want to be heard" with the desire "to be heard."

This distinction has limited practical consequences for elected officials, since they still need to be open to constituent input whenever it comes – as well they should. It would be an unwise elected official who discounted constituent communication because the constituent really only wanted latent rather than actual input. But it would be a wise elected official, indeed, who recognized that his or her constituents, and the American people generally, are decent, intelligent folk who happen to live in an era of abundant activity options. More than ever, as the saying goes, politics is a sideshow in the circus of life. Accordingly, people do not want to be forced into deliberating the ever more detailed and technocratic policy matters that frequent the political arena today. They want someone else to do this for them without a lot of fuss and bluster. But they want to know that they could be influential if they wanted to be. Elected officials should do everything they can to take public input seriously when it comes, but they should not expect it to come often.

MIDDLE-OF-THE-ROAD POLICIES
WILL NOT DO THE TRICK

One final clarification involves an important alternative argument best associated with the writing of Morris Fiorina (1999) but also found in the work of E. J. Dionne (1991), Jacobs and Shapiro (2000), and others. Fiorina believes Americans' dissatisfaction with their government is easy to explain: "Ordinary people are by and large moderate in their views. . . . Meanwhile, political and governmental processes are polarized, the participants self-righteous and intolerant, their rhetoric emotional and excessive. The moderate center is not well represented" (411). The story is appealing. Moderate people are provided with extreme representatives, which results in an acute case of dissatisfaction with government. No doubt some truth resides in these claims.[7] At times, Fiorina's ideas overlap

and Verba's argument one step further. People not only want to know that they can participate if they so desire; they also want to know that elected officials will take them seriously and not react self-interestedly. Simply knowing the channels are open does not go far enough for most Americans.

[7] Though it is interesting to note that a few decades ago the claim was just the opposite, that people were upset with the government because it was providing them with moderate policies when they wanted more extreme policies (see Miller 1974).

with ours. For example, we applaud his emphasis on political "rhetoric" and, more generally, "governmental processes." But there are also important differences, the most obvious of which is that policy space is the driving element of Fiorina's theory. He believes that the people who are debating (and deciding on) policies in the American political system do not share the policy views of the ordinary people. If they did, he claims, then ordinary people would be much more content with their government.

We believe Fiorina's account puts too much emphasis on policy positions and people's placement on policy space. Our findings in Part I lead us to believe that policy is only part of the story, frequently a small part. More specifically, Fiorina believes the people have sincere, even deeply felt, moderate policy positions; we believe, on the other hand, that people's consistent middle-of-the-road responses on specific policy issues are frequently traceable to the fact that a moderate answer is the safest to give to a survey question dealing with an issue about which the respondent does not care. Americans are not extremists, to be sure, but uncertainty and apathy frequently masquerade as moderation. Like Fiorina, we believe people are put off by the sights and sounds of elites debating policy specifics. Unlike Fiorina, we believe the reason they are put off is not that the debate has the wrong policy tone but, rather, that the debate is taking place at all, particularly since the debate almost always deals with issues about which most people do not care and that therefore they assume is being orchestrated by someone with self-serving interests. People's funk would not end if the government were suddenly to adopt more moderate policies (indeed, the people already perceive government policy outputs to be middle-of-the-road; see Fig. 1.3), just as it would not end if parties and interest groups all took a giant step toward the policy middle.

Convincing evidence for this last assertion, owing to its status as a counterfactual, is impossible to produce, but think back to the strong negative reactions of people to their New England town meeting experiences. These meetings were not dominated by wild-eyed national-party activists. They were meetings of neighbors, relatives, and acquaintances. The agenda was not unnecessarily inflammatory but, rather, consisted of the issues the town needed to decide in order to function. Yet the disgust and vitriol of the people was palpable. People dislike political conflict because they think solving problems is easier than it actually is. Divisive parties may exacerbate people's dislike of politics; they do not create it. It is easy to demonize party activists and those involved in interest groups, but they are often merely ordinary people who care enough to move off of top dead center.

FUTURE RESEARCH

With these clarifications in mind, we conclude with suggestions for future research. The obvious request is for more empirical research on the consequences of people's involvement in politics generally and in deliberation and group joining specifically. As is evident from our brief survey in Chapter 8, research in this area has caught hold lately and shows great promise, but much remains to be done. So many dependent variables and so many different forms of popular involvement exist that researchers will be kept busy for quite some time. But if these empirical studies are not undertaken, the political system could be reshaped to meet the preferences of elite theorists rather than the preferences of ordinary people. The early empirical research clearly indicates that, no matter how well intentioned the theorists may be, their notions of the kind of political system the people would view as more preferable and more legitimate is as incorrect as possible.

But it is not enough to undertake empirical research if the results are ignored or at least downplayed, and when it comes to research suggesting that additional public involvement in politics may not be such a good idea, there seems to be a tendency of scholars to go into denial. Examples abound. Though Cronin's (1989: 228) survey evidence shows "Americans overwhelmingly endorse leaving the job of making laws to their elected representatives," his account of direct democracy is clearly sympathetic, and he clings to the unsubstantiated belief that "a country willing to share more political power with its citizens will find a citizenry willing to participate in the workings of government" (ix–x). Cronin advocates letting people vote directly more than they do now, even though his findings question people's desire to do so. As mentioned earlier, Etzioni (1996: 221–2) recognizes that what he calls "Navajo democracy," talking and talking until everyone in the group is in agreement, "worked only if the moral agenda was quite limited and the social bonds and normative preexisting understandings . . . were strong." In other words, it works only when it is not needed (just as Mansbridge found). But this finding does not deter Etzioni from promoting a broad-based communitarian reform agenda. Similarly, Conover, Crewe, and Searing

(1991) read their evidence as saying "communitarian forms of citizenship flourish more among people who regard themselves as friends and neighbors rather than as strangers" (825), but they refuse to believe that "communal citizenship is only feasible in very small and very homogeneous communities" (826). And March and Olsen (1995: 63) concede (similar to Etzioni) that democratic governance will work only by "removing certain issues from the agenda" but persist in making the usual claims for the miracles of full participation.

Some of the most insightful empirical work in the area has been produced by Nina Eliasoph, Jane Mansbridge, and Morris Fiorina. All of them conducted painstaking field research on people in groups that came together for some purpose; all are shrewd observers of human nature; and all have written creative accounts of their observations. Though it was not their intention, collectively they present a scathing account of the ability of various forms of participation to produce meaningful and beneficial political experiences. Regarding group participation, Eliasoph (1998: 27) concludes, "If I were a citizen searching for a public forum in which to learn how to participate . . . and clarify my thoughts about the wider world, volunteer groups would not usually [be] good places to search." Mansbridge (1983), in observing decision making in New England town meetings as well as in a communal, community help group, discovered essentially the same thing: "If . . . interests on an issue are similar the face-to-face assembly . . . can help resolve misunderstandings and produce mutually beneficial solutions," but "in moments of genuine conflict, face-to-face contact among citizens encourages suppression of the conflict [thereby accentuating] rather than redressing the disadvantage of those with least power in society" (276–7). For his part, Fiorina (1999: 408), after observing a controversial issue play through his own small town, was equipped to explain "why participatory democracy makes Americans unhappy."

In spite of their own carefully collected evidence that participation on anything other than agreeable and noncontentious (that is, nonpolitical) issues is problematic, these scholars find it difficult to break out of the mind-set that the solution is still to get these very people who do not want to participate on difficult issues to participate. Eliasoph (1998), for example, calls for "confessional talk shows on television" (260), for people in grassroots groups to write newspaper columns (262), and for creating "public spheres for political conversation" (234) – all this right after she acknowledges that "the

people I met . . . did not want to talk politics" (230). Mansbridge
(1983) is more willing to see the real dangers of participatory democracy in anything other than "unitary" settings, but she does not
want to do so, calling this conclusion "bitter" (293) and "depressing"
(295). She argues that we need to reject "the cynical doctrine that
interests always conflict" so we can then use participatory practices
in these (allegedly numerous) nonadversarial situations (298). And
Fiorina (1999), shortly after recognizing the public's utter distaste
for participatory democracy, concludes that "the answer may lie in
going further down the path of popular participation" (414).[8] The
logic for all these scholars seems to be that the people dislike government because they are too involved in it, but that we can fix this
situation by getting them even more involved in government.

The reluctance of scholars and others to acknowledge the problems of getting the people, most of whom want to avoid conflict-
laden political settings, more involved in precisely those situations is
understandable in that it moves us away from the comfortable "if
people would just participate then everything would be okay" view
of politics. It is too bad that political participation, especially "strong"
and rich participation such as deliberation, is not a magic bullet that,
among other things, would lead to better policy decisions, a more
legitimate government, and tolerant, other-regarding people. It is far
from that. And pretending that it does have these consequences does
no favors for the American people.

Fiorina (1999) wants to address forthrightly the negative implications of people being deeply involved in politics but demurs, saying
he feels boxed in because "there is no turning back; any argument
to restrict popular participation would be met with incredulity, if
not ridicule" (414). We are certainly not arguing that popular participation be restricted, only that those who care about American
democracy be clear-headed in their assessments of the advantages
and disadvantages of increasing popular participation. Unfortunately, there appears to be a fairly pervasive tendency to avoid questioning assumptions about the value of ordinary people participating
in politics.

It is a sad commentary on our profession that those outside
the world of political punditry usually have a better feel for the
American people's attitude toward government than those inside it.

---

[8] At several points, however, Fiorina seems more comfortable with majoritarian
rather than deliberative, participatory procedures.

Pundits make statements such as "self government is not a drab necessity but a joy to be treasured" (Dionne 1991: 354), when in fact the people will tell you that self-government is not a treasure, that it is not a joy, that it *is* drab, and that they are not even sure it is necessary. Nonpundits are more likely to make statements such as the one novelist John Updike gives to his character in *Rabbit Redux*: "I don't think about politics . . . that's one of my goddam precious American Rights, not to think about politics." This is precisely the attitude of a large number of people. The evidence is clear that Americans do not want to spend more time involved in politics regardless of the particular form this involvement would take. This lack of desire makes it unlikely that efforts to rub people's noses in politics will produce better decisions, better people, or a more legitimate political system. American politics will not be improved by pretending the people are something they are not; it will be improved by first determining the people's preferences and then initiating the delicate process of molding democratic processes to suit people's preferences while simultaneously molding people's preferences to suit realistic democratic processes.

Appendix A

NATIONAL SURVEY

The data sets used throughout most of this book are part of the Democratic Processes project funded by the National Science Foundation (grant SES-97-09934). The telephone-survey data were collected by the Gallup Organization from mid-April to mid-May 1998. Gallup generated a random-digit-dial sample that provided equal access to all operating telephones. The standard methodology of the Gallup poll – contacting respondents with a three-call design using the "youngest male-oldest female" respondent selection procedure – was used. If a respondent was not reached in a household on the first call, Gallup called back two other times. If someone answered the phone, the interviewer asked to speak with the youngest male, eighteen years of age or older, who was at home at the time. If no male was available, the interviewer asked to speak with the oldest female, eighteen years of age or older, who was at home at the time. The average length of the interviews was 28 minutes and had a 53 percent response rate. The data have been weighted to match the sample with the population (adults in the United States, eighteen or older) based on the most recent U.S. Census. A total of 1,266 people completed the survey.

The survey items and scales used in the regression analyses in Chapters 3 and 6 were standardized to range from 0 to 1, making comparisons across variables easier. See King (1986) and Luskin (1991) for a discussion of how to interpret scales using this method of standardizing variables.

Age: Coded as reported age.

Income: "Was your total household income in 1997, before taxes, above or below $35,000? ... I am going to mention a number of income categories. When I come to the category that describes your total household income before taxes in 1997, please stop me." Responses were coded 1 = under $5,000, 2 = $5,000 to less than $10,000, 3 = $10,000 to less than $15,000, 4 = $15,000 to less than $20,000, 5 = $20,000 to less than $25,000, 6 = $25,000 to less than $30,000, 7 = $30,000 to less than $35,000, 8 = $35,000 to less than $40,000, 9 = $40,000 to less than $50,000, 10 = $50,000 to less than $60,000, 11 = $60,000 to less than $70,000, 12 = $70,000 to less than $100,000, 13 = $100,000 and over.

Race: "What is your race? Are you white, African-American, Asian or some other race?" Coded 0 = white, 1 = people of color.

Gender: 0 = male, 1 = female.

Education: "What is the highest level of education you have completed?" Coded 1 = less than high school, 2 = some high school, 3 = high school graduate, 4 = some technical school, 5 = technical school graduate, 6 = some college, 7 = college graduate, 8 = post graduate or professional degree.

Efficacy is a scale created by summing responses to two questions: "People like you have a say about what the government does" and "Public officials care a lot about what people like you think." Possible responses were agree or disagree, coded so that efficacious responses were assigned a 1 and inefficacious responses a 0 (alpha = 0.42).

The political knowledge index was created by summing correct responses to four factual questions: "Now, I have a few questions concerning various public figures. We want to see how much information about them gets out to the public from television, newspapers and the like. The first name is Al Gore. What job or political office does he now hold? [1 = correctly identifies Gore as the Vice President] What about Tony Blair? [1 = correctly identifies Blair as Prime Minister of the United Kingdom]," "Who has the final responsibility to decide if a law is constitutional or not? Is it the President, the Congress, the Supreme Court, or don't you know?" [1 = the Supreme Court], and "Which party currently has the most members in the U.S. Senate?" [1 = Republicans].

Party identification was coded 1 = strong Democrat, 2 = not very strong Democrat, 3 = Independent leaning toward the Democrats, 4 = Independent, 5 = Independent leaning toward the Republicans, 6 = not very strong Republican, 7 = strong Republican. Democrat was coded 1 if strong or not very strong Democrat, else 0. Republican was coded 1 if strong or not very strong Republican, else 0.

Personal financial condition: "We are interested in how people are getting along financially these days. Would you say that you are better off financially, worse off or just about the same as you were a year ago?" Responses were coded 1 = worse off, 2 = same, 3 = better off.

Country's financial condition: "We would like to know your views about the nation's financial well-being. Is the nation better off, worse off, or about the same financially as it was a year ago?" Responses were coded 1 = worse off, 2 = same, 3 = better off.

Perceived policy gap was measured by taking the absolute value of respondents' self-placement on the ideology scale minus their perceptions of the recent policies of the national government: "We hear a lot of talk these days about liberals and conservatives. Some people hold extremely liberal political views. Think of them as a 1 on a seven-point scale. Other people hold extremely conservative political views. Think of them as a 7 on a seven-point scale. And, of course, there are people in between at 2, 3, 4, 5, or 6. Using the one-to-seven scale, with 1 defined as extremely liberal and 7 as extremely conservative, how do you rate . . . Yourself? . . . The recent policies of the national government in Washington?" Respondents were also asked to rate the Democratic party and the Republican party.

Perceived process gap was measured by taking the absolute value of respondents' self-placement on the process scale minus their perception of the national government. Actual question wording is in the text and respondents were asked, "Which number from 1 to 7 best represents . . . How you think government *should* work? . . . How you think the national government in Washington *actually* works?" Respondents were also asked how the Democratic party thinks government should work and how the Republican party thinks government work.

Stealth democracy is an additive index based on the following questions: "Elected officials would help the country more if they would stop talking and just take action on important problems"; "What people call 'compromise' in politics is really just selling out on one's principles"; "Our government would run better if decisions were left up to successful business people"; "Our government would run better if decisions were left up to non-elected, independent experts rather than politicians or the people." Responses were coded 4 = strongly agree, 3 = agree, 2 = disagree, 1 = strongly disagree.

Negative view of disagreement was measured using the following questions: "When people argue about political issues, you feel uneasy and uncomfortable" (response options were strongly disagree, disagree, agree, strongly agree); after being asked what was the "most important problem facing the country," respondents were asked, "Thinking about the American people, do you think most Americans, some Americans, or very few Americans think [most important problem response] is the single biggest problem facing the country today?" (response options were very few Americans, some Americans, most Americans); "How interested are you in politics and national affairs?" (response options were very interested, somewhat interested, slightly interested, and not at all interested).

Approval of various parts of the government: "Now, please tell me if you strongly approve, approve, disapprove or strongly disapprove of the way different entities have been handling their job lately. How about . . . The political system overall? . . . The federal government? . . . Your state government? . . . Congress? . . . President Bill Clinton? . . . The Supreme Court?" Responses were coded 1 = strongly disapprove, 2 = disapprove, 3 = approve, 4 = strongly approve.

Approval of Ross Perot's message: "Regardless of what you thought of Ross Perot as a person, did you strongly approve, approve, disapprove, or strongly disapprove of what Ross Perot had to say when he ran for president?" Responses were coded 1 = strongly disapprove, 2 = disapprove, 3 = approve, 4 = strongly approve.

Vote choice in 1996: Following a question asking respondents whether they had voted in the 1996 election, voters were asked, "Did you vote for the Democrat Bill Clinton, the Republican Bob Dole, or the Independent Ross Perot?"

Support for reforms: Ban political parties – "Political parties should be banned from politics"; campaign finance limits – "Limits should be placed on how much money can be spent in political campaigns"; more ballot initiatives – "People should be allowed to vote directly on policies through ballot initiatives and the like much more often than they do now"; new political party – "What we need is a new national party to run candidates for office"; devolve power to states – "Power should be shifted from the federal government to the state and local governments"; term limits – "Members of Congress should be allowed to stay in office as long and as often as they're elected" (reverse coded); ban interest group contact – "Interest groups should be prohibited from contacting members of Congress." Responses were coded 4 = strongly agree, 3 = agree, 2 = disagree, 1 = strongly disagree.

Compliance with the law: "People should obey the law even if it goes against what they think is right." Responses were coded 4 = strongly agree, 3 = agree, 2 = disagree, 1 = strongly disagree.

Power: "Groups in our political system differ in how much power they have. Please tell me if the group I mention has too much, about the right amount, or not enough power. How about... Political parties?... Special interest groups?... The national government in Washington?... Your state government?... Ordinary people?" Responses coded 1 = not enough power, 2 = about the right amount, 3 = too much power.

Emotions: "I would now like to know how you feel about different parts of the American political system. First, tell me if any of the following aspects of our political system have made you proud. How about... The American people?... The national government in Washington?... Your state government? Now, have any of them made you angry? How about... The American people?... The national government in Washington?... Your state government?" Responses coded 0 = no, 1 = yes.

Characterizations of the American people and elected officials: "Next, I would like you to think about how you would characterize two groups – the American people and elected officials in Washington. First, let's think about being informed. If 1 is extremely uninformed and 7 is extremely informed, with 2, 3, 4, 5, and 6 in between, where would you place... The American people?... The elected officials in Washington?" "Now if 1 is extremely selfish and 7 is extremely unselfish, where would you place... The American people?... The elected officials in Washington?" "Next, if 1 is extremely divided among themselves on political issues and 7 is extremely united, where would you place... The American people?... The elected officials in Washington?" "Finally, let's think about intelligence. If 1 is extremely unintelligent and 7 is extremely intelligent, where would you place... The American people?... The elected officials in Washington?"

Trust: "Do you think most people would try to take advantage of you if they got a chance, or do you think they would try to be fair?" 1 = try to take advantage, 2 = try to be fair. "Generally speaking, would you say that most people can be trusted, or would you say that you can't be too careful in dealing with people?" 1 = most people can be trusted, 2 = can't be too careful.

Attitudes toward government: Response options strongly disagree, disagree, agree, strongly agree. "Our basic governmental structures are the best in the world and should not be changed in a major fashion." "You are generally satisfied with the public policies the government has produced lately." "The president needs a lot of staffers and assistants to get his work done." "Government officials should debate more because they are too likely to rush into action without discussing all sides." "The American government used to be able to get the job done, but it can't seem to any more." "Our government would work best if it were run like a business." "Congress needs to have committees to get its work done." "The current political system does a good job of representing the interests of all Americans, rich or poor, white or black, male or female."

Attitudes toward intermediary linkages: Response options strongly disagree, disagree, agree, strongly agree. "Special interest groups have too much control over what the government does." "The media does a good job letting the government know what the American people are concerned about." "The media should quit focusing on all the negative news because it makes things seem worse than they are."

Attitudes toward the American people: Response options strongly disagree, disagree, agree, strongly agree. "People just don't have enough time or knowledge about politics to make decisions about important political issues." "If the American people decided political issues directly instead of relying on politicians, the country would be a lot better off."

FOCUS GROUPS

The eight focus group sessions were conducted in the fall and winter of 1997 in four communities: Omaha, Nebraska; Bangor, Maine; San Marcos, California; and Atlanta, Georgia. Each focus group consisted of 6 to 12 participants who were recruited either by professional recruiters (in California by the Social and Behavioral Research Institute at California State University, San Marcos, and in Georgia by TDM Research of Birmingham, Alabama) or by advertisements, flyers, random telephone calls, and announcements at various civic and social meetings (Nebraska and Maine). Although the focus-group participants were not a random sample, they varied in age, race, socioeconomic status, and political leanings. Interested readers may contact the authors for a more detailed description of the focus-group participants (see also Krueger 1988; Morgan 1988; Stewart and Shamdasani 1990). Each session lasted approximately two hours and participants were paid from $20 to $50 for their time. The sessions were tape-recorded.

The moderator worked from a list of broad questions. Deviations from the order of the list were common, although all of the main questions were asked at some point in all of the focus groups. An assistant tape-recorded the sessions and kept track of participants' comments with pen and paper. The tape recordings were later transcribed. We analyzed the transcripts systematically, first by examining the connections people made among various political objects, and then by organizing the comments topically.

The focus-group question protocol follows:

1. As a way to get started, let's talk about how our government works. What do you like and what do you dislike about the way the government works in the United States?

    Probe: What do you think makes it work and not work sometimes?

2. Now let's move away from thinking about how the government *actually* works and think about how you would *like* to see the government work. I *really* want you to be imaginative here. In a perfect world, what would the ideal government be? If you were designing a system from scratch, what would it look like?

    Probe: Who would make the important decisions?

             How much say would the people have in what the government does?

             Would elected officials have more or less power?

    Probe: Would you feel comfortable leaving political decisions completely up to the institutions without having any input from the American people?

3. Now I'd like us to talk about the two main parts of our political system – the American people and the institutions of government – to find out what you think are their strengths and weaknesses. First, what do you see as the strengths and weaknesses of ordinary Americans in terms of their ability to make good political decisions?

    Probe: Are they smart, informed, energetic, interested in politics or are they dumb, uninformed, lazy, politically naive, uninterested?

    Probe: Do you think the American people generally agree with each other about how to solve the problems facing the nation?

Follow-up: Next, what do you see as the strengths and weaknesses of the institutions of government in terms of their ability to make good political decisions?

Probe: Are they representative, fair to ordinary people, and efficient or are they biased, tilted toward only certain interests, and wasteful?

Follow-up: Some people advocate moving toward a total direct democracy where people vote directly on important political deci-sions and we wouldn't even need to have elected officials anymore. Much like a large New England town meeting, the American people would be making all of the decisions themselves. What do you think of this idea?

Probe: Would the decisions be better or worse in a direct democracy than they are now?

Follow-up: There are other groups that play a part in our political system besides ordinary people and government institutions. For example, there are political parties and interest groups. What are the strengths and weaknesses of political parties and interest groups in America as they exist nowadays?

Follow-up: Another group that plays a role in our government is unelected, nonpartisan issue experts who often work on policy. Some people have said we should rely on these nonpartisan experts to make the tough decisions in our country, rather than relying on elected officials or ordinary people. What do you think of this idea?

Probe: Would it bother you to have unelected experts making
the decisions?
Do you think the American people would lose some of
their influence if decisions were left up to these experts?
Would these experts do better than elected officials?
Better than ordinary people?

4. Some people prefer having the national government more pow-erful, whereas others prefer giving more influence to state and local governments. What are your feelings about giving state and local gov-ernment more influence?

Probe: Would it be better if state and local governments had
more power or the national government had more
power?

5. A lot of people think government is inefficient and that it really ought to be run like a business. What do you think of this idea?

6. Finally, we get the sense that people are really upset with our political system, but rarely are they asked what they think needs to be done to make it better. We want to know what you think needs to be done to improve the political system. Do we need something major done to get the government back on track? [Examples might include banning political parties and interest groups or having just a one house legislature rather than the House and the Senate.] Or do you think the changes just need to be small – like campaign finance reform?

Appendix B

Coding and Frequencies for Most Important Problem Facing the
Country Question

Label	Frequency	Percent
Apathy	4	0.3
Breakdown of family	15	1.2
Budget/budget deficit	42	3.3
Corruption in politics/government	70	5.5
Crime	82	6.5
Decline in values/morals	78	6.2
Drugs/drug use	73	5.8
Economics	27	2.1
Education/system/finance	61	4.8
Ethics	3	0.3
Government has too much control	21	1.6
Government spending	22	1.8
Greed	6	0.5
Health care	17	1.3
Homelessness	16	1.3
Immigration	7	0.5
Juveniles	9	0.7
Lack of leadership	12	0.9
Lack of discipline	4	0.3
Lack of religion/belief in God	19	1.5
Lack of jobs	33	2.6
Lack of honesty	14	1.1
Media	14	1.1
Minimum wage/low paying jobs	7	0.6
Parenting/child rearing	14	1.1
President/Bill Clinton	53	4.2

(*continued*)

Coding and Frequencies for Most Important Problem Facing the
Country Question (*continued*)

Label	Frequency	Percent
Poverty	29	2.3
Racism	23	1.8
Social Security	21	1.6
Taxes	26	2.0
Too much emphasis on president/personal life	15	1.2
Violence	46	3.6
Welfare system	27	2.1
Nothing	1	0.1
Other	200	15.8
Don't know	154	12.2
Refused	3	0.2
Total	1,268	100

Source: Democratic Processes Survey, Gallup Organization, 1998.

References

"A Balanced-Budget Deal Won, a Defining Issue Lost." 1997. *Congressional Quarterly Weekly Report* (2 August): 1831–6.

Abramson, Jeffrey. 1994. *We, the Jury.* New York: Basic Books.

Ackerman, Bruce. 1980. *Social Justice in the Liberal State.* New Haven: Yale University Press.

1989. "Why Dialogue?" *Journal of Philosophy* 86: 1–21.

Aldrich, John H. 1983. "A Downsian Spatial Model with Party Activism." *American Political Science Review* 77: 974–90.

1995. *Why Parties? The Origin and Transformation of Party Politics in America.* Chicago: University of Chicago Press.

Alesina, Alberto, and Romain Wacziarg. 2000. "The Economics of Civic Trust." In *Disaffected Democracies*, Susan J. Pharr and Robert D. Putnam, eds. Princeton: Princeton University Press.

Alford, John R., and John R. Hibbing. 2001. "Sucker Aversion." Unpublished manuscript, Rice University, Houston, Texas.

Almond, Gabriel, and Sidney Verba. 1963. *The Civic Culture.* Princeton: Princeton University Press.

Alvarez, R. Michael, and Charles H. Franklin. 1994. "Uncertainty and Political Perceptions." *Journal of Politics* 56: 671–88.

Alvarez, R. Michael, and Jonathan Nagler. 1995. "Economics, Issues and the Perot Candidacy: Voter Choice in the 1992 Presidential Election." *American Journal of Political Science* 39: 714–44.

Alvarez, R. Michael, and Matthew Schousen. 1993. "Policy Moderation in Conflicting Expectations." *American Politics Quarterly* 21: 410–38.

Ansolabehere, Stephen, and Shanto Iyengar. 1995. *Going Negative: How Political Advertisements Shrink and Polarize the Electorate.* New York: Free Press.

Arnold, Douglas. 1990. *The Logic of Congressional Action.* New Haven, Conn.: Yale University Press.

Asch, Solomon. 1951. "Effects of Group Pressure on Modification and Distortion of Judgment." In *Groups, Leadership and Men*, Harold Guetzkow, ed. Pittsburgh: Carnegie Press.

Austen-Smith, David. 1990. "Information Transmission in Debate." *American Journal of Political Science* 34: 124–52.

Austen-Smith, David, and Jeffrey S. Banks. 1996. "Information Aggregation, Rationality, and the Condorcet Jury Theorem." *American Political Science Review* 90: 34–45.

Austen-Smith, David, and William H. Riker. 1987. "Asymmetric Information and the Coherence of Legislation." *American Political Science Review* 81: 897–918.

Avineri, Shlomo, and Avner de-Shalit. 1992. *Communitarianism and Individualism*. New York: Oxford University Press.

Axelrod, Robert. 1997. "The Dissemination of Culture: A Model with Local Convergence and Global Polarization." *Journal of Conflict Resolution* 41: 203–26.

Bach, Stanley, and Steven S. Smith. 1988. *Managing Uncertainty in the House of Representatives*. Washington: Brookings Institution.

Baker, Lisa, Richard Koestner, Nicolay M. Worren, Gaeten F. Losier, and Robert J. Vallerand. 1995. "False Consensus Effects for the 1992 Canadian Referendum." *Canadian Journal of Behavioral Science* 27: 1–22.

Barber, Benjamin R. 1984. *Strong Democracy: Participatory Politics for a New Age*. Berkeley: University of California Press.

  1998. *A Passion for Democracy*. Princeton: Princeton University Press.

Barkow, Jerome H., Leda Cosmides, and John Tooby. 1992. *The Adapted Mind*. New York: Oxford University Press.

Baumgartner, Frank R., and Bryan D. Jones. 1993. *Agendas and Instability in American Politics*. Chicago: University of Chicago Press.

Becker, Theodore Lewis, and Christa Daryl Slaton. 2000. *The Future of Teledemocracy*. Westport, Conn.: Praeger.

Beem, Christopher. 1999. *The Necessity of Politics: Reclaiming American Public Life*. Chicago: University of Chicago Press.

Beer, Samuel H. 1966. "The British Legislature and the Problem of Mobilizing Consent." In *Lawmakers in a Changing World*, E. Frank, ed. Englewood Cliffs, N.J.: Prentice-Hall.

Bell, Daniel A. 1999. "Democratic Deliberation: The Problem of Implementation." In *Deliberative Politics: Essays on Democracy and Disagreement*, Stephen Macedo, ed. Oxford: Oxford University Press.

Benhabib, Seyla. 1994. "Deliberative Rationality and Models of Democratic Legitimacy." *Constellations* 1: 26–52.

Bennett, Stephen Earl. 1990. "The Dimensions of Americans' Political Information." Paper presented at the annual meeting of the American Political Science Association, San Francisco, August.

Bentham, Jeremy. 1839. *The Works of Jeremy Bentham*, John Bowring, ed. Edinburgh: William Tait Publishers.

Berman, S. 1997. "Civil Society and the Collapse of the Weimar Republic." *World Politics* 49: 401–29.

Berry, J. M., K. E. Portney, and K. Thomson. 1993. *The Rebirth of Urban Democracy*. Washington: Brookings Institution.

Bianco, William T. 1994. *Trust: Representatives and Constituents*. Ann Arbor: University of Michigan Press.

Blau, P. M. 1974. "Parameters of Social Structure." *American Sociological Review* 39: 615–35.

Blinder, Alan S. 1997. "Is Government Too Political?" *Foreign Affairs* 76: 115–26.

Bohman, James. 1996. *Public Deliberation.* Cambridge: MIT Press.

Born, Richard. 1994. "Split Ticket Voters, Divided Government, and Fiorina's Policy-Balancing Model." *Legislative Studies Quarterly* 19: 95–115.

Bowler, Shaun, Todd Donovan, and Caroline J. Tolbert. 1998. *Citizens as Legislators.* Columbus: Ohio State University Press.

Brady, David W., and Sean M. Theriault. 2001. "A Reassessment of Who's to Blame: A Positive Case for the Public Evaluation of Congress." In *What Is It about Government That Americans Dislike?*, John R. Hibbing and Elizabeth Theiss-Morse, eds. Cambridge: Cambridge University Press.

Brehm, John. 1993. *The Phantom Respondents.* Ann Arbor: University of Michigan Press.

Brehm, John, and Wendy Rahn. 1997. "Individual-Level Evidence for the Causes and Consequences of Social Capital." *American Journal of Political Science* 41: 999–1023.

Brinkley, Alan. 1997a. "The Assault on Government." In *New Federalist Papers*, Alan Brinkley, Nelson W. Polsby, and Kathleen M. Sullivan, eds. New York: W. W. Norton.

1997b. "The Challenge to Representative Democracy." In *New Federalist Papers*, Alan Brinkley, Nelson W. Polsby, and Kathleen M. Sullivan, eds. New York: W. W. Norton.

Broder, David S. 1996. "So Much for a Civil 1995." *Washington Post Weekly* (8–14 January 1996): 4.

1997. "It Turns Out We're Not Such a Nation of Civic Slugs after All." *Lincoln Journal Star* (17 December 1997): 8B.

1999. "Bradley Follows His Story Line." *Lincoln Journal Star* (28 July 1999): 6B.

2000. *Democracy Derailed: Initiative Campaigns and the Power of Money.* New York: Harcourt.

Brody, Richard A., and Benjamin I. Page. 1972. "The Assessment of Policy Voting." *American Political Science Review* 66: 450–8.

"Building the Perfect Citizen." 1998. *Economist* (22 August 1998): 21–22.

Burke, Edmund. 1949 [1755–1777]. *Burke's Politics*, Ross J. S. Hoffman and Paul Levack, eds. New York: Alfred Knopf.

1955 [1791]. *Reflections on the Revolution in France.* New York: Liberal Arts Press.

Butler, David, and Austin Ranney. 1994. *Referendums around the World.* Washington, D.C.: American Enterprise Institute Press.

Caldeira, Gregory A. 1986. "Neither the Purse nor the Sword." *American Political Science Review* 80: 1209–26.

Caldeira, Gregory A., and James L. Gibson. 1992. "The Etiology of Public Support for the Supreme Court." *American Journal of Political Science* 36: 635–64.

Campbell, Angus, Philip E. Converse, Warren E. Miller, and Donald E. Stokes. 1960. *The American Voter.* New York: John Wiley.

Cappella, Joseph N., and Kathleen Hall Jamieson. 1997. *Spiral of Cynicism.* New York: Oxford University Press.

Carey, James. 1987. "The Press and the Public Discourse." *The Center Magazine* (March/April 1987): 4–16.

Carman, Christopher, and Christopher Wlezien. 1999. "Ideological Placements and Political Judgments of Government Institutions." Paper delivered at the annual meeting of the Midwest Political Science Association, Chicago, Illinois, April.

Chambers, Simone. 1996. *Reasonable Discourse: Jurgen Habermas and the Politics of Discourse.* Ithaca, N.Y.: Cornell University Press.

Chanley, Virginia, Thomas J. Rudolph, and Wendy M. Rahn. 2001. "Public Trust in Government in the Reagan Years and Beyond." In *What Is It about Government That Americans Dislike?* John R. Hibbing and Elizabeth Theiss-Morse, eds. Cambridge: Cambridge University Press.

Citrin, Jack. 1974. "Comment: The Political Relevance of Trust in Government." *American Political Science Review* 68: 973–88.

———. 1996. "Who's the Boss? Direct Democracy and Popular Control of Government." In *Broken Contract*, Stephen C. Craig, ed. Boulder: Westview.

Cohen, Joshua. 1989. "Deliberation and Democratic Legitimacy." In *The Good Polity*, Alan Hamlin and Philip Pettit, eds. Oxford: Basil Blackwell.

Cohen, R. L. 1985. "Procedural Justice and Participation." *Human Relations* 38: 643–63.

Coleman, James. 1988. "Social Capital in the Creation of Human Capital." *American Journal of Sociology* 94: 95–120.

———. 1990. *Foundations of Social Theory.* Cambridge, Mass.: Harvard University Press.

Condorcet, Marquis de. 1994 [1785]. *Essai sur l'application de l'analyse a la probabilite des decisions rendues a la pluralite des voix.* Trans. Iain McLean and Fiona Hewitt. Paris.

Conover, Pamela Johnston, and Stanley Feldman. 1981. "The Origins and Meaning of Liberal/Conservative Self-Identification." *American Journal of Political Science* 25: 617–45.

Conover, Pamela Johnston, Ivor M. Crewe, and Donald D. Searing. 1991. "The Nature of Citizenship in the United States and Great Britain." *Journal of Politics* 53: 800–32.

Constant, Benjamin. 1988 [1819]. "The Liberty of the Ancients Compared with That of the Moderns." In *Benjamin Constant: Political Writings*, Biancamaria Fontana, ed. Cambridge: Cambridge University Press.

Converse, Philip E. 1964. "The Nature of Belief Systems in Mass Publics." In *Ideology and Discontent*, David E. Apter, ed. New York: Free Press.

Cook, Clive. 2000. "In the Crowded Center, Disagreement Is Vital." *National Journal* (29 July): 2443–4.

Cooper, Joseph. 1999. *Congress and the Decline of Public Trust.* Boulder: Westview Press.

Craig, Stephen C. 1993. *The Malevolent Leaders: Popular Discontent in America.* Boulder: Westview.

Craig, Stephen C., ed. 1996. *Broken Contract: Changing Relationships between Americans and Their Government.* Boulder, Colo.: Westview Press.

Crewe, Ivor, and Martin Harrop. 1986. *Political Communications: The General Election Campaign of 1983.* Cambridge: Cambridge University Press.

Crick, Bernard. 1992. In *Defense of Politics*, 4th ed. Chicago: University of Chicago Press.

Cronin, Thomas. 1989. *Direct Democracy.* Cambridge: Harvard University Press.

Dahl, Robert A. 1956. *A Preface to Democratic Theory.* Chicago: University of Chicago Press.

1970. *After the Revolution: Authority in a Good Society.* New Haven: Yale University Press.

1989. *Democracy and Its Critics.* New Haven: Yale University Press.

Dalager, Jon K. 1996. "Voters, Issues, and Elections." *Journal of Politics* 58: 486–515.

Davidson, Roger, David M. Kovenock, and Michael K. O'Leary. 1968. *Congress in Crisis: Politics and Congressional Reform.* Belmont, Calif.: Wadsworth.

Dawson, Richard E. 1973. *Public Opinion and Contemporary Disarray.* New York: Harper and Row.

della Porta, Donatella. 2000. "Social Capital, Beliefs in Government, and Political Corruption." In *Disaffected Democracies,* Susan J. Pharr and Robert D. Putnam, eds. Princeton: Princeton University Press.

Delli Carpini, Michael X., and Scott Keeter. 1996. *What Americans Know about Politics and Why It Matters.* New Haven: Yale University Press.

Dewey, John. 1927. *The Public and Its Problems.* New York: Holt, Rinehart and Winston.

Dionne, E. J., Jr. 1991. *Why Americans Hate Politics.* New York: Simon and Schuster.

2000. "Scrap the System." *Washington Post Weekly* (13 November): 27.

Doise, Willem, Alain Clemence, and Fabio Lorenzi-Cioldi. 1993. *The Quantitative Analysis of Social Representations.* London: Harvester Wheatsheaf.

Dow, Jay, and Michael Munger. 1990. "Public Choice in Political Science." *PS: Political Science and Politics* 23: 604–10.

Downs, Anthony. 1957. *An Economic Theory of Democracy.* New York: Harper and Row.

Dryzek, John S. 1990. *Discursive Democracy.* Cambridge: Cambridge University Press.

2000. *Deliberative Democracy and Beyond.* New York: Oxford University Press.

Durr, Robert H., John B. Gilmour, and Christina Wolbrecht. 1997. "Explaining Congressional Approval." *American Journal of Political Science* 41: 175–207.

Dworkin, Ronald. 1989. "Liberal Community." *California Law Review* 77: 479–504.

Dye, Thomas R. 1966. *Politics, Economics, and the Public.* Chicago: Rand McNally.

Eagly, Alice H., and Shelly Chaiken. 1993. *The Psychology of Attitudes.* New York: Harcourt Brace Jovanovich.

Easton, David. 1965. *A Framework for Political Analysis.* Englewood Cliffs, N.J.: Prentice-Hall.

Eliasoph, Nina. 1998. *Avoiding Politics.* Cambridge: Cambridge University Press.

Elshtain, Jean Bethke. 1995. *Democracy on Trial.* New York: Basic Books.

Ely, John Hart. 1980. *Democracy and Distrust.* Cambridge: Cambridge University Press.

Enelow, James, and Melvin J. Hinich. 1984. *The Spatial Theory of Voting: An Introduction.* Cambridge: Cambridge University Press.

Etzioni, Amitai. 1972. "Minerva: An Electronic Town Hall." *Policy Sciences* 3: 457–74.

1996. *The New Golden Rule.* New York: Basic Books.

Fallows, James. 1996. *Breaking the News: How the Media Undermine American Democracy.* New York: Pantheon.

Fenno, Richard, F. Jr. 1977. "U.S. House Members in Their Constituencies: An Exploration." *American Political Science Review* 71: 883–917.

1978. *Home Style.* Boston: Little, Brown.

Finifter, Ada. 1970. "Dimensions of Political Alienation." *American Political Science Review* 64: 389–410.

Fiorina, Morris P. 1977. *Congress: Keystone of the Washington Establishment.* New Haven: Yale University Press.

1981. *Retrospective Voting in American National Elections.* New Haven: Yale University Press.

1996. *Divided Government,* 2nd ed. Boston: Allyn and Bacon.

1999. "The Dark Side of Civic Engagement." In *Civic Engagement in American Democracy,* Theda Skocpol and Morris P. Fiorina, eds. Washington: Brookings Institution.

Fishkin, James S. 1991. *Democracy and Deliberation.* New Haven: Yale University Press.

1995. *The Voice of the People.* New Haven: Yale University Press.

Fiske, Susan T., and Shelley E. Taylor. 1991. *Social Cognition,* 2nd ed. New York: McGraw-Hill.

Foerstel, Karen. 2000. "Grass Greener after Congress." *Congressional Quarterly Weekly Report* 58 (11 March): 515–19.

Folger, R. 1977. "Distributive and Procedural Justice." *Journal of Personality and Social Psychology* 35: 108–19.

Frantzich, Stephen E. 1999. *Citizen Democracy.* Lanham, Md.: Rowman and Littlefield.

Fraser, Nancy. 1989. "What's Critical about Critical Theory? The Cases of Habermas and Gender." In *Unruly Practices: Power, Discourse, and Gender in Contemporary Social Theory,* Nancy Fraser, ed. Minneapolis: University of Minnesota Press.

1992. "Rethinking the Public Sphere: A Contribution to the Critique of Actually Existing Democracy." In *Habermas and the Public Sphere,* Craig Calhoun, ed. Cambridge: MIT Press.

Frohock, Fred M. 1997. "The Boundaries of Public Reason." *American Political Science Review* 91: 833–44.

Frymer, Paul. 1994. "Ideological Consensus within Divided Party Government." *Political Science Quarterly* 109: 287–311.

Funk, Carolyn L. 2001. "Dr. Jekyll and Mr. Hyde: Public Views of Debate in the Political System." In *What Is It about Government That Americans Dislike?* John R. Hibbing and Elizabeth Theiss-Morse, eds. Cambridge: Cambridge University Press.

Gallup. 2001. http://www.gallup.com.

Gamble, Barbara S. 1997. "Putting Civil Rights to a Popular Vote." *American Journal of Political Science* 41: 245–69.

Gamson, William A. 1968. *Power and Discontent.* Homewood, Ill.: Dorsey.

Gangl, Amy. 2000. "It Isn't Fair: Do Perceptions of Procedural Justice in Evaluations of Congress Matter More Than Getting What You Want?" Paper presented at the annual meeting of the Midwest Political Science Association, Chicago, Illinois, April.

Geer, John G. 1989. *Nominating Presidents*. New York: Greenwood.

Gerber, Elisabeth. 1999. *The Populist Paradox: Interest Group Influence and the Promise of Direct Legislation*. Princeton: Princeton University Press.

Germond, Jack W., and Jules Witcover. 1994. *Mad as Hell: Revolt at the Ballot Box, 1992*. New York: Warner Books.

Gerring, John. 1998. *Party Ideologies in America, 1828–1996*. Cambridge: Cambridge University Press.

Gibson, James L. 1989. "Understandings of Justice: Institutional Legitimacy, Procedural Justice, and Political Tolerance." *Law and Society Review* 23: 469–86.

———. 1991. "Institutional Legitimacy, Procedural Justice, and Compliance with Supreme Court Decisions." *Law and Society Review* 25: 631–5.

———. 1998. "A Sober Second Thought: An Experiment in Persuading Russians to Tolerate." *American Journal of Political Science* 42: 819–50.

Gibson, James L., Gregory A. Caldeira, and Vanessa A. Baird. 1998. "On the Legitimacy of National High Courts." *American Political Science Review* 92: 343–58.

Glynn, Carroll J., Ronald E. Ostman, and Daniel G. McDonald. 1995. "Opinion, Perceptions and Social Reality." In *Public Opinion and the Communication of Consent*, Theodore L. Glasser and Charles T. Salmon, eds. New York: Guilford Press.

Glynn, Carroll J., Susan Herbst, Garrett J. O'Keefe, and Robert Y. Shapiro. 1999. *Public Opinion*. Boulder: Westview.

Goodsell, Charles. 1994. *The Case for Bureaucracy*, 3rd ed. Chatham: Chatham House.

Gould, Jack. 1940. *New England Town Meetings: Safeguard of Democracy*. Battleboro, Vt.: Stephen Daye Press.

Greenberg, Edward S. 1986. *Workplace Democracy: The Political Effects of Participation*. Ithaca, N.Y.: Cornell University Press.

Greenberg, Edward S., and Benjamin I. Page. 1997. *The Struggle for Democracy*, 3rd ed. New York: Longman.

Grossman, Lawrence K. 1995. *The Electronic Republic*. New York: Penguin Books.

Guinier, Lani. 1994. *The Tyranny of the Majority*. New York: Free Press.

Guth, Werner, and Reinhard Tietz. 1990. "Ultimatum Bargaining Behavior: A Survey and Comparison of Experimental Results." *Journal of Economic Psychology* 11: 417–49.

Gutmann, Amy, and Dennis Thompson. 1996. *Democracy and Disagreement*. Cambridge: Harvard University Press.

Habermas, Jurgen. 1973. *Theory and Practice*. Boston: Beacon Books.

———. 1984. *A Theory of Communicative Action*, vol. 1. Boston: Beacon Press.

———. 1987. *A Theory of Communicative Action*, vol. 2. Boston: Beacon Press.

———. 1996. *Between Facts and Norms*. Cambridge, Mass.: MIT Press.

Hampson, Rick. 1996. "Decline of the Town Meeting." *Lincoln Journal Star* (14 October 1996): 2A.

Hansen, Susan B. 1997. "Talking about Politics: Gender and Contextual Effects on Political Proselytizing." *Journal of Politics* 59: 73–103.

Hardin, Russell. 1999. "Deliberation: Method, Not Theory." In *Deliberative Politics: Essays on Democracy and Disagreement*, Stephen Macedo, ed. Oxford: Oxford University Press.

2000. "The Public Trust." In *Disaffected Democracies*, Susan J. Pharr and Robert D. Putnam, eds. Princeton: Princeton University Press.

Hartz, Louis. 1955. *The Liberal Tradition in America*. New York: Harcourt, Brace and World.

Headlam, James Wycliffe. 1933. *Election by Lot at Athens*, 2nd ed. Cambridge: Cambridge University Press.

Hess, David. 1998. "Congress Hibernating Till Fall: With Approval Ratings Up, Why Mess with Success." *Houston Chronicle* (19 March 1998): 8A.

Hetherington, Marc J. 1999. "The Effect of Political Trust on the Presidential Vote, 1968–1996." *American Political Science Review* 93: 311–26.

Hetherington, Marc J., and John D. Nugent. 2001. "Explaining Public Support for Devolution: The Role of Political Trust." In *What Is It about Government That Americans Dislike?* John R. Hibbing and Elizabeth Theiss-Morse, eds. Cambridge: Cambridge University Press.

Hibbing, John R. 1982. *Choosing to Leave*. Washington: University Press of America.

Hibbing, John R., and Elizabeth Theiss-Morse. 1995. *Congress as Public Enemy*. Cambridge: Cambridge University Press.

1996. "Civics Is Not Enough: Teaching Barbarics in K–12." *PS: Political Science and Politics* 29: 57–62.

1998. "The Media's Role in Public Negativity toward Congress." *American Journal of Political Science* 42: 475–98.

2001. *What Is It about Government That Americans Dislike?* Cambridge: Cambridge University Press.

Hibbing, John R., and Eric Tiritilli. 2000. "Public Disapproval of Congress Can Be Dangerous to Majority Party Candidates." In *Change and Continuity in House Elections*, David W. Brady, John Cogan, and Morris P. Fiorina, eds. Stanford: Stanford University Press.

Hightower, Jim. 1997. *There's Nothing in the Middle of the Road but Yellow Stripes and Dead Armadillos*. New York: Harper Collins.

Hinich, Melvin J., and Michael Munger. 1994. *Ideology and the Theory of Political Choice*. Ann Arbor: University of Michigan Press.

Hinich, Melvin J., and Peter C. Ordeshook. 1970. "Plurality Maximization and Vote Maximization." *American Political Science Review* 64: 772–91.

Hotelling, Harold. 1929. "Stability in Competition." *Economic Journal* 39: 41–57.

Huckfeldt, Robert, and John Sprague. 1995. *Citizens, Contexts, and Social Communication*. Cambridge: Cambridge University Press.

Huckfeldt, Robert, Paul A. Beck, Russell J. Dalton, and J. Levine. 1995. "Political Environments, Cohesive Social Groups, and the Communication of Public Opinion." *American Journal of Political Science* 39: 1025–54.

"Ineffectual, Unloved, Exhausted." 1985. *Economist* (2 March 1985): 40.

Ivins, Molly. 1992. *Molly Ivins Can't Say That, Can She?* New York: Random House.

1998. "Members of Congress Working Hard for Those Who Bought Them Off." *Lincoln Journal-Star* (26 June 1998): 6B.

Jacobs, Lawrence R., and Robert Y. Shapiro. 2000. *Politicians Don't Pander*. Chicago: University of Chicago Press.

Janis, Irving. 1982. *Groupthink*. Boston: Houghton Mifflin.

Johnson, James. 1998. "Arguing for Deliberation: Some Skeptical Considerations." In *Deliberative Democracy*, Jon Elster, ed. Cambridge: Cambridge University Press.

Johnson, Thomas J., Carol E. Hays, and Scott P. Hays. 1998. *Engaging the Public: How Government and the Media Can Reinvigorate Democracy*. Lanham, Md.: Rowman and Littlefield.

Kalven, Harry, Jr., and Hans Zeisel. 1970. *The American Jury*. Chicago: University of Chicago Press.

Kaplowitz, Stan A., Edward L. Fink, Dave D'Alessio, and G. Blake Armstrong. 1983. "Anonymity, Strength of Attitude and the Influence of Public Opinion Polls." *Human Communication Research* 10: 5–25.

Kay, Alan F. 1998. *Locating Consensus for Democracy*. Albany, N.Y.: Johnson Press.

Kazee, Thomas. 1994. *Who Runs for Congress?* Washington: Congressional Quarterly Press.

Kazin, Michael. 1995. *The Populist Persuasion*. New York: Basic Books.

Keohane, Robert O. 2001. "Governance in a Partially Globalized World." *American Political Science Review* 95: 1–13.

Kerbel, Matthew Robert. 1999. *Remote and Controlled*, 2nd ed. Boulder: Westview.

Kernell, Samuel. 1978. "Explaining Presidential Popularity." *American Political Science Review* 72: 506–22.

Kerr, N. L., R. J. MacCoun, and G. P. Kramer. 1996. "Bias in Judgment." *Psychological Review* 103: 687–719.

Kettering Foundation. 1991. *Citizens and Politics: A View from Main Street America*. Dayton, Ohio: Kettering Foundation.

Key, V. O., Jr. 1966. *The Responsible Electorate*. Cambridge, Mass.: Harvard University Press.

Kidd, Quentin. 2001. *American Government: Readings from across Society*. New York: Longman.

Kimball, David C., and Samuel C. Patterson. 1997. "Living Up to Expectations: Public Attitudes toward Congress." *Journal of Politics* 59: 701–28.

Kinder, Donald R., and D. Roderick Kiewiet. 1979. "Economic Discontent and Political Behavior." *American Journal of Political Science* 23: 495–527.

King, Anthony. 1997. *Running Scared*. New York: Free Press.

King, David C. 1997. "The Polarization of American Parties and Mistrust of Government." In *Why People Don't Trust Government*, Joseph S. Nye, Jr., Philip D. Zelikow, and David C. King, eds. Cambridge: Harvard University Press.

King, Gary. 1986. "How Not to Lie with Statistics." *American Journal of Political Science* 39: 666–87.

Knack, Stephen. 2001. "Election-Day Registration: The Second Wave." *American Politics Research* 29: 65–78.

Kraus, Jeffrey. 2000. "Book Review of Citizen Participation in Resource Allocation." *American Political Science Review* 94: 954–5.

Krehbiel, Keith. 1997. Personal communication.

Krosnick, Jon A. 1990. "Government Policy and Citizen Passion." *Political Behavior* 12: 59–92.

Krueger, Richard. 1988. *Focus Groups: A Practical Guide for Applied Research*. Newbury Park, Calif.: Sage.

Kryzanek, Michael J. 1999. *Angry, Bored, Confused*. Boulder: Westview.

Kuklinski, James, Ellen Riggle, Victor Ottati, Norbert Schwarz, and Robert Wyer, Jr. 1991. "The Cognitive and Affective Bases of Political Tolerance Judgments." *American Journal of Political Science* 35: 1–27.

Kuklinski, James, Paul J. Quirk, Jennifer Jerit, and Robert F. Rich. 2001. "The Political Environment and Citizen Decision Making: Information, Motivation, and Policy Tradeoffs." *American Journal of Political Science* 45: 410–24.

La Due Lake, Ronald, and Robert Huckfeldt. 1998. "Social Capital, Social Networks, and Political Participation." *Political Psychology* 19: 567–84.

Lane, Robert E. 1965. "The Politics of Consensus in an Age of Affluence." *American Political Science Review* 59: 874–95.

Lascher, Edward L., Jr., Michael G. Hagen, and Steven A. Rochlin. 1996. "Gun Behind the Door? Ballot Initiatives, State Policies and Public Opinion." *Journal of Politics* 58: 760–75.

Latane, Bibb, and John M. Darley. 1970. *The Unresponsive Bystander: Why Doesn't He Help?* Englewood Cliffs, N.J.: Prentice-Hall.

Lawrence, Robert Z. 1997. "Is It Really the Economy, Stupid?" In *Why People Don't Trust Government,* Joseph S. Nye, Jr., Philip D. Zelikow, and David C. King, eds. Cambridge, Mass.: Harvard University Press.

Lerner, S. C. 1981. "Adapting to Scarcity and Change." In *The Justice Motive in Social Behavior,* M. J. Lerner and S. C. Lerner, eds. New York: Plenum Press.

"Letters to the Editor." 1998. *Houston Chronicle* (21 April): 25A.

Levi, Margaret. 1996. "Social and Unsocial Capital: A Review Essay of Robert Putnam's 'Making Democracy Work.'" *Politics and Society* 24: 45–55.

1997. *Consent, Dissent, and Patriotism.* Cambridge: Cambridge University Press.

1998. "A State of Trust." In *Trust and Governance,* Valerie Braithwaite and Margaret Levi, eds. New York: Russell Sage Foundation.

Levitin, Teresa, and Warren E. Miller. 1979. "Ideological Interpretations of Presidential Elections." *American Political Science Review* 73: 751–71.

Light, Paul G. 1985. *Artful Work: The Politics of Social Security Reform.* New York: Random House.

Lijphart, Arend. 1997. "Unequal Participation: Democracy's Unresolved Dilemma." *American Political Science Review* 91: 1–14.

Lind, E. Allan, and Tom R. Tyler. 1988. *The Social Psychology of Procedural Justice.* New York: Plenum Press.

Lippmann, Walter. 1955. *Essays in the Public Philosophy.* Boston: Little, Brown.

Lipset, Seymour Martin. 1960. *Political Man.* New York: Doubleday.

Lipset, Seymour Martin, and William Schneider. 1987. *The Confidence Gap: Business, Labor and Government in the Public Mind.* Baltimore: Johns Hopkins University Press.

Loewenberg, Gerhard. 1971. *Modern Parliaments: Change or Decline?* Chicago: Aldine-Atherton.

Loewenberg, Gerhard, and Samuel C. Patterson. 1979. *Comparing Legislatures.* Boston: Little, Brown.

Lupia, Arthur, and Mathew D. McCubbins. 1998. *The Democratic Dilemma.* Cambridge: Cambridge University Press.

Luskin, Robert. 1991. "*Abusus non tollit usum.* Standardized Coefficients, Correlations, and R^2s." *American Journal of Political Science* 35: 1032–46.

Luttbeg, Norman R., and Michael M. Gant. 1995. *American Electoral Behavior 1952–1992.* Itasca, Ill.: F. E. Peacock.

MacDonald, Gus. 1986. "Election 500." In *Political Communications: The General Election Campaign of 1983,* Ivor Crewe and Martin Harrop, eds. Cambridge: Cambridge University Press.

Macedo, Stephen. 1999. *Deliberative Politics: Essays on Democracy and Disagreement.* Oxford: Oxford University Press.

MacKuen, Michael. 1990. "Speaking of Politics: Individual Conversational Choice, Public Opinion, and the Prospects for Deliberative Democracy." In John A. Ferejohn and James H. Kuklinski, eds., *Information and Democratic Processes.* Urbana: University of Illinois Press.

Magleby, David. 1984. *Direct Legislation.* Baltimore: Johns Hopkins University Press.

Manin, Bernard. 1987. "On Legitimacy and Political Deliberation." *Political Theory* 15: 338–68.

Mansbridge, Jane J. 1983. *Beyond Adversary Democracy.* Chicago: University of Chicago Press.

March, James G., and Johann Olsen. 1984. "The New Institutionalism: Organizational Factors in Political Life." *American Political Science Review* 78: 734–49.

March, James G., and Johan P. Olsen. 1995. *Democratic Governance.* New York: Free Press.

Marcus, George, John L. Sullivan, Elizabeth Theiss-Morse, and Sandra Wood. 1995. *With Malice Toward Some: How People Make Civil Liberties Judgments.* Cambridge: Cambridge University Press.

Margolis, Jane. 1992. "Piranhas, Monsters, and Jugglers: The Psychology of Gender and Academic Discourse." *On Teaching and Learning* 4: 5–26.

Margolis, Michael. 1977. "From Confusion to Confusion: Issues and Voters, 1952–1972." *American Political Science Review* 71: 31–43.

Marks, Gary, and Norman Miller. 1987. "Ten Years of Research on the False-Consensus Effect: An Empirical and Theoretical Review." *Psychological Bulletin* 102: 72–90.

Martin, Paul S., and Michele P. Clairbourn. 2000. "Trusting and Joining? An Empirical Test of the Social Capital Hypothesis." Unpublished manuscript. University of Wisconsin, Madison.

Martinez, Michael, and David Hill. 1999. "Did Motor Voter Work?" *American Politics Quarterly* 27: 296–315.

Mathews, David. 1994. *Politics for People: Finding a Responsible Public Voice.* Urbana: University of Illinois Press.

Mathews, Richard K. 1995. *If Men Were Angels: James Madison and the Heartless Empire of Reason.* Lawrence: University of Kansas Press.

Mayhew, David R. 1974. *Congress: The Electoral Connection.* New Haven: Yale University Press.

McCauley, C., C. L. Stitt, K. Woods, and D. Lipton. 1973. "Group Shift to Caution at the Race Track." *Journal of Experimental Social Psychology* 9: 80–6.

McClosky, Herbert. 1964. "Consensus and Ideology in American Politics." *American Political Science Review* 58: 361–82.

McCombs, Maxwell, and Amy Reynolds. 1999. *The Poll with a Human Face.* Mahwah, N.J.: Lawrence Erlbaum Press.

McGraw, Kathleen, Elaine Willey, and William Anderson. 1999. "It's the Process, Stupid! Procedural Considerations in Evaluations of Congress." Paper presented at the annual meeting of the Midwest Political Science Association, Chicago, Illinois, April.

McKelvey, Richard D. 1975. "Policy Related Voting and Electoral Equilibrium." *Econometrica* 43: 815–43.

McLeod, Jack M., William P. Eveland, Jr., and Edward M. Horowitz. 1998. "Going beyond Adults and Voter Turnout." In *Engaging the Public*, Thomas J. Johnson, Carol E. Hays, and Scott P. Hays, eds. Lanham, Md.: Rowman and Littlefield.

Mendelberg, Tali. 2002. "The Deliberative Citizen: Theory and Evidence." In *Research in Micropolitics*, vol. 6, Michael Delli Carpini, Leonie Huddy, and Robert Y. Shapiro, eds. New York: Elsevier.

Mendelberg, Tali, and John Oleske. 2000. "Race and Public Deliberation." Paper presented at the annual meeting of the Midwest Political Science Association, Chicago, April.

Merrill, Samuel III, and Bernard Grofman. 1999. *A Unified Theory of Voting*. Cambridge: Cambridge University Press.

Milbrath, Lester, and M. L. Goel. 1977. *Political Participation*, 2nd ed. Chicago: Rand McNally.

Milgrim, Stanley. 1974. *Obedience to Authority: An Experimental View*. New York: Harper Colophon.

Mill, John Stuart. 1975 [1861]. *Three Essays*, Richard Wolheim, ed. London: Oxford University Press.

  1977 [1859, 1861]. *Collected Writings*, vol. 19, J. M. Robson, ed. Toronto: University of Toronto Press.

Miller, Arthur H. 1974. "Political Issues and Trust in Government, 1964–1970." *American Political Science Review* 68: 951–72.

Miller, Matthew. 1991. "Do People Really Know Best?" *Omaha World-Herald* (10 December 1991): 27.

Miller, Warren E., and Donald E. Stokes. 1963. "Constituency Influence in Congress." *American Political Science Review* 57: 45–56.

Monroe, Alan D. 1979. "Consistency between Public Preferences and National Policy Decisions." *American Politics Quarterly* 7: 3–18.

Montgomery, Robert L. 1992. "Social Influence and Conformity: A Transorientational Model." In *Social Judgment and Intergroup Relations: Essays in Honor of Muzafer Sherif*, Donald Granberg and Gian Sarup, eds. New York: Springer-Verlag.

Morgan, David. 1988. *Focus Groups as Qualitative Research*. Newbury Park, Calif.: Sage.

Morin, Richard. 1996. "Tuned Out, Turned Off." *Washington Post Weekly* (5–11 February 1996): 6–8.

Morin, Richard, and Claudia Deane. 2001. "Better Late than Never." *Washington Post Weekly* (1 January): 14.

Morone, James A. 1990. *The Democratic Wish*. New York: Basic Books.

Morrell, Michael. 1999. "Citizens' Evaluations of Participatory Democratic Procedures." *Political Research Quarterly* 52: 293–322.

Morris, Dick. 1999. *Vote.com*. Los Angeles: St. Martin's.

Morris, Jonathan, and Marie Witting. 2001. "Congressional Partisanship, Bipartisanship and Public Opinion: An Experimental Analysis." *Politics and Policy* 29: 47–68.

Moscovici, Serge. 1992. "The Discovery of Group Polarization." In *Social Judgments and Intergroup Relations: Essays in Honor of Muzafer Sherif*, Donald Granberg and Gian Sarup, eds. New York: Springer-Verlag.

Mueller, John. 1973. *War, Presidents, and Public Opinion*. New York: Wiley.

1999. *Capitalism, Democracy and Ralph's Pretty Good Grocery*. Princeton: Princeton University Press.

Mullen, Brian, J. L. Atkins, D. S. Champion, C. Edwards, D. Hardy, J. E. Story, and M. Vanderklok. 1985. "The False Consensus Effect: A Meta-Analysis of 115 Hypothesis Tests." *Journal of Experimental Social Psychology* 21: 262–83.

Mullen, Brian, and Li-tze Hu. 1988. "Social Projection as a Function of Cognitive Mechanisms: Two Meta-Analytic Integrations." *British Journal of Social Psychology* 27: 333–56.

Muller, Edward N. 1972. "A Partial Test of a Theory of Potential for Political Violence." *American Political Science Review* 66: 928–59.

Murphy, Kevin. 2000. "Who Cares?" *Experience* (Fall): 41–4.

Mutz, Diana C. 1992. "Impersonal Influence in American Politics." *The Public Perspective: A Roper Center Review of Public Opinion and Polling* 4 (November/December): 19–21.

1997. "Mechanisms of Momentum: Does Thinking Make It So?" *Journal of Politics* 59: 104–25.

1998. *Impersonal Politics*. Cambridge: Cambridge University Press.

2000. "The Consequences of Cross-Cutting Networks for Political Participation." Paper presented at the annual meeting of the Midwest Political Science Association, Chicago, April.

2001. "Cross-Cutting Social Networks." Unpublished manuscript. Ohio State University.

Mutz, Diana C., and Jeffrey J. Mondak. 2001. "The Workplace as a Context for Cross-Cutting Political Discourse." Unpublished manuscript. Ohio State University.

Myers, D. G., and G. D. Bishop. 1970. "Discussion Effects on Racial Attitudes." *Science* 169: 778–9.

Naisbitt, John. 1984. *Megatrends: Ten New Directions Transforming Our Lives*. New York: Warner Books.

Newton, Kenneth. 1999. "Social and Political Trust in Established Democracies." In *Critical Citizens*, Pippa Norris, ed. New York: Oxford University Press.

Newton, Kenneth, and Pippa Norris. 2000. "Confidence in Public Institutions: Faith, Culture, or Performance." In *Dissaffected Democracies*, Susan J. Pharr and Robert D. Putnam, eds. Princeton: Princeton University Press.

Nie, Norman, Sidney Verba, and John Petrocik. 1976. *The Changing American Voter*. Cambridge, Mass.: Harvard University Press.

Niemi, Richard G., and Herbert R. Weisberg. 1976. *Controversies in American Voting Behavior*. San Francisco: W. H. Freeman.

Noelle-Neuman, Elisabeth. 1984. *The Spiral of Silence: Public Opinion – Our Social Skin*. Chicago: University of Chicago Press.

Norris, Pippa. 1996. "Does Television Erode Social Capital? A Reply to Putnam." *PS: Political Science and Politics* 29: 474–80.

Nye, Joseph S., Jr. 1997. "Introduction: The Decline of Confidence in Government." In *Why People Don't Trust Government*, Joseph S. Nye, Jr., Philip D. Zelikow, and David C. King, eds. Cambridge, Mass.: Harvard University Press.

Nye, Joseph S., Jr., and Philip D. Zelikow. 1997. "Conclusion: Reflections, Conjectures, and Puzzles." In *Why People Don't Trust Government*, Joseph S. Nye, Jr., Philip D. Zelikow, and David C. King, eds. Cambridge, Mass.: Harvard University Press.

Ordeshook, Peter C. 1970. "Extensions to a Mathematical Model of the Electoral Process and Implications for the Theory of Responsible Parties." *Midwest Journal of Political Science* 14: 43–70.

Ornstein, Norman J. 2000. "Deliberative Democracy Headed for the Dark Side?" *State Legislatures* 26 (January): 8–11.

Orren, Gary. 1997. "Fall from Grace: The Public's Loss of Faith in Government." In *Why People Don't Trust Government*, Joseph S. Nye, Jr., Philip D. Zelikow, and David C. King, eds. Cambridge, Mass.: Harvard University Press.

Packenham, Robert A. 1970. "Legislatures and Political Development." In *Legislatures in Developmental Perspective*, Allan Kornberg and Lloyd D. Musolf, eds. Durham: Duke University Press.

Page, Benjamin I. 1996. *Who Deliberates?* Chicago: University of Chicago Press.

Page, Benjamin I., and Richard A. Brody. 1972. "Policy Voting and the Electoral Process: The Vietnam War Issue." *American Political Science Review* 66: 979–95.

Page, Benjamin I., and Calvin Jones. 1979. "Reciprocal Effects of Policy Preferences, Party Loyalties, and the Vote." *American Political Science Review* 73: 1071–89.

Page, Benjamin I., and Robert Y. Shapiro. 1992. *The Rational Public: Fifty Years of Trends in Americans' Policy Preferences*. Chicago: University of Chicago Press.

Parker, Martin. 1997. "Dividing Organizations and Multiplying Identities." In *Ideas of Difference: Social Spaces and the Labor of Division*, Kevin Hetherington and Rolland Murro, eds. Oxford: Blackwell.

Pateman, Carole. 1970. *Participation and Democratic Theory*. Cambridge: Cambridge University Press.

Patterson, Samuel C., and Gregory A. Caldeira. 1990. "Standing Up for Congress: Variations in Public Esteem since the 1960s." *Legislative Studies Quarterly* 15: 25–47.

Patterson, Thomas. 1980. *The Mass Media Election*. New York: Praeger.

Peel, Mark. 1998. "Trusting Disadvantaged Citizens." In *Trust in Governance*, Valerie Braithwaite and Margaret Levi, eds. New York: Russell Sage Foundation.

Petty, Richard E., and John T. Cacioppo. 1981. *Attitudes and Persuasion: Classic and Contemporary Approaches*. Dubuque, Iowa: William C. Brown.

Pharr, Susan J. 2000. "Officials' Misconduct and Public Distrust." In *Disaffected Democracies*, Susan J. Pharr and Robert D. Putnam, eds. Princeton: Princeton University Press.

Phillips, Kevin. 1995. *Arrogant Capital*. Boston: Little, Brown.

Piven, Frances Fox, and Richard A. Cloward. 1988. *Why Americans Don't Vote.* New York: Pantheon Books.

——— 1996. "Northern Bourbons: A Preliminary Report on the National Voter Registration Act." *PS: Political Science and Politics* 29: 39–42.

"Poll: Voters Choose Persona over Issues." 1999. *Lincoln Journal-Star* (17 December): 7A.

Polsby, Nelson W. 1993. "Where Do You Get Your Ideas?" *PS: Politics and Political Science* 26: 83–7.

——— 1997. "Term Limits." In *New Federalist Papers*, Alan Brinkley, Nelson W. Polsby, and Kathleen M. Sullivan, eds. New York: W. W. Norton.

Pomper, Gerald M. 1972. "From Confusion to Clarity: Issues and American Voters, 1952–1972." *American Political Science Review* 66: 415–28.

Poole, Keith T., and Howard Rosenthal. 1997. *Congress: A Political-Economic History of Roll Call Voting.* New York: Oxford University Press.

Popkin, Samuel L. 1991. *The Reasoning Voter.* Chicago: University of Chicago Press.

Putnam, Robert D. 1993. *Making Democracy Work: Civic Traditions in Modern Italy.* Princeton: Princeton University Press.

——— 1995. "Bowling Alone: America's Declining Social Capital." *Journal of Democracy* 6: 65–78.

——— 2000. *Bowling Alone: The Collapse and Revival of American Community.* New York: Simon and Schuster.

Putnam, Robert D., Susan J. Pharr, and Russell J. Dalton. 2000. "Introduction: What's Troubling the Trilateral Democracies?" In *Disaffected Democracies*, Susan J. Pharr and Robert D. Putnam, eds. Princeton: Princeton University Press.

Rabinowitz, George, and Stuart Macdonald. 1989. "A Directional Theory of Issue Voting." *American Political Science Review* 83: 93–121.

Rapaport, Ronald, Alan I. Abramowitz, and John McGlennon. 1986. *The Life of the Parties.* Lexington: University of Kentucky Press.

Rauch, Jonathan. 1994. "The Hyperpluralism Trap." *The New Republic* (6 June 1994): 22–5.

Rawls, John A. 1971. *A Theory of Justice.* Cambridge: Harvard University Press.

RePass, David E. 1971. "Issue Salience and Party Choice." *American Political Science Review* 65: 389–400.

Ridout, Travis N., and Rodolpho Espino. 2000. "What Is It about Joining a Group That Makes People Trust Others More?" Paper presented at the annual meeting of the Midwest Political Science Association, Chicago, April.

Riker, William. 1982. *Liberalism against Populism.* San Francisco: W. H. Freeman.

Rosen, Jeffrey. 2000. "Judge Not: The Supreme Court Puts Itself in Harm's Way." *The New Republic* 11 December: 17.

Rosenberg, Morris. 1954–5. "Some Determinants of Political Apathy." *Public Opinion Quarterly* 18: 349–66.

Rosenstone, Steven J., and John Mark Hansen. 1993. *Mobilization, Participation, and Democracy in America.* New York: Macmillan.

Rosenthal, Alan. 1998. *The Decline of Representative Democracy.* Washington: Congressional Quarterly Press.

Ross, Lee, David Greene, and Pamela House. 1977. "The 'False Consensus Effect': An Egocentric Bias in Social Perception and Attribution Processes." *Journal of Experimental and Social Psychology* 13: 277–90.

Rousseau, Jean Jacques. 1946 [1762]. *The Social Contract and Discourses*, G. D. H. Cole, translator and editor. New York: E. P. Dutton.

    1947 [1762]. *The Social Contract*, Ernest Barker, ed. London: Oxford University Press.

Sandel, Michael. 1982. *Liberalism and the Limits of Justice*. Cambridge: Cambridge University Press.

    1984. *Liberalism and Its Critics*. New York: New York University Press.

    1996. *Democracy's Discontent*. Cambridge: Harvard University Press.

Sanders, Lynn M. 1997. "Against Deliberation." *Political Theory* 25: 347–76.

Schauer, Frederick. 1999. "Talking as a Decision Procedure." In *Deliberative Politics: Essays on Democracy and Disagreement*, Stephen Macedo, ed. Oxford: Oxford University Press.

Schedler, Andreas. 1997. *The End of Politics?* New York: St. Martins.

Scholz, John T., and Mark Lubell. 1998. "Trust and Taxpaying: Testing the Heuristic Approach to Collective Action." *American Journal of Political Science* 42: 398–417.

Schudson, Michael. 1998. *The Good Citizen: A History of American Civic Life*. New York: Free Press.

Schumpeter, Joseph. 1961. *Capitalism, Socialism, and Democracy*. New York: Harper and Row.

Sears, David O., and John Maconahay. 1973. *The Politics of Violence*. Boston: Houghton Mifflin.

Seelye, Katharine Q. 1998. "Americans Take a Dim View of the Government, Survey Finds." *New York Times* (10 March 1998): A15.

Sherif, Muzafer. 1935. "A Study of Some Social Factors in Perception." *Archives of Psychology* 27, no. 187: 1–60.

    1937. "An Experimental Approach to the Study of Attitudes." *Sociometry* 1: 90–8.

Simon, Adam F., and Tracy Sulkin. 2000. "Assessing Deliberation in Small Groups." Paper presented at the annual meeting of the Midwest Political Science Association, Chicago, April.

Simonsen, William, and Mark D. Robbins. 2000. *Citizen Participation in Resource Allocation*. Boulder, Colo.: Westview.

Sniderman, Paul M., and Thomas Piazza. 1993. *The Scar of Race*. Cambridge, Mass.: Harvard University Press.

Sniderman, Paul M., Louk Hagendoorn, and Markus Prior. 2000. "The Banality of Extremism: Exploratory Studies in Political Persuasion." Paper presented at the annual meeting of the Midwest Political Science Association, Chicago, April.

Solomon, Burt. 2000. "We the Mob." *National Journal* 32 (1 July): 2140–3.

Spence, David B. 1999. "The Benefits of Agency Policymaking: Perspectives from Positive Theory." Unpublished paper, University of Texas.

Stark, Steven. 1995. "Too Representative Government." *Atlantic Monthly* (May 1995): 92–106.

Stewart, David, and Prem Shamdasani. 1990. *Focus Groups: Theory and Practice*. Newbury Park, Calif.: Sage.

Stimson, James. 1995. "Opinion and Representation." *American Political Science Review* 89: 179–83.

Stokes, Donald. 1963. "Spatial Models of Party Competition." *American Political Science Review* 57: 368–77.

Stokes, Susan C. 1998. "Pathologies of Deliberation." In *Deliberative Democracy*, Jon Elster, ed. Cambridge: Cambridge University Press.

Stolle, Dietland. 1998. "Bowling Together, Bowling Alone: The Development of Generalized Trust in Voluntary Associations." *Political Psychology* 19: 497–526.

Stoner, J. A. F. 1961. "A Comparison of Individual and Group Decisions Involving Risk." Master's thesis, School of Industrial Management, Massachusetts Institute of Technology.

Stouffer, Samuel. 1955. *Communism, Conformity, and Civil Liberties*. New York: Doubleday.

Stringer, Peter, and Laurie Thomas. 1996. "Of Cats and Clouds." In *The Construction of Group Realities: Culture, Society, and Personal Construct Theory*, Deborah Kalekin-Fishman and Beverly M. Walker, eds. Malabar: Krieger Publishing.

Suksi, Markku. 1993. *Bringing in the People*. Dordrecht, The Netherlands: Martinus Nijhoff Publishers.

Sullivan, John L., James Piereson, and George E. Marcus. 1982. *Political Tolerance and American Democracy*. Chicago: University of Chicago Press.

Sunstein, Cass. 2001. *Republic.com*. Princeton: Princeton University Press.

Tannen, Deborah. 1994. *Gender and Discourse*. Oxford: Oxford University Press.

Taylor, Charles. 1992. "Atomism." In *Communitarianism and Individualism*, Shlomo Avineri and Avner de-Shalit, eds. Oxford: Oxford University Press.

"Televising the Highest Court." 2000. *New York Times* (5 December): A30.

Theriault. Sean M. 1998. "Moving Up or Moving Out: Career Ceilings and Congressional Retirement." *Legislative Studies Quarterly* 23: 419–34.

Thibaut, John, and Laurens Walker. 1975. *Procedural Justice: A Psychological Analysis*. Hillsdale, N.J.: Erlbaum.

Tilker, Harvey. 1970. "Socially Responsible Behavior as a Function of Observer Responsibility and Victim Feedback." *Journal of Personality and Social Psychology* 14: 95–100.

Tocqueville, Alexis de. 1951. *Democracy in America*, vol. 1. New York: Alfred Knopf.

Tolchin, Susan J. 1999. *The Angry American: How Voter Rage Is Changing the Nation*. Boulder: Westview.

Tufte, Edward R. 1975. "Determinants of the Outcomes of Midterm Congressional Elections." *American Political Science Review* 69: 812–26.

Tyler, Tom R. 1990. *Why People Obey the Law*. New Haven: Yale University Press.

1994. "Psychological Models of the Justice Motive: Antecedents of Distributive and Procedural Justice." *Journal of Personality and Social Psychology* 67: 850–63.

2001. "The Psychology of Public Dissatisfaction with Government." In *What Is It about Government That Americans Dislike?* John R. Hibbing and Elizabeth Theiss-Morse, eds. Cambridge: Cambridge University Press.

Tyler, Tom R., and G. Mitchell. 1994. "Legitimacy and the Empowerment of Discretionary Legal Authority." *Duke Law Journal* 43: 703–814.

Tyler, Tom R., Karen Rasinski, and N. Spodick. 1985. "The Influence of Voice on Satisfaction with Leaders." *Journal of Applied Social Psychology* 15: 700–25.

Ulbig, Stacy G., and Carolyn L. Funk. 1999. "Conflict Avoidance and Political Participation." *Political Behavior* 21: 280–96.

Uslaner, Eric M. 1993. *The Decline of Comity in Congress.* Ann Arbor: University of Michigan Press.

2001. "Is Washington Really the Problem?" In *What Is It about Government That Americans Dislike?* John R. Hibbing and Elizabeth Theiss-Morse, eds. Cambridge: Cambridge University Press.

van Mill, David. 1996. "The Possibility of Rational Outcomes from Democratic Discourse and Procedures." *Journal of Politics* 58: 734–52.

Verba, Sidney. 1961. *Small Groups and Political Behavior.* Princeton: Princeton University Press.

Verba, Sidney, and Norman Nie. 1972. *Participation in America: Political Democracy and Social Equality.* New York: Harper and Row.

Verba, Sidney, Kay Lehman Schlozman, and Henry E. Brady. 1995. *Voice and Equality.* Cambridge: Harvard University Press.

Wahlke, John C. 1971. "Policy Demands and System Support." *British Journal of Political Science* 1: 271–90.

Wahlke, John C., Heinz Eulau, William Buchanan, and LeRoy Ferguson. 1962. *The Legislative System.* New York: Wiley.

Walker, Jack L. 1966. "A Critique of the Elitist Theory of Democracy." *American Political Science Review* 60: 285–95.

Wattenberg, Martin P. 1981. "The Decline of Political Partisanship in the United States." *American Political Science Review* 75: 941–50.

Weberg, Brian. 2000. "Instant Democracy for Everyone." *State Legislatures* 26: 17–20.

Wilentz, Sean, 1993. "Vox Populi." *New Republic* (9 August 1993): 29–35.

Will, George. 1992. *Restoration: Congress, Term Limits and the Recovery of Deliberative Democracy.* New York: Free Press.

Wilson, James Q. 1975. "The Riddle of the Middle Class." *The Public Interest* 39: 125–9.

Wolfe, Alan. 1998. *One Nation, after All.* New York: Viking Books.

Wolfensberger, Donald. 1999. *Congress and the People: Deliberative Democracy on Trial.* Baltimore: Johns Hopkins University Press.

Wolff, Robert Paul. 1970. *In Defense of Anarchism.* New York: Anchor Books.

Wright, James D. 1976. *The Dissent of the Governed: Alienation and Democracy in America.* New York: Academic.

Young, Iris Marion. 1996. "Communication and the Other: Beyond Deliberative Democracy." In *Democracy and Difference*, Seyla Benhabib, ed. Princeton: Princeton University Press.

Young, Iris Marion. 2000. *Inclusion and Democracy.* New York: Oxford University Press.

Zaller, John R. 1986. "Analysis of Information Items in the 1985 NES Pilot Study." Report to the NES Board of Overseers. Unpublished manuscript. University of California, Los Angeles.

1992. *The Nature and Origins of Mass Opinion.* Cambridge: Cambridge University Press.

Index

abortion, 16, 17, 59, 62, 223, 234
Abramowitz, Alan I., 54
Abramson, Jeffrey, 173, 191n, 194
accountability of government, 2, 4,
    138–139, 141, 143–144, 145–147,
    148, 149, 150, 181, 216–217, 227,
    238–240
Ackerman, Bruce, 184n, 191
Adams, John, 218n
Adams, John Q., 218n
Afghanistan, 2–4, 64
Aldrich, John H., 23n, 54
Alesina, Alberto, 18
Alford, John R., 221n, 235
Almond, Gabriel, 171, 239n–240n
Alvarez, R. Michael, 21n, 22n, 72n
American National Election Study,
    25n
American people: compared with
    elected officials, 109–111;
    emotional reactions toward,
    107–109; perceived consensus of,
    132–133, 147; perceived political
    capabilities of, 91, 112–121,
    124–128; perceived power of, 102,
    107, 129; reservations about
    empowering, 126–127;
    trustworthiness of, 113–114
American Political Science
    Association, 89n
Anderson, William, 49
Ansolabehere, Stephen, 55n, 147n,
    157

apathy, 117, 120, 231, 241
approval of government, 4, 34, 64,
    67–71, 79–82, 98–102, 151; see also
    Congress; presidency; Supreme
    Court
Arnold, Douglas, 155n
Asch, Solomon, 195
Austen-Smith, David, 193n, 207n,
    231n
Avineri, Shlomo, 89n, 179
Axelrod, Robert, 185–186

Bach, Stanley, 212
Baird, Vanessa A., 236n
Baker, Lisa, 132n
ballot initiatives, 7, 43, 50, 58, 75,
    76, 89, 90–91, 105, 129, 164;
    public hesitancy toward, 91
Banks, Jeffrey S., 193n
Barber, Benjamin, 125, 167, 173,
    178, 184, 200, 226n
Barkow, Jerome H., 221n, 235
Baumgartner, Frank, 57n, 194n
Becker, Theodore Lewis, 125, 165,
    229n
Beem, Christopher, 185
Beer, Samuel H., 174n
Bell, Daniel A., 233
Benhabib, Seyla, 174
Bennett, Stephen Earl, 22n
Bentham, Jeremy, 212, 213
Berman, S., 186
Berry, J. M., 200